P9-BZC-421

NEW PATTERNS
OF MANAGEMENT

RENSIS LIKERT

*Director, Institute for Social Research
and Professor of Psychology and Sociology
The University of Michigan*

MCGRAW-HILL BOOK COMPANY

New York   Toronto   London   1961

NEW PATTERNS OF MANAGEMENT

11 12 13 14 – M P – 9 8

37850

TO J. G. L.

PREFACE

This volume is intended for persons concerned with the problems of organizing human resources and activity. It is written especially for those who are actively engaged in management and supervision and for students of administration and organization. It presents a newer theory of organization based on the management principles and practices of the managers who are achieving the best results in American business and government. It draws also upon research done in voluntary organizations.

The few partial tests of the theory suggest that important increases in organizational effectiveness and productivity can be achieved through its use. Moreover, there is evidence of increased human satisfaction for members of the organizations applying the theory.

The research upon which the proposed theory is based has been carried on intensively since 1947. It has gone forward in both centers of the Institute for Social Research, namely, the Survey Research Center and the Research Center for Group Dynamics. Brief summaries of the general pattern of the research findings are presented and used as the basis for the theory.

To maintain a relatively consistent orientation, the focus of this volume is largely on the problems of business enterprises. People interested in other kinds of institutions, such as schools, hospitals, labor unions, professional and voluntary organizations, should, however, experience no difficulty in applying the general principles of the theory to their organizations.

This volume has been made possible by the companies and other organizations in which the research was done. We who have done the research and all those who benefit from it owe a deep debt of gratitude to these companies, their managements and employees. Their generous support and wholehearted cooperation contributed indispensably to the successful conduct of the research.

At times the assistance of particular persons has been of crucial importance. For example, the entire program of research was launched in 1947 by funds provided by the Office of Naval Research under the imaginative and forward-looking leadership of Admiral Harold G. Bowen and

Captain Victor A. Conrad. The faith and courage of F. Bruce Gerhard made it possible to conduct the clerical experiment which has yielded fundamental insights. The extension of the research to include labor unions occurred because of the initiative of Joseph H. Willitts and Leland C. DeVinney of the Rockefeller Foundation.

This book draws heavily upon the research and thinking of the staff of the Institute for Social Research. Angus Campbell, Director of the Survey Research Center, and Dorwin Cartwright, former Director and now Research Coordinator of the Research Center for Group Dynamics, have provided valuable stimulation and constructive criticism. The past and present directors of the Organizational Behavior and Organizational Change Programs of research, namely, Daniel Katz, Robert L. Kahn, Stanley E. Seashore, and Floyd C. Mann, have been a major source of ideas and valuable suggestions. I have benefited greatly also from the work and advice of Alvin Zander, Director of the Research Center for Group Dynamics, and from John R. P. French, Jr., Ronald Lippitt, Donald Pelz, and Arnold Tannenbaum. Similarly, I feel a deep debt to all those other persons, some of whom are now with other institutions, who conducted or aided in the studies which I have drawn upon so extensively and which have guided my thinking. The citations and bibliography reflect the importance of their contributions.

In addition to the members of the Institute staff, many persons have read parts or all of the manuscript and have given me many excellent suggestions. Charles W. L. Foreman, S. F. Leahy, Donald Grant, Mason Haire, John Paul Jones, James Marshall, Douglas McGregor, Irwin Rose, and Robert Schwab have been especially helpful.

Jane Likert, my wife, has edited the manuscript and has significantly shortened and clarified the material presented.

Margaret M. Johnson has prepared the bibliography and index in addition to giving other indispensable help in the preparation of this volume.

Helen M. Gault, Edwin Taylor, and Russell Trubey have conscientiously reproduced copies of the chapters through what seemed to them—and to me—countless revisions. Their assistance is deeply appreciated.

For permission to quote from their publications and to use some of the material published previously I am grateful to the following: American Management Association, American Philosophical Society, American Psychological Association, Harper & Brothers, *Harvard Business Review*, Harvard University Graduate School of Business Administration, Holt, Rinehart and Winston, Inc., League of Women Voters of the United States, Life Insurance Agency Management Association, McGraw-Hill Book Company, Inc., North-Holland Publishing Co., *Personnel Psychology*, Public Service Administration, The Society for the Psychological Study of Social Issues, Tavistock Publications, and John Wiley & Sons, Inc.

Rensis Likert

CONTENTS

Chapter I

INTRODUCTION

Managers with the best records of performance in American business and government are in the process of pointing the way to an appreciably more effective system of management than now exists. With the assistance of social science research, it is now possible to state a generalized theory of organization based on the management practices of these highest producers. The over-all characteristics of this management system are presented in this volume.

Important forces and resources are accelerating this new development. Others are delaying it. One of the accelerating forces likely to grow in importance in the United States is the competition from the industrially developed countries throughout the world. We are already experiencing this competition and are apt to feel its effects even more acutely in the next decade. Other highly developed countries are using modern industrial technology with skills approaching ours and in some instances equal to ours. With lower labor and salary costs and other lower fixed costs, they can compete with us in world markets on very favorable terms. One way of holding a satisfactory share of the market, domestically and abroad, will be to increase the productivity of our enterprises.

One important source of increased productivity will be the full development and skillful application of the form of social organization which the highest-producing managers are using increasingly.

Another factor likely to accelerate the development of a better system of managing the human resources of an organization are certain changes taking place in the American society. Supervisors and managers report in interviews that people are less willing to accept pressure and close supervision than was the case a decade or two ago. The trend in America, generally, in our schools, in our homes, and in our communities, is toward giving the individual greater freedom and initiative. There are fewer direct, unexplained orders in schools and homes, and youngsters are participating increasingly in decisions which affect them.

These fundamental changes in American society create expectations among employees as to how they should be treated. Expectations pro-

1

foundly affect employee attitudes, since attitudes depend upon the extent to which our experiences meet our expectations. If experience falls short of expectations, unfavorable attitudes occur. When our experience is better than our expectations, we tend to have favorable attitudes. This means, of course, that if expectations in America are changing in a particular direction, experience must change in the same direction and at the same or at a greater rate. Otherwise, the attitudinal response of people to their experience will be unfavorable.

Another development providing impetus to the trend toward greater use of participation in business and government is the substantial increase in the educational level of the labor force. In 1940, the proportion of workers with a high school or college education was 39.1 per cent. By 1950 it had increased to 50.3 and by 1959 to 62.0 per cent. The trend seems likely to continue if one can judge by the aspirations of parents for their children's education. As people acquire more education, their expectations rise as to the amount of responsibility, authority, and income they will receive. Also, a longer exposure to the values of an educational system which places emphasis on participation and individual initiative increases the likelihood that these values will be accepted by the individual and carried over into the working situation.

Coupled with the cultural trend in American homes, schools, and communities is an increasing concern about mental health and an emphasis on the growth of individuals into healthy, emotionally mature adults. These developments are also creating pressures in business and government which may well lead to important changes in the management system. Argyris (1957c) has a volume devoted to the dilemma which management faces in endeavoring to adhere to accepted management principles and at the same time to fulfill the personality needs of the emotionally mature people which our homes and schools are trying hard to produce.

Another factor likely to accelerate the formulation and use of a newer theory of management is the growing state of readiness for it. In our interviews and discussions with middle and top management, we have been impressed with the number of people who display a restless dissatisfaction with the theories and practices prevalent today.

Finally, in the larger companies, there are increasing numbers of people with training in diverse, complex technologies and highly specialized skills and professions. The great increase in research and development, the rapid growth of new fields of engineering, such as nuclear, electronics, missiles, and plastics, the increased use of more complex forms of mathematics and statistics, and the introduction of large computers illustrate current developments. It is not at all uncommon for subordinates or staff to know far more about an important matter than does the chief. The chief, by himself, can no longer make the best decision based on the best technical facts. The problems are often so complex that no one subordinate has all the technical information required. To marshal all the relevant information bearing on a decision, it is usually necessary to involve experts from several different fields. As a consequence, there is much greater need for cooperation and participation in managing the enterprise than when technologies were simple and the chief possessed all the technical knowledge needed. To meet the demands created by our more complex technologies and much larger and diverse enterprises, more complex systems of organizing human effort are being created. The theory proposed in this volume extends this development.

Several decades ago Taylor (1911) pointed to the fact that human variability in performance could be used to discover better ways of doing work. The social sciences and their capacity to measure human and organizational variables are making possible the extension of this fundamental idea from the organization of the work itself to the problem of building the most productive and satisfying form of human organization for conducting any enterprise.

Measurements now made available by social science research reveal that managers achieving better performance (i.e., greater productivity, higher earnings, lower costs, etc.) differ in leadership principles and practices from those achieving poorer performance. This variation reflects important differences in basic assumptions about ways of managing people.

The full significance of the contribution of the high-producing managers to the creation of a better management system is not recognized even by the managers themselves. Each has made his changes gradually over time, often by intuition and, as a consequence, tends not to be entirely aware of the magnitude of the changes he, himself, has introduced. Nor is he fully aware that his improvements and insights, and those of other successful managers as well, are beginning to form a general pattern.

Social science research is providing systematic evidence that such a pattern is emerging. It is also providing a body of organized data from which a valid statement of this better management system can be made. This volume presents a suggested formulation of this newer system.

Chapters 2, 3, and 4 summarize research findings which show the general pattern of management used by the high-producing managers in contrast to that used by the other managers. This summary of the research results is highly condensed and does not include all the qualifications that a rigorous statement of the research would require. It reflects, however, generalizations and over-all patterns which the author believes to be valid.

Attention is turned next, in Chapters 5 and 6, to a consideration of why this general pattern is not more widely recognized and accepted as the best way to manage.

Chapter 7 states a general principle of supervision which helps to explain the causes of differing results from the same supervisory procedures. It also points to the necessity of using broad principles rather than specific procedures.

Chapter 8 presents an over-all statement of a newer management system based on a systematic integration of the principles and practices used by the high-producing managers. In Chapter 9, tests are made of some of the important dimensions of this management system.

Results of a large study of a national voluntary organization are summarized in Chapter 10. A major finding of this study is used to elaborate an important dimension of the newer management system.

Chapters 11 and 12 develop in some detail major dimensions of the proposed newer theory for organizing human behavior. Chapter 13 discusses the value of measurements of the human dimensions of an organization and the use of these measurements in operating under the newer theory.

Chapter 14 suggests that the various systems of management and control that have evolved in the course of time can be examined from a comparative viewpoint. The orderly array of relationships that appear when this comparative approach is used provides additional material to show the nature of the newer system of management and to suggest appropriate operating procedures for applying the newer theory in specific situations.

The final chapter touches briefly on some of the problems likely to be encountered in any attempt to apply the theory and suggests ways of coping with them.

Most of the research findings on which the newer theory is based have come from studies in business. But application of the theory is not limited to these enterprises. It is equally applicable to other kinds of organized human activity, such as schools, voluntary associations, unions, hospitals, governmental agencies, scientific and professional organizations, and the like. The specific procedures will vary with the organization, but the basic theory can be applied to all.

The material presented in this book draws heavily on the work of the two centers of the Institute for Social Research: the Survey Research Center and the Research Center for Group Dynamics. The over-all results of this research are, generally speaking, quite consistent with the findings of other investigators in the United States, Europe, India, and Japan. Unfortunately, it has not been possible in this volume to discuss even briefly all this other important research. References to some of it, however, will be found throughout the text. The bibliography may help also to fill in the gaps.

Chapter 2

LEADERSHIP AND ORGANIZATIONAL PERFORMANCE

How best to organize the efforts of individuals to achieve desired objectives has long been one of the world's most important, difficult, and controversial problems. Many people have worked hard to find better ways, but progress has beeen slow. In recent years, a new approach is being made based on advances in research methodology. It is now possible to measure such dimensions of organizational functioning as motivational forces, communication effectiveness, and decision-making processes. Rigorous, quantitative research can now be used in place of the cruder methods available previously. The sample-interview survey, controlled field experiments, and refined methods of statistical and mathematical analysis are some of the tools useful in such research.

The Institute for Social Research began, in 1047, a large-scale program of research, using these new methodologies to study the complex human problems of administration.[1] A series of related studies has been conducted to discover the organizational structure and the principles and methods of leadership and management which result in the best performance. The general design of most of the studies has been to measure and examine the kinds of leadership and related variables employed by the best units in an organization in contrast to those used by the poorest. In more recent years, some experiments have also been undertaken in companies to apply and test the findings of the earlier studies.

In carrying forward this research, several criteria have been used to evaluate administrative effectiveness. These include:

[1] This program was given generous support during its formative years by the Office of Naval Research. Other major sources of basic support include the Rockefeller Foundation, the Carnegie Corporation, the Schwartzhaupt Foundation, and the National Institutes of Health. Funds for numerous specific research ventures have been provided by several other foundations and by the firms and organizations in which the research was done.

5

· Productivity per man hour or some similar measure of the organization's success in achieving its productivity goals
· Job satisfaction and other satisfactions derived by members of the organization
· Turnover, absence, and similar measurements
· Costs
· Scrap loss
· Employee and managerial motivation

Since 1947, studies have been conducted or are now under way in a wide variety of industries: automotive, chemical, delivery service, electronics and electrical instruments, electric appliances and equipment, food, heavy machinery, insurance, paper, petroleum, public utilities, railroads, and textiles. Studies have also been made in hospitals and government agencies. Data have been obtained from tens of thousands of employees doing widely different kinds of jobs, ranging from operations involving unskilled workers to laboratories doing highly specialized scientific research.

This and the next two chapters will summarize some of the major findings of these studies. No attempt will be made to present all the results. The general conclusions, however, are supported by comparable results from other studies the Institute for Social Research has made and are consistent with the results obtained by other investigators.

Employee-centered or Job-centered Supervision

Many companies base their operations upon theories which state that it is management's responsibility to:

1. Break the total operation into simple, component parts or tasks
2. Develop the best way to carry out each of the component parts
3. Hire people with appropriate aptitudes and skills to perform each of these tasks
4. Train these people to do their respective tasks in the specified best way
5. Provide supervision to see that they perform their designated tasks, using the specified procedure and at an acceptable rate as determined by such procedures as timing the job
6. Where feasible, use incentives in the form of individual or group piece rates

Supervisors who base their activity on this concept of management are more often found to be in charge of units producing at a *low* rather than a high level; that is, those supervisors whose units have a relatively poor production record tend to concentrate on keeping their subordinates busily engaged in going through a specified work cycle in a prescribed way and at a satisfactory rate as determined by time standards (item 5 above).

Supervisors with the best records of performance focus their primary attention on the human aspects of their subordinates' problems and on endeavoring to build effective work groups with high performance goals.

Supervisors with the latter orientation will be called "employee-centered"; those with the former orientation will be called "job-centered." Figure 2-1 presents the findings from one study. It illustrates the pattern

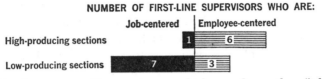

Fig. 2-1. "Employee-centered" supervisors are higher producers than "job-centered" supervisors.

of results from several different studies in widely different kinds of work, such as clerical, sales, and manufacturing (Bose, 1957; Ganguli, 1957; Kahn, 1956; Katz & Kahn, 1951; Katz & Kahn, 1952; Katz, Maccoby, & Morse, 1950; Likert & Willits, 1940).

The point of view of an assistant manager of a low-production department illustrates job-centered supervision: "This interest-in-people approach is all right, but it's a luxury. I've got to keep pressure on for production, and when I get production up, then I can afford to take time to show an interest in my employees and their problems."

Contrast this with the point of view of a manager of a high-producing division (R. Likert, 1952b):

One way in which we accomplish a high level of production is by letting people do the job the way they want to so long as they accomplish the objectives. I believe in letting them take time out from the monotony. Make them feel that they are something special, not just the run of the mill. As a matter of fact, I tell them if you feel that job is getting you down get away from it for a few minutes. . . . If you keep employees from feeling hounded, they are apt to put out the necessary effort to get the work done in the required time.

I never make any decisions myself. Oh, I guess I've made about two since I've been here. If people know their jobs I believe in letting them make decisions. I believe in delegating decision-making. Of course, if there's anything that affects the whole division, then the two assistant managers, the three section heads and sometimes the assistant section heads come in here and we discuss it. I don't believe in saying that this is the way it's going to be. After all, once supervision and management are in agreement there won't be any trouble selling the staff the idea.

My job is dealing with human beings rather than with the work. It doesn't matter if I have anything to do with the work or not. The chances are that people will do a better job if you are really taking an interest in them. Knowing the names is important and helps a lot, but it's not enough. You really have to know each individual well, know what his problems are. Most of the time I discuss matters with employees at their desks rather than in the office. Sometimes I sit on a waste paper basket or lean on the files. It's all very informal. People don't seem to like to come into the office to talk.

In addition to their orientation toward employees, the performance goals of supervisors are also important in affecting productivity. Kahn (1956) found that foremen in charge of high-producing units are both employee-centered and seen by their employees as feeling that achieving a high level of production was one of the most important parts of their job. If a high level of performance is to be achieved, it appears to be necessary for a supervisor to be employee-centered and at the same time to have high performance goals and a contagious enthusiasm as to the importance of achieving these goals. Other data bearing on this point will be examined in Table 2-1, page 10.

Figure 2-2 shows that there is a marked *inverse* relationship between the average amount of "unreasonable" pressure the men in a department

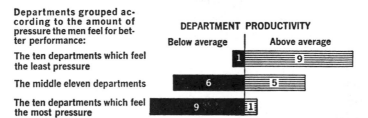

Departments grouped according to the amount of pressure the men feel for better performance:

DEPARTMENT PRODUCTIVITY

Below average | Above average

The ten departments which feel the least pressure — 1 | 9

The middle eleven departments — 6 | 5

The ten departments which feel the most pressure — 9 | 1

Fig. 2-2. Relationship between unreasonable pressure men feel for high performance and department productivity.

feel and the productivity of the department. Feeling a high degree of unreasonable pressure is associated with low performance, according to unpublished data from a study conducted by Stanley E. Seashore and Basil Georgopoulos. The data in Figure 2-2 are from thirty-one geographically separated departments, all of which perform essentially the same operation. The question asked was, "On the job, do you feel any pressure for better performance over and above what you, yourself, think is reasonable?" The answers could vary from "I feel a great deal of pressure" to "I feel no pressure at all." The results shown in Figure 2-2 are in keeping with the finding that low productivity is associated with job-centered supervision.

Unreasonable pressure for better performance is also associated with a low level of confidence and trust in the supervisor. The greater the amount of unreasonable pressure the men feel from the supervisor for better performance, the less confidence and trust the men have in that supervisor.

Consistent with the inverse relationship between unreasonable pressure for better performance and the amount of work turned out is the finding that conflict between supervisors and employees is associated with low productivity. Georgopoulos (1957) found an appreciable relationship between the amount of conflict employees felt existed between them and their supervisors and the level of production of the employees. The greater the conflict was felt to be, the lower was the level of production.

Supportive Managerial Behavior and Productivity

General rather than close supervision is more often associated with a high rather than a low level of productivity. This relationship, found in a study of clerical workers, is shown in Figure 2-3 for supervisors. Similar

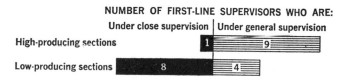

Fig. 2-3. Low-production section heads are more closely supervised than high-production heads.

results were also found for nonsupervisory employees (Katz et al., 1950). Comparable findings have been obtained in other studies. In a large public utility, for example, it was found that those supervisors who were rated as "immediately promotable" by their superiors were much more frequently seen by their subordinates as using general rather than close supervision (Mann & Dent, 1954a). The high-producing supervisors and managers make clear to their subordinates what the objectives are and what needs to be accomplished and then give them freedom to do the job. The subordinates can pace themselves and can use their own ideas and experience to do the job in the way they find works best. Supervisors in charge of low-producing units tend to spend more time with their subordinates than do the high-producing supervisors, but the time is broken into many short periods in which they give specific instructions, "Do this, do that, do it this way, etc."

The differences between these two methods can be illustrated by an example cited recently by Estes (1960), "the difference between getting a janitor to agree to keep the floors clean, as contrasted with sweeping routinely every half hour with a 20-inch broom 10 strokes to a minute."

Table 2-1 is based on data from a study of life insurance agency management. It contrasts the proportion of favorable answers about their managers made by agents in ten of the best agencies in the United States and answers obtained from ten mediocre agencies. Not all agents commented on each variable. Consequently, these data show for each variable the proportion of favorable answers of those who commented. The

TABLE 2-1 *

RELATIONSHIP OF AGENCY PERFORMANCE TO MANAGEMENT PRACTICES SHOWN BY
FAVORABLE COMMENTS OF AGENTS ON MANAGERS' BEHAVIOR
IN "SUPERIOR" AND "MEDIOCRE" AGENCIES

| Trait of manager | Favorable comments as per cent of total comments | | |
	"Superior" agencies	"Mediocre" agencies	Difference
Group A—The manager's attitude toward his agents:			
Unselfish in dealings with agents........	100%	26%	74%
Cooperative with agents..............	92	35	57
Sympathetic toward agents.............	88	32	56
Interested in agents' success...........	100	54	46
Democratic toward agents.............	81	36	45
Sincere in dealings with agents.........	91	55	36
Eager to help agents voluntarily........	70	47	23
Fair and just to all agents.............	67	48	19
Willing to help agents when requested...	96	89	7
Honest in business dealings............	92	85	7
Group B—The manager's attitude toward the agencies' task:			
Enthusiastic about the importance of the work	95%	50%	45%
Group C—The manager's professional skill:			
Capable planner and organizer.........	35%	5%	30%
Capable personal salesman............	91	67	24
Capable recruiter, trainer, office manager, etc.	38	22	16
Knows life insurance..................	93	85	8
Group D—The manager's personality:			
Friendly personality..................	93%	63%	30%
Has "good personality"...............	95	90	5
"Fine fellow" personality..............	100	100	0

* From R. Likert and J. M. Willits, *Morale and agency management*, Vol. II. Hartford, Conn.: Life Insurance Agency Management Assn., 1940.

greater the difference in favorable comments, the more the variable involved is associated with agency success. Those managers who are seen by their agents as "unselfish," "cooperative," "sympathetic," "democratic," and "interested in the agent's success" are much more apt to be in charge of superior agencies than are managers whose agents see them as being the opposite. "Honesty," "fairness," and "willingness to help when asked" apparently are also necessary since they have a positive relation to success even though the relationship is much less marked.

The managers in charge of the superior agencies were convinced that life insurance plays a valuable and significant role in the society and were able to transmit this conviction to their agents. Contagious enthusiasm about the importance of the work has a marked relationship to the success of an agency (Table 2-1) and points to the importance of the manager's attitudes toward the goals of the organization. A conviction that the mission or task has value adds to the likelihood of high levels of performance.

Organizational skills and technical knowledge or competence (e.g., planner, organizer, trainer, "skilled in selling," "knows life insurance") also have a positive relationship to agency success, but this relationship is less marked than with many of the human dimensions. In the studies conducted by the Institute for Social Research, there is evidence that technical competence contributes to supervisory success in situations where the job is not highly standardized. When methods departments have standardized the operation, the technical knowledge of the supervisor becomes less important in affecting the productivity of his unit.

As we have just seen, genuine interest and unselfish concern on the part of a superior in the success and well-being of his subordinates have a marked effect on their performance. This relationship is manifest in all the ways in which superiors and subordinates interact. For example, Figure 2-4, based on a study of railroad maintenance-of-way crews,

FOREMEN'S REACTION TO A POOR JOB
(as reported by their men)

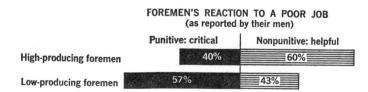

Fig. 2-4. The high-producing foreman is helpful and understanding when his men do a poor job.

shows that high-producing foremen tend either to ignore the mistakes their men make, knowing that the men have learned from the experience, or to use these situations as educational experiences by showing how to do the job correctly. The foremen of the low-producing sections, on the other hand, tend to be critical and punitive when their men make mistakes (Katz, Maccoby, Gurin, & Floor, 1951).

Further evidence of the importance of the superior's genuine concern for the success and well-being of his subordinates comes from this same study. It was found that those superiors who take time to train subordinates for better jobs achieve a higher level of performance than those supervisors who feel that this is a waste of time or that it may result in losing able subordinates through promotion. Similarly, sincere concern by a superior in the personal problems of his subordinates is associated with high performance. It is often assumed that anything which takes a worker away from his job will reduce the amount of work he turns out. This is not always the case. Time taken from the subordinate's job to discuss his personal problems with a sympathetic superior is time well spent. It results in improved performance if the interest of the boss is viewed by the subordinate as genuine and not as an intrusion on privacy. These results are typical of the findings from many studies.

Figures 2-1 to 2-4 and Table 2-1 are based on measurements taken at a particular point in time. Consequently, they show that a relationship exists, but do not tell the extent to which one or the other variable is causal. A high-producing section, for example, may make the supervisor employee-centered, whereas a low-producing section may cause him to be job-centered. Or it may be that employee-centered supervision causes a high level of productivity. Or it may partly cause high productivity and in part be caused by it. The data in the figures do not answer this question.

Other evidence, however, suggests a tentative explanation. As supervisors are shifted from job to job, they tend to carry with them their habitual attitudes toward the supervisory processes and toward their subordinates. For example, in one of the companies involved in this research program, it was found that switching managers of high- and low-production divisions produced some interesting results. The high-production managers were found to raise the productivity of the low-production divisions faster than the former high-production divisions slipped under the low-producton managers. The company, as a consequence, endeavored to raise the general level of productivity by periodically shifting the managers. It was found that each of the managers, when shifted, tended to adhere to his habitual orientation toward his subordinates, irrespective of the productivity level of his division at the time. High-producing managers maintained their employee-centered, general supervision. Low-producing managers, even when placed in charge of high-producing divisions, continued to use job-centered, close supervision. These results and data from field experiments indicate that supervisory attitudes and behavior tend to be major causal influences.

Better Productivity Measurements Needed

The relationships between the level of productivity and the managerial principles and practices, which we have examined in the preceding pages, show considerable variability from situation to situation. Although all the different research findings support the same general conclusion as to the kind of leadership which yields the best performance, there is a wide range in the relationships.

Some of the many factors responsible for this variability will be discussed in Chapters 6 and 7. One in particular, however, should be mentioned here. The research findings show that *the more accurate the measurements of productivity, the sharper and more marked are the relationships between productivity and management principles and practices.* Thus, for example, productivity ratings of different units appear to be least accurate when based only on the judgments of the superior. The data indicate that these productivity ratings by superiors tend to be inaccurate because the superior bases his judgment less on the actual productivity of each supervisor's unit and more on his perception of how the supervisor manages his unit. Superiors tend to rate favorably those supervisors whose pattern of supervision corresponds to the pattern which the superior feels should be used to obtain the best production. Thus, if a superior feels that job-centered supervision yields the best results, he will rate highest those supervisors who use this kind of supervision.

When the ratings of the different units are based on time standards and are expressed as a percentage of these standards, the ratings are usually better than when based on judgment but they still have large errors. The most accurate and comparable ratings are those obtained when the same kind of work is done with the same technology by people with equivalent aptitude. We have been fortunate to find some of these situations and to obtain data from them, situations in which there were parallel divisions or plants doing the same operation and employing the same technology.

The fact that the magnitude of the relationships increases as the accuracy of the measurements becomes greater is important, for it enables us to have greater confidence in the conclusions drawn on the preceding pages. Some of the relationships which at first glance do not appear to be as large as might be expected are smaller than the true relationship because of errors in the productivity measurements of the department or of the individual worker. These errors attenuate the observed relationship below its true value.

Some General Factors and Productivity

The extent to which some general, nonsupervisory factors were or were not associated with productivity proved surprising to us. For example, the development of favorable attitudes among employees toward a company does not appear in itself to bring high productivity. As Figure 2-5 shows, in a study of a large company, employees in high-productivity sections were found to have no more favorable attitudes toward the company than the employees in the low-producing sections (Katz et al., 1950). This study has been repeated and with similar results. In other

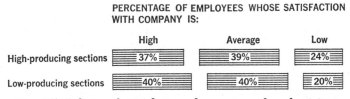

Fig. 2-5. Relation of attitude toward company and productivity.

studies where the productivity of *individuals* was related to attitude toward the company, a very low positive relationship has usually been obtained but the relationships are so slight as to be negligible (Katz & Kahn, 1952). These studies show that, within a company, those employees who have favorable attitudes toward the company are no more likely, with the present system of management, to be high producers than are those who have unfavorable attitudes.

Although these favorable attitudes do not automatically become converted into high productivity, they have value since they are associated with less absence and less turnover (Mann & Baumgartel, 1953a). Favorable attitudes toward a company are also likely to assist a company in recruiting superior employees in a tight labor market. But while employees may like the place—much as they would like a country club—the conversion of favorable attitudes into high productivity depends upon how well supervisors, managers, and the line organization perform their leadership tasks.

Recreation and similar programs can be worthwhile, but here again, the amount of good a company derives from them depends upon how well supervision and management are performing their functions. The gain from such welfare programs is not automatic, as Figure 2-6 shows (Katz et al., 1950).

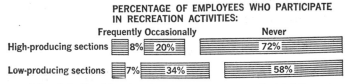

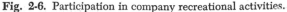

Fig. 2-6. Participation in company recreational activities.

High-producing employees do not always have more favorable attitudes than low-producing employees toward performance ratings when such ratings are linked to merit increases. A study in a large company showed that the employees in the more productive sections had no more favorable attitudes toward the rating system than did the employees in the sections which were low in productivity. In one of two large departments studied, as Figure 2-7 shows, the employees in the high-producing

PERCENTAGE OF EMPLOYEES WHO HOLD:

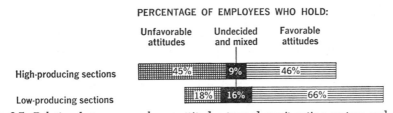

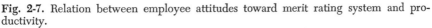

Fig. 2-7. Relation between employee attitudes toward merit rating system and productivity.

sections were actually much less favorable in their attitudes toward the merit rating system than were the employees in the low-producing sections (Katz et al., 1950). Evidently, motivational forces, in addition to the desire to be rewarded for better performance, are involved in reactions to rating systems linked to merit increases. Data from other studies indicate that one of these other motivational forces is the desire to have no conditions superimposed upon the work group which cause competition and discriminatory cleavages among members of the group. To have a friendly, supportive relationship day in and day out with one's colleagues is more important to most people than relatively minor financial rewards.

Another surprising relationship was the finding that the more productive employees engaged in highly routine jobs are *less* satisfied with the work than are less productive workers (Figure 2-8; Katz et al., 1950;

PERCENTAGE OF EMPLOYEES WHOSE
INTRINSIC JOB SATISFACTION IS:

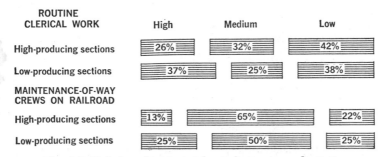

Fig. 2-8. Relation of intrinsic job satisfaction to productivity.

Katz et al., 1951). As tasks become more varied and require greater training and skill, the relationship appears to change progressively from the negative to positive (Hoppock, 1935; Katz & Kahn, 1952; Super, 1939). For professional work there is a positive relationship between job satisfaction and performance.

When jobs are excessively routine, the monotony and loss in satisfaction with the work seem to affect productivity adversely. The validity of this conclusion was demonstrated by the results when one of the companies applied the findings to its own operation. The jobs of the employees were made more varied and less specialized. This reduced the extent of functionalization, the number of separate tasks, and the number of separate sections required for the entire operation. With the reduction in the number of sections, one entire hierarchical layer of management was no longer needed. Not only were these salaries saved, but the productivity of the clerical employees increased because of greater variety in the work. Similar changes, often called job enlargement, have been made in other companies and brought about corresponding improvement (Mann & Hoffman, 1960; Walker & Guest, 1952).

Supervisory Behavior and Attitudes

Supervisory behavior which yields a high level of productivity also yields favorable attitudes on such job-related matters as supervision, working conditions, compensation, and the work itself. In a large public utility, as Figure 2-9 shows, the employees in work groups with favorable

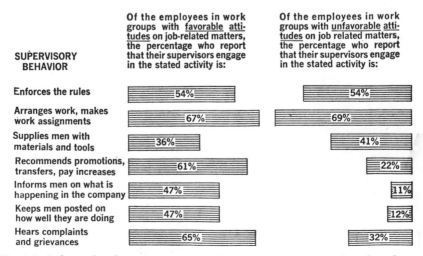

Fig. 2-9. Relationship between supervisory behavior and the attitudes of workers on job-related matters.

SUPERVISORY BEHAVIOR:

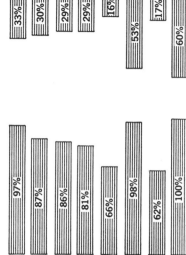

Of the employees in work groups with favorable attitudes on job-related matters, the percentage who report that their supervisors engage in the stated activity is:

Of the employees in work groups with unfavorable attitudes on job-related matters, the percentage who report that their supervisors engage in the stated activity is:

Supervisory behavior	Favorable	Unfavorable
Supervisor thinks of employees as human beings rather than as persons to get the work done	97%	33%
Supervisor will go to bat or stand up for me	87%	30%
Supervisor usually pulls for the men or for both the men and the company, rather than for himself or company only	86%	29%
Supervisor takes an interest in me and understands my problems	81%	29%
Supervisor is really part of the group; interests are the same as those of the people in the group	66%	16%
Feel free to discuss important things about job with supervisor	98%	53%
Supervisor likes to get our ideas and tries to do something about them	62%	17%
Does some good to discuss important things about job with supervisor	100%	60%

Fig. 2-10. Relationship between supervisory behavior and the attitudes of workers on job-related matters.

attitudes on job-related matters and the employees in groups with un-favorable attitudes indicate about equally often that their supervisor per-forms such functions as "enforces the rules," "arranges work and makes assignments," and "supplies men with material and tools" (Katz, 1949). But the employees in work groups with favorable job-related attitudes, much more frequently than those in groups with unfavorable attitudes, state their supervisors indicate a real interest in the well-being of their employees. These supervisors "recommend promotions, transfers, pay increases," "inform men on what is happening in the company," "keep men posted on how well they are doing," and "hear complaints and grievances."

Other data (unpublished) obtained in this study are shown in Figure 2-10. The items in this figure reveal that supervisors of work groups with favorable job-related attitudes are much more interested in their subordi-nates as persons than are the supervisors in charge of work groups with unfavorable job-related attitudes. Moreover, the men in the work groups with favorable job-related attitudes are much more likely to see their su-pervisors as "really part of the group" than are the men in groups with unfavorable attitudes (66 to 16 per cent).

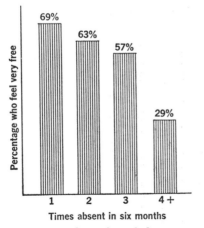

Fig. 2-11. Relationship of absence to feeling free to discuss job problems with supervisor (white-collar men).

When other criteria of performance are used, such as absence or the extent to which higher management considers the supervisor "promotable," similar patterns of findings emerge. As Figure 2-11 shows, supervisors who make the men feel free to discuss job problems with them have appreciably less ab-sence in their work group than do supervisors who display the opposite behavior (Mann & Baumgartel, 1953a).

The item "Supervisor usually pulls for the men or both the men and the com-pany, rather than for himself or the company only" (Figure 2-10) charac-teristically shows a marked relationship to job-related attitudes (Morse, 1953).

This item is also found to have a marked relationship to productivity, to promotability of the supervisor as judged by higher levels of management (Figure 12-12), and to similar perform-ance variables (Mann & Dent, 1954a).

It is significant that nonsupervisory employees, in describing what the supervisor should do, place more emphasis on "pulling for the men or both the men and the company" than do supervisors in response to the same question. Moreover, in describing what they wish their supervisors to do, higher levels of management place even less emphasis than supervisors on "pulling for the men or both the men and the company" and more emphasis on "pulling for the company." With each successively higher level of management (at least to middle management) superiors tend to place more emphasis than do the subordinates on

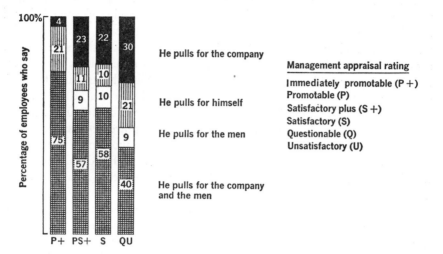

Fig. 2-12. Relationship of promotability of supervisor to employees' feelings as to supervisor's identification.

the desirability of having the supervisor concerned primarily with pressing for higher production, better quality, and lower costs (Brooks, 1955; Fleishman, Harris, & Burtt, 1955; Gordon, 1955; Jacobson, 1951). Management appears to be urging supervisors to behave in a manner likely to yield poorer results in the long run even though short-run improvement may be achieved (see also Chapter 5).

Regardless of the criterion used to evaluate performance, the results show, as we have seen, that on the average, those supervisors who achieve the best in performance differ in their supervisory behavior and attitudes in several important respects from those whose performance is the poorest. The same basic patterns and differences are obtained whether productivity, absence, turnover, employee satisfaction, or the judged promotability of the supervisor is used to appraise performance.

It does not follow from these results, however, that the various criteria used to evaluate performance display consistent interrelationships, that productivity and employee satisfaction, for example, are always positively related. In some instances they may be. In other situations there may be little or no relationship, and in still other circumstances the relationship may be negative: where one is high, the other is low. The reasons for these varying relationships among the criteria will be discussed further in Chapters 5, 6, and 13.

Freedom and Productivity

Classical management theories emphasize that the particular job and work cycle for each rank-and-file employee is to be clearly specified and that he should be closely supervised to be sure that he adheres to the task as specified. Implicit, if not explicit, in this theory is the concept that rank-and-file employees cannot be trusted to do a full day's work, that such employees will abuse any freedom given them by ceasing to work or by engaging in wasteful activity. But as we have seen, data directly opposite to this assumption are found when specific measurements of general supervision in contrast to close supervision are obtained (Figure 2-3). Employees who feel more free to set their own work pace prove to be more productive than those who lack this sense of freedom. This relationship is found in widely different kinds of working situations. For example, in a service operation, workers were asked, "How free do you feel to set your own pace?" The answers to this question ranged over five choices from "I am completely free" to "No freedom at all." When the men's answers by departments were related to departmental productivity, the results shown in Figure 2-13 were obtained. As will be ob-

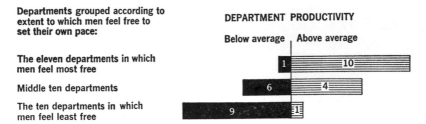

Fig. 2-13. Relationship between freedom men feel to set own work pace and department productivity.

served, in the 11 departments in which the men feel the greatest freedom, 10 are above average in productivity. In contrast, of the 10 departments lowest in the amount of freedom felt, 9 are below average in productivity.

The common assumption that nonsupervisory employees, given increased freedom, will loaf and not produce does not seem to be borne out by the evidence. Their behavior depends upon the conditions accompanying the freedom. Managers who achieve high performance in their units accompanied by a sense of freedom supervise by setting general goals and objectives and providing less specific direction than do the managers of low-producing units (Kahn, 1958; Katz & Kahn, 1951; Mann and Dent, 1954a; Mann & Dent, 1954b). They use more participation and achieve higher involvement, greater interest in the work, and more responsibility for it than do the low-producing managers.

Freedom in doing one's work is associated with higher productivity at the supervisory as well as at the nonsupervisory level. Figure 2-14 shows

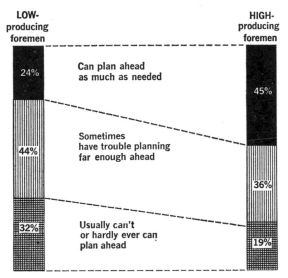

Fig. 2-14. Foreman's autonomy and productivity.

that giving supervisors more freedom to plan ahead is related to productivity.

Scientists show a similar response to freedom (Meltzer, 1956). The productivity of scientists is influenced, as might be expected, by the resources they have available as well as by their freedom. When both freedom and funds are low, there is, of course, relatively little scientific publication (Figure 2-15). As both freedom and research funds increase, the productivity increases. The increase in productivity, as available funds increase, is greatest for those scientists who are completely free to choose their problems. [These data are from a national sample of physiologists (Gerard, 1958; Meltzer, 1958).]

In another study Pelz also obtained evidence that freedom under certain conditions is associated with high performance by research scientists. Pelz (1957, pp. 33–35) describes his findings as follows:

It is possible to picture three rather distinct types of scientific leaders . . . "underdirective," "overdirective," and "participative." The underdirective leader assumes that his scientists know what they are doing. He leaves them pretty much alone, giving help only when asked. His leadership role is passive. The overdirective leader, in contrast, assumes personal direction for all the work being performed in the laboratory. His scientists are so many extra hands to execute his ideas, students who follow in the footsteps of the professor.

The participative leader, in contrast to the first type, is active rather than passive. He does not leave his subordinates alone. But he avoids dominating

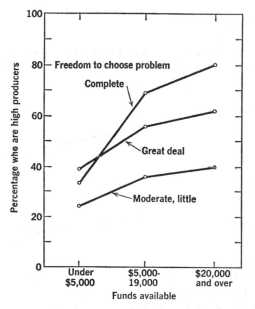

Fig. 2-15. Publications as related to research funds and freedoms. (*After D. C. Pelz, Motivation of the engineering and research specialist, General Management Series*, No. 186, *American Management Association, New York, 1957. By permission of the publishers.*)

the scene like the second type. He tries to get people to rely on their own initiative. He may use group discussion rather than the individual-to-individual conferences which the other two types of leaders use.

One of the factors which differentiates these types is the amount of freedom the leader allows his subordinates. In the government organization for medical research, we measured the dependence or independence which the scientists in different groups had with respect to their chief. A "group" was defined as two or more scientists, roughly on the same job level or grade, reporting to a common chief. Because of the large differences in supervision given to the younger as against the older scientists, we studied the data separately for "junior" and "senior" levels, the senior level consisting of individuals with five or more years of experience beyond a Ph.D.

Four patterns of relations between the scientist and the chief are shown for the junior-level scientists [Figure 2-16]. At one extreme is "dependence"; in this type of relationship, none of the scientists makes his own decisions on what projects to undertake; all report that the chief has considerable influence on their work. At the opposite extreme is "independence," in which the reverse is true; many of the subordinates make their own decisions, and report the chief as having little influence on their work. There are two intermediate categories. Under "separation," neither the subordinate nor the chief has much to say; under "mutual influence," both have a good deal to say. Along the vertical

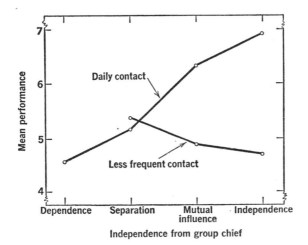

Fig. 2-16. The relationship of scientific performance to independence from group chief and contact with chief. (*After D. C. Pelz, Motivation of the engineering and research specialist, General Management Series, No. 186, American Management Association, New York, 1957. By permission of the publishers.*)

axis is the average standing on scientific performance as measured by the ranking technique described earlier.

Our first analysis with this scale was disappointing. Persons in the four categories showed little difference from each other in terms of scientific performance. But further scrutiny brought out an interesting pattern. We separated the scientists into those who have frequent contact with their chief (once a day, on the average, or more often) and those who have infrequent contact with them (only a few times a week, or less often). For those who see him weekly [lower curve of Figure 2-16], the performance curve is flat among the four categories and even declines with independence. But, for those who see their chief daily, the highest performance is shown by those who have considerable independence in pursuing their own work, but at the same time maintain close daily relations with the chief.

What goes on in these daily encounters? We aren't sure, exactly; this is one of the areas that we are pushing further in our current studies. In all probability, the chief—by frequent inquiries—shows his interest in and enthusiasm for the work, and this is something on which a young scientist thrives. The chief may offer hints as to methods; he may refer to relevant articles; he may simply express his confidence in the progress that is being made. His very presence may serve as a motivating factor, causing the young scientist to push ahead as rapidly as he can, knowing that the chief will take pleasure in the results.

We are becoming more and more convinced that this active interest in the ongoing work, combined with a hands-off policy concerning its direction, is one of the most fruitful things that a research chief can do—particularly with his younger personnel. But this is not an easy thing for a leader to do. A competent chief who keeps in touch with his subordinates' work finds it natural to impose his own ideas. Or, if he wants to give them a free hand, it is all too easy to leave them isolated. To achieve the proper balance is a feat which requires a great deal of skill in human relationships.

Similar results were obtained when we examined data on the men above this chief—the head of a larger branch or laboratory. When the immediate chief gives freedom but the branch chief maintains frequent contact, performance remains high. Apparently, the chief of the larger unit can also serve as a source of this stimulation which flows during contact between scientist and chief.

The results in Figure 2-10 add a very important condition to the conclusion that freedom in doing one's work leads to high performance; namely, the probabilities are that freedom will lead to high performance only when there is a great deal of interaction between the individual, his colleagues, and his superior. Young scientists who make their own decisions independently from their chiefs and who do not see their chiefs daily are appreciably poorer in scientific performance than those scientists who have the same independence but who see the chief at least once a day.

Interaction with one's colleagues shows a relationship to scientific performance comparable with interaction with the chief. Pelz (1957) found that those scientists who are "isolates" and who see their colleagues less often than two or three times a week are appreciably less productive than those scientists who see their colleagues more often. Evidently freedom without the stimulation and fresh orientation as well as the motivation which comes from interaction with other scientists tends, on the average, to lead to poor performance. These interactions apparently provide both intellectual stimulation and the motivation which comes from expectations of others as to our performance.

The conclusion that freedom is effective only in situations in which there is high interaction is borne out by other data. In a study of life insurance agencies (Likert & Willits, 1940), evidence was obtained indicating that agents under a commission form of compensation and left entirely to themselves with complete freedom tended to be poor salesmen. Interaction and stimulation from supervisors and peers was necessary to achieve high performance. Evidently, if freedom is to contribute to high performance, the individual must be a part of an active social system where there is frequent contact and interaction. This interaction motivates the individual. He knows and accepts what is expected of him and often takes a major role in setting the goals himself. When the individual has the required skills and the high performance goals and motivation arising from interaction between the individual, his peers, and his superior, freedom appears to result in improved performance. Further data on this appear in Chapter 9.

Pelz (1957) has also obtained evidence that frequent interaction between a scientist and the group of colleagues from whom he feels he gets the greatest stimulation and help contributes to the level of the scientist's creativity when these colleagues differ from him in previous experience and professional goals. Infrequent contact with such colleagues or frequent interaction with colleagues whose professional goals and previous experience are similar is associated with a lower level of creativity. Evidently, the stimulation of diversity yields new insights and fosters creativity.

When the analysis is based on the *one* colleague seen by the scientist as providing greatest significance to his work, a different pattern is obtained. If the scientist sees the colleague frequently and if he and the colleague have common goals, the creativity of the scientist is likely to be high. If he sees such a colleague less often, or if the colleague, although seen frequently, differs from him in goals, the scientist's creativity is lower.

These findings suggest that although diversity stimulates new ideas, the support and understanding of one's closest colleague or his chief are necessary to carry the ideas to fruition. Often new ideas are so unorthodox that other scientists may at first reject them. To persist in the face of opposition from one's peers apparently requires the motivation that comes from the encouragement of one's closest associate or chief.

Some Conclusions

In this chapter, we have briefly summarized some of the findings emerging from research on organizational performance. The data show the great importance of the quality of leadership. For every criterion, such as productivity, absence, attitudes, and promotability of the supervisor, the same basic patterns of supervision yielded the best results. Supervision and the general style of leadership throughout the organization are usually much more important in influencing results than such general factors as attitudes toward the company and interest in the job itself.

In the next chapter we shall examine the contribution to effective performance of the supervisors' skill in group methods of leadership and the influence of group loyalty and group goals upon the results achieved.

Chapter 3

GROUP PROCESSES AND ORGANIZATIONAL PERFORMANCE

Research in organizations is yielding increasing evidence that the superior's skill in supervising his subordinates *as a group* is an important variable affecting his success: the greater his skill in using group methods of supervision, the greater are the productivity and job satisfactions of his subordinates.

Nonsupervisory employes of a public utility were asked, "Do group discussions do any good?" and could check one of the alternatives listed: "Yes, the supervisor likes to get our ideas and tries to do something about them," "No, not really, it's just talk," "No, we don't get a real hearing for our own ideas." When their answers were related to their attitudes on job-related matters, a marked relationship was found (Mann & Dent, 1954a). (Job-related attitudes include those toward the work itself, supervision, working conditions, pay, promotion, etc.) For both blue-collar and white-collar employees, those with favorable job-related attitudes were much more likely to feel that group discussions did some good, that their supervisor liked to get their ideas and tried to do something about them (Figure 3-1).

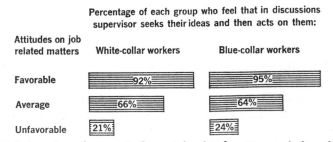

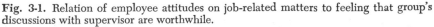

Fig. 3-1. Relation of employee attitudes on job-related matters to feeling that group's discussions with supervisor are worthwhile.

The frequency of work-group meetings, as well as the attitude and behavior of the superior toward the ideas of subordinates, affects the extent to which employees feel that the supervisor is good at handling people. These results are shown in Figure 3-2. Of those who report that the superior holds meetings frequently and that he "likes to get our ideas and tries to do something about them," 74 per cent feel that their superior is good in dealing with people. On the other hand, of those who say their boss seldom holds meetings and when he does, "it's just talk, we don't really get a hearing for our ideas," 12 per cent feel that their supervisor is

I. Of the workers in work groups where the men feel that the supervisor likes to get their ideas and tries to do something about the ideas, the percentage who feel the supervisor is good in dealing with people is:

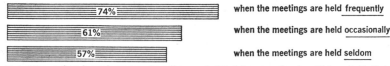

74% — when the meetings are held frequently

61% — when the meetings are held occasionally

57% — when the meetings are held seldom

II. But of the workers in work groups where the men feel that the supervisor is not interested in their ideas, that it is just talk, and that they don't really get a hearing for their ideas, the percentage who feel the supervisor is good in dealing with people is:

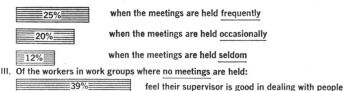

25% — when the meetings are held frequently

20% — when the meetings are held occasionally

12% — when the meetings are held seldom

III. Of the workers in work groups where no meetings are held:

39% — feel their supervisor is good in dealing with people

Fig. 3-2. The proportion of workers who feel that their supervisor is good at dealing with people as affected by the frequency of the supervisor's use of work-group meetings and his use of ideas which emerge in the meetings.

good in dealing with people. Of those who say that their supervisor *never* holds meetings, 39 per cent feel that he is good in dealing with people.

These data demonstrate that if a superior is not genuinely interested in his subordinates' ideas and prepared to act upon them, he is better off not having group meetings to discuss work problems. The data in Figure 3-2 are from nonsupervisory employees in a large public utility. Almost identical results have been obtained in other studies involving quite different kinds of work. Moreover, the same pattern is obtained at different hierarchical levels. Superiors at every level influence their subordinates' evaluation of them by the frequency with which they hold meetings and the extent to which they display interest in the ideas of their subordinates and make use of these ideas.

Typical of the relationships between the judged performance of a supervisor and the frequency with which he holds group meetings to discuss work-related problems are the data shown in Figure 3-3. Supervisors

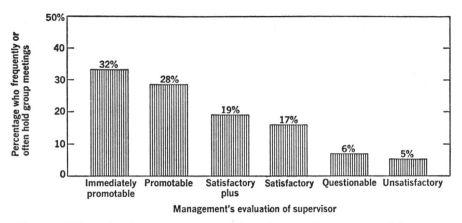

Fig. 3-3. Relationship between management's evaluation of supervisor and frequency with which he holds group meetings.

who are evaluated highly by management make much more frequent use of group meetings to deal with work-related problems than do supervisors who receive a mediocre or poor rating (Mann & Dent, 1954).

Supervisors who "consider employees as individuals rather than merely persons to get the work out" and who, when dealing with problems, "identify primarily with employees or with both company and employees rather than identifying primarily with the company" develop greater pride in their work groups than supervisors who behave otherwise (Morse, 1953). A supportive attitude on the part of the superior, as well as the constructive use of group meetings, is necessary to develop group pride and loyalty.

Another important relationship is shown in Figure 3-4. Foremen of

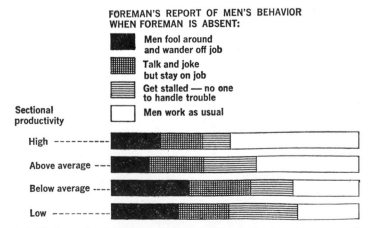

Fig. 3-4. High-productivity work groups perform well when foreman is absent.

high-production work groups report much more frequently than do the foremen of low-production groups that their work groups perform well when the foremen are absent. High-production supervisors apparently develop within the work group the expectation, the capacity, and the goals required to function effectively whether or not the foreman is present (Institute for Social Research, 1951).

Group Loyalty and Organizational Performance

In several studies involving such widely different kinds of work as clerical, manufacturing, sales, and delivery service, the loyalty of nonsupervisory employees toward their work group and pride in its ability to produce are found to have a low positive relationship with productivity (Kahn, 1956; Katz et al., 1950; Likert & Willits, 1940; Seashore, 1954). Figure 3-5, which presents results for clerical workers and railroad main-

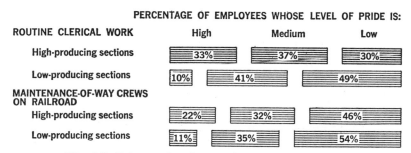

Fig. 3-5. Relation of pride in work group to productivity.

tenance-of-way crews (Katz et al., 1950; Katz et al., 1951), illustrates the magnitude of this relationship. Work groups with greater pride in their capacity to produce or with greater loyalty and attraction to the group tend to be the groups producing at a higher level. [In India, Bose (1957) found similar results.]

In the study of the clerical operations, the workers and supervisors who displayed pride in their work group made such comments as, "We have a good group," "We work together well," or "We help out each other." One supervisor said about her group, "They all have definite assign ments and they're a nice cooperative crowd. They just jump in and d things and never bother me. They have a responsibility toward the group."

High peer-group loyalty (loyalty among the workers toward one another irrespective of their attitude toward their supervisor) is not necessarily associated with high productivity. There is substantial evidence, both from operating experience and from the more precise measurement obtained in research projects, that work groups can have goals which will influence productivity and cost either favorably or adversely. The power and tendency of work groups to restrict production have been found in many studies. One of the most important conclusions, for example, emerging from the famous Western Electric study by Mayo and his associates showed that industrial organizations almost always have an "informal organization" which consists of all or most of the subordinate members of work groups. The goals of this "informal organization" often tended to restrict production, to increase absence, and in other ways to run counter to the general objectives of the organization (Mayo, 1931; Roethlisberger & Dickson, 1939; Whitehead, 1938).

These findings have been confirmed in many studies conducted since the original Western Electric project. Studies have shown that group goals which lead to unnecessary waste and at least some restriction in output are widespread in our industrial and governmental organizations. This restriction and waste occurs among white-collar workers as well as among blue-collar workers (French & Zander, 1949). It occurs among unorganized workers, as well as organized (Mathewson, 1931). It occurs at the nonsupervisory level and at higher levels. The armed services also provide evidence of this phenomenon (Stouffer et al, 1949). Several of these studies have been summarized by such writers as Argyris (1957c), Dubin (1951), Roethlisberger (1941), Viteles (1953), and W. F. Whyte (1955).

The research findings from these studies also provide extensive evidence that productivity can be increased substantially and waste correspondingly lessened when the goals of work groups shift so as to become more consistent with the objectives of the organization. This was probably the most striking result of the original Western Electric study. When the attitudes of the girls in the first Relay Assembly Room gradually shifted from opposition to the objectives of the company to greater acceptance of these objectives, a substantial increase in production occurred and important information about the total operation of which management had been unaware began to flow (Roethlisberger & Dickson, 1939.)

Work groups which have high peer-group loyalty and common goals appear to be effective in achieving their goals. If their goals are the achievement of high productivity and low waste, these are the goals they will accomplish (Lewin, 1958). If, on the other hand, the character of their supervision causes them to reject the objectives of the organization and set goals at variance with these objectives, the goals they establish can have strikingly adverse effects upon productivity (Zaleznik, Christenson, & Roethlisberger, 1958). Analyses by Seashore (1954) provide impressive evidence of the power of the goals of cohesive groups.[1] His study showed that the greater the peer-group loyalty, the greater the influence which the goals of the group have on the performance of members of the group. Thus, in work groups with high peer-group loyalty, the variations in productivity from worker to worker are less than in work groups with low peer-group loyalty. This relationship, based on data from a company manufacturing heavy machinery, is shown in Figure 3-6. Moreover,

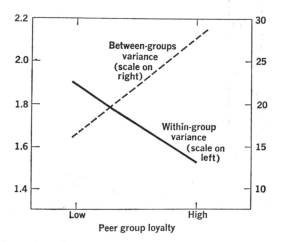

Fig. 3-6. Relationship of peer-group loyalty to variance on actual productivity.

as the data in the figure show, the greater the peer-group loyalty, the greater are the differences between the groups in the level of productivity. Increased peer-group loyalty evidently is associated with greater motivational pressure to produce at the level which the group feels is appropriate. (Further evidence on this point appears in the table on page 42.)

This conclusion is borne out by the results in Figure 3-7. In this analysis, work groups were divided into two clusters, based roughly on the extent to which the work groups accept or reject company goals. The relationship was then examined between the level of peer-group loyalty and the productivity of each of these two clusters. As was expected, the data show that among the work groups which tend to accept company goals, high peer-group loyalty is associated with higher productivity. On the

---

[1] Seashore defined his measurement of group loyalty as group cohesiveness and used questions dealing with the following dimensions: whether workers feel a part of the group, want to stay in the group, stick together, help each other, and get along together. These dimensions are essentially the same as those used in the other studies and referred to here as peer-group loyalty.

other hand, among the work groups which tend to reject company goals, high peer-group loyalty is associated with lower productivity (Seashore, 1954).

As we observed in Figure 3-6, work groups with high peer-group loyalty are, on the average, somewhat more productive. This indicates that

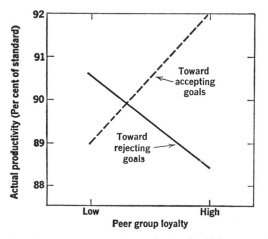

Fig. 3-7. Relationship of peer-group loyalty to productivity when motivation is toward accepting versus rejecting company goals.

among groups with high peer-group loyalty there are more groups with high performance goals than with low. Supervisors who have the skill to build high peer-group loyalty evidently tend to have the leadership ability to create relatively high performance goals. This would suggest that there should be a fairly marked relationship between peer-group loyalty and attitudes toward the supervisor. This proves to be the case. In work groups with high peer-group loyalty, attitudes toward the supervisor are appreciably more favorable than in work groups with low peer-group loyalty ($r = +0.50$ to $+0.70$). This relationship is shown in Figure 3-8 (from unpublished data collected by S. E. Seashore and Basil Georgopoulos). Peer-group loyalty also has been found to have a fairly marked relationship with a combined index of attitudes toward supervision and attitudes toward the company. Thus, Seashore (1954) found that work groups with high peer-group loyalty had more favorable attitudes toward supervision and toward the company than work groups with low peer-group loyalty. The relationship he obtained is slightly less marked than that shown in Figure 3-8.

As might be expected from the preceding results, work groups with high peer-group loyalty tend to have more favorable attitudes toward production than do groups with low peer-group loyalty. Thus, groups with greater peer loyalty differ from groups with less peer loyalty in having higher production goals. Their opinion as to what is reasonable production is higher and is more nearly the same as that of their foreman

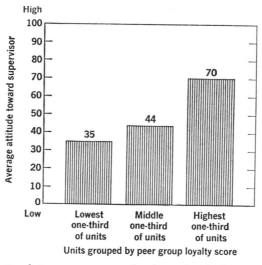

Fig. 3-8. Relation between peer-group loyalty and attitude toward supervisor.

(Katz et al., 1951; unpublished data collected by R. L. Kahn). Moreover, the groups with high peer loyalty have a more favorable attitude toward the high producer (R. Likert, 1958b; Morse, 1953).

High peer-group loyalty is associated also with less anxiety on matters related to the job (Figure 3-9). Evidently, when an individual is a mem-

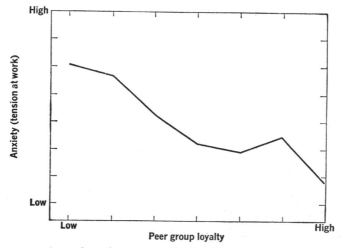

Fig. 3-9. Relationship of peer-group loyalty to feeling of tension at work.

ber of a group with high peer-group loyalty, he feels that he has greater
support and security and, consequently, feels less anxiety, even when
restricting production, than do those persons in groups with low peer-
group loyalty (Seashore, 1954).

Group Factors Contributing to Performance

Several reasons may account for the higher productivity of work groups
with high peer-group pride and loyalty. One is that workers in these
groups show more cooperation in getting the work done than do members
of groups with low peer-group loyalty. In the high-loyalty groups, there
tends to be a flow of work back and forth between the workers, depending upon the load. In groups with low peer-group loyalty, there is more
feeling that each worker is on his own, that how he gets along in his work
is his own responsibility.

The effect upon productivity when workers help one another is shown
in Figure 3-10. When foremen in a company manufacturing heavy equip-

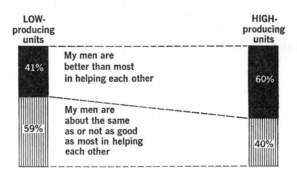

Fig. 3-10. Relationship of group solidarity to productivity (foreman's report).

ment were asked, "How does your section compare with other sections in
the way the men help each other on the job?" the answers showed a
marked relationship to the productivity of the sections. The foremen of
high-production sections reported much more often than the foremen of
low-production groups that their men helped one another (Katz & Kahn,
1952).

Workers in the high-production work groups not only have greater
peer-group loyalty and help one another more, but give this help on their
own initiative. The willingness of the groups with high peer-group loyalty
to help one another seems to come from better interpersonal relationships
developed by the foreman's effective leadership. This atmosphere seems
to be fostered by leadership which uses group methods of supervision [2]

[2] Group methods of supervision are discussed in Chapters 8, 11, and 12.

and which develops in the entire group a sense of responsibility for getting the total job done.

Low levels of peer-group loyalty are found when the foreman deals with workers individually and makes individual work assignments. One supervisor of a low-productive clerical group described his pattern of supervision as follows: "I apportion out the work to the people in my section and generally supervise the work handled. If a clerk is out, I have to make arrangements to have her work done. The work must go on even though there are absences. This involves getting work redistributed to those who are there."

In contrast to these specific individual assignments, the supervisors of groups with high productivity and high group loyalty more often create a sense of group responsibility for getting the work done. Thus, one of these supervisors reported: "We use the honor system. There are a certain number of girls and a certain amount of work comes in. We leave it up to each girl to take her share and get it done" (Katz et al., 1950).

Another factor contributing to the higher level of productivity of groups with high peer-group loyalty is their lower rate of absence from the job. As Figure 3-11 shows, persons in groups with high peer-group loyalty are much less likely to be absent from work than persons in groups with low peer-group loyalty. This chart is based on data from white-collar workers (Mann & Baumgartel, 1953a). Similar results were obtained for blue-collar workers. Apparently the warm, friendly reaction and security which one gets or fails to get from his work group profoundly affects his desire to be present in the group.

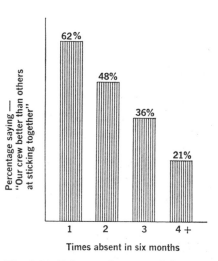

Fig. 3-11. Relation of group solidarity to absence (white-collar men).

As we have seen in the preceding pages, groups with high peer-group loyalty display a consistently different pattern from that shown by groups with a low degree of loyalty. In addition to the differences mentioned, the following characteristics have been found: The members of groups with greater peer loyalty are more likely to have:

1. Greater identification with their group and a greater feeling of belonging to it

2. More friends in the group and in the company rather than outside the company

3. Better interpersonal relations among the members of the work group

4. A more favorable attitude toward their jobs and their company

5. Higher production goals and more actual production with less sense of strain or pressure

As the importance of group influences has been recognized and as more precise measurements have been obtained, there is increasing evidence which points to the power of group influences upon the functioning of organizations. In those situations where the management has recognized the power of group motivational forces and has used the kinds of leadership required to develop and focus these motivational forces on achieving the organization's objectives, the performance of the organization tends to be appreciably above the average achieved by other methods of leadership and management. Members of groups which have common goals to which they are strongly committed, high peer-group loyalty, favorable attitudes between superiors and subordinates, and a high level of skill in interaction clearly can achieve far more than the same people acting as a mere assemblage.

These results are consistent also with the findings of other researchers. Argyris (1957c), Cartwright and Zander (1960), Viteles (1953), and W. F. Whyte (1955) have reported or summarized the results of a number of other studies consistent with the findings reported here. The recent study by Zaleznik, Christenson, and Roethlisberger (1958) adds impressive confirmation as does Marrow's report based on operating experience as well as experimental research (French et al., 1958; Marrow, 1957).

Studies in the armed services also yield evidence as to the importance of peer-group loyalty in influencing performance (Merton & Lazarsfeld, 1950; Stouffer et al., 1949). For example, an abstract [3] of Goodacre's study (1953) reports:

. . . Men in squads making high scores on the criterion problem reported a significantly greater number of men in their squads "buddying around" together on the post after duty hours, and taking the initiative to give orders to other men during the problem, although they had no authority to do so. The men in the high scoring squads also reported fewer disagreements with the way their squad leader ran the problem, more satisfaction with the present positions held by the men in their squads, more pride in their squad, and the feeling that their squad was one to which more men would like to belong.

Similar results have been obtained in research in the Army on the importance of stable anchorage in a friendly face-to-face group as a factor

[3] *Human Organization Clearinghouse Bull.*, 1954, 3(1), 29.

influencing the capacity of the soldier to function effectively under the stress of battle conditions. Those soldiers who faced the stress of combat as members of a small, well-knit group with loyalty among the members performed better and were less likely to break down than those soldiers who lacked group support. Poor performance occurred when soldiers were sent into combat as individual replacements in an outfit new to them or when their group was not well knit because of poor leadership (A. M. Rose, 1951).

Corroborative Research Findings

Research and experience in other countries also provide corroborative evidence. For example, the studies being conducted by the Tavistock Institute in England on the human factors affecting the productivity of coal miners provide evidence as to the importance of the work group. With mechanization of the English coal mines came the "longwall" method of mining. This method organizes the work in such a way that the traditional face-to-face working teams of miners is completely disrupted. Instead of the usual small team of two to four men doing all the operations involved in extracting the coal, the longwall method used about 40 workmen, spread over three shifts. The work is broken down into a standard series of component operations that follow each other in rigid succession. The entire cycle is spread over three work shifts of 7½ hours each, so that a total cycle is completed only once every 24 hours. Two of the shifts, "cutting" and "ripping," generally use 10 men each, and the third shift, "filling," uses 20 men. Reorganizing the work and giving up the small face-to-face group led to serious problems of absenteeism, turnover, and sickness among miners, including psychosomatic disorders. Quite spontaneously, sporadic and rather guarded innovations in work organization modifying the "longwall" method have occurred during the past several years. Though differing from each other, these innovations have involved restoration of the face-to-face work group with responsible autonomy, greater work-group cohesiveness, and greater job satisfaction. Trist and Bamforth (1951, p. 38), in an analysis of the disappointing results obtained in England from increased mechanization of the mines, state the following conclusion with regard to the longwall method of coal getting:

The immediate problems are to develop formal small-group organization on the filling shift and to work out an acceptable solution to the authority questions in the cutting team. But it is difficult to see how these problems can be solved effectively without restoring responsible autonomy to primary groups throughout the system and ensuring that each of these groups has a satisfying sub-whole as its work task, and some scope of flexibility in work pace.

The substantially better results obtained from the shortwall method of mining substantiates Trist and Bamforth's conclusion. As Wilson (1951) points out, the improved productivity and increased worker satisfaction come from organizing the work so that it is conducted by stable, well-knit teams.

Revans (1957) has demonstrated marked relationships between the size of an enterprise and such variables as absence, accidents, and strikes. He found that both the total size of the enterprise and the size of the work groups within the organization are related to the above variables. He has found that for coal mining, quarries, hospitals, and telephone exchanges, the larger the unit, the less favorable are the results so far as absence, sickness, accidents, and strikes are concerned. Two reports dealing with the adverse effects of increased size have been published by the Acton Society Trust (1953; 1957). Other material dealing with the relation of size to the functioning of an organization appears in *Large-scale Organisation* (Milward, 1950).

Group forces are important not only in influencing the behavior of individual work groups with regard to productivity, waste, absence, and the like, they also affect the behavior of entire organizations. Georgopoulos (1957) has demonstrated that group forces in the form of group standards or norms are related to the performance of industrial organizations. Moreover, he presents evidence to show that "for the study of organizational effectiveness in large-scale organizations, the group, and not the individual performer, is the proper unit of research and analysis" (Georgopoulos, 1957, p. 150). He found that the variability between work groups was almost six times as much as the variability between workers within groups. Meltzer (1956) similarly found that for many variables related to the performance of any organization, analyses reflecting the situation for groups yield clearer and more significant differences than analyses dealing only with the measurements for individuals.

The preceding discussion demonstrates that there is a growing body of evidence indicating that significantly better results are obtained when an organization uses its manpower as members of well-knit, effectively functioning work groups with high performance goals than when its members are supervised on an individual man-to-man basis. As the data in this chapter also indicate, this pattern of organizational functioning tends, at present, to be the exception rather than the rule. The use of the coordinated efforts of well-integrated work groups to achieve organizational objectives apparently requires greater leadership skills and a different philosophy of management than that generally prevailing today. The highest-producing managers, much more than other managers, sense the power of group processes and are making greater use of them.

An Experimental Study

In addition to surveys comparing the behavior of high- and low-producing managers, the Institute for Social Research has conducted experiments on leadership, management, and organizational effectiveness. The experiments in industrial plants bear out the relationships between productivity and such variables as leadership principles and skills and group loyalty which have been examined in this chapter. For example, Coch and French conducted an experiment involving variations in group-participation procedure. They describe their results as follows (Coch & French, 1948, pp. 520–522):

The first variation involved participation through representation of the workers in designing the changes to be made in the jobs. The second variation consisted of total participation by all members of the group in designing the changes. Two experimental groups received this total participation treatment. A fourth (control) group was used as a control and treated in the customary manner.

The control group went through the usual factory routine when they were changed. The production department modified the job, and a new piece rate was set. A group meeting was then held in which the control group was told that the change was necessary because of competitive conditions, and that a new piece rate had been set. The new piece rate was thoroughly explained by the time study man, questions were answered, and the meeting dismissed.

Experimental group 1 was changed in a different manner. Before any changes took place, a group meeting was held with all the operators to be changed. The need for the change was presented as dramatically as possible, showing two identical garments produced in the factory; one was produced in 1946 and had sold for 100 per cent more than its fellow in 1947. The group was asked to identify the cheaper one and could not do it. This demonstration effectively shared with the group the entire problem of the necessity of cost reduction. A general agreement was reached that a savings could be effected by removing the "frills" and "fancy" work from the garment without affecting the folders' opportunity to achieve a high efficiency rating. Management then presented a plan to set the new job and piece rate:

1. Make a check study of the job as it was being done.
2. Eliminate all unnecessary work.
3. Train several operators in the correct methods.
4. Set the piece rate by time studies on these specially trained operators.
5. Explain the new job and rate to all the operators.
6. Train all operators in the new method so they can reach a high rate of production within a short time.

The group approved this plan (though no formal group decision was reached), and chose the operators to be specially trained. A sub-meeting with the "special" operators was held immediately following the meeting with the entire group. They displayed a cooperative and interested attitude and immediately presented many good suggestions. This attitude carried over into the working out of the details of the new job; and when the new job and piece rates were set, the "special" operators referred to the results as "our job," "our rate," etc. The new job and piece rates were presented at a second group meeting to all the operators involved. The "special" operators served to train the other operators on the new job.

Experimental groups 2 and 3 went through much the same kind of change meetings. The groups were smaller than experimental group 1, and a more intimate atmosphere was established. The need for a change was once again made dramatically clear; the same general plan was presented by management. However, since the groups were small, all operators were chosen as "special" operators; that is, all operators were to participate directly in the designing of the new jobs, and all operators would be studied by the time study men. It is interesting to note that in the meetings with these two groups, suggestions were immediately made in such quantity that the stenographer had great difficulty in recording them. The group approved of the plans, but again no formal group decision was reached.

The results are shown in Figure 3-12 and demonstrate the effectiveness of participation on production.

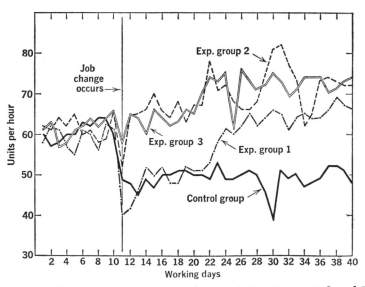

Fig. 3-12. The effect of participation on production. (*After Lester Coch and J. R. P. French, Jr., Overcoming resistance to change, Human Relations,* 1948, **1**(4), 512–532. *By permission of the publishers.*)

As a further test of these results, the group used initially as the control group was exposed to the full participative approach when it underwent another change several months after the original experiment. When treated like experimental groups 2 and 3, this group showed a productivity record identical with that shown by experimental groups 2 and 3. Figure 3-13 shows these curves.

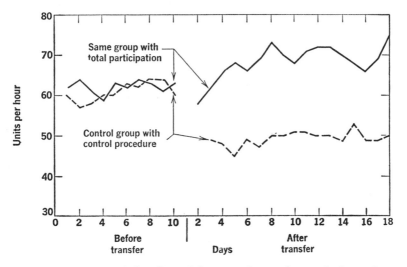

Fig. 3-13. A comparison of the effect of the control procedure with the total participation procedure on the same group. (*After Lester Coch and J. R. P. French, Jr., Overcoming resistance to change, Human Relations, 1948, 1(4), 512-532. By permission of the publishers.*)

In each part of the experiment data were obtained which show the force of group standards in determining the level of production. The following is also taken from Coch & French (1948, pp. 529-530):

Probably the most important force affecting the recovery under the control procedure was a group standard, set by the group, restricting the level of production to 50 units per hour. Evidently this explicit agreement to restrict production is related to the group's rejection of the change and of the new job as arbitrary and unreasonable. Perhaps they had faint hopes of demonstrating that standard production could not be attained and thereby obtain a more favorable piece rate. In any case there was a definite group phenomenon which affected all the members of the group. . . .

An analysis was made for all groups of the individual differences within the group in levels of production. In Experiment I the 40 days before change were compared with the 30 days after change; in Experiment II the 10 days before change were compared to the 17 days after change. As a measure of variability, the standard deviation was calculated each day for each group. The average daily standard deviations before and after change were as follows:

GROUP VARIABILITY

	Before change	After change
Experiment I:		
Control group	9.8	1.9
Experimental 1	9.7	3.8
Experimental 2	10.3	2.7
Experimental 3	9.9	2.4
Experiment II:		
Control group	12.7	2.9

There is indeed a marked decrease in individual differences within the control group after their first transfer. In fact the restriction of production resulted in lower variability than in any other group. Thus, we may conclude that the group standard at 50 units per hour set up strong, group-induced forces. . . .

The table of variability also shows that the experimental treatments markedly reduced variability in the other four groups after transfer.

Coch and French found, in their different groups, changes in employee attitudes and reactions to supervision and management corresponding with the changes which occurred in productivity. For the control group they found (Coch & French, 1948, pp. 522–523):

. . . Resistance developed almost immediately after the change occurred. Marked expressions of aggression against management occurred, such as conflict with the methods engineer, expressions of hostility against the supervisor, deliberate restriction of production, and lack of cooperation with the supervisor. There were 17 per cent quits in the first 40 days. Grievances were filed about the piece rate, but when the rate was checked, it was found to be a little "loose."

For experimental group 1 they reported:

. . . During the 14 days, the attitude was cooperative and permissive. They worked well with the methods engineer, the training staff, and the supervisor. . . . There was one act of aggression against the supervisor recorded in the first 40 days.

For experimental groups 2 and 3 they found:

. . . They worked well with their supervisors and no indications of aggression were observed from these groups. There were no quits in either of these groups in the first 40 days.

These results [4] of Coch and French confirm the power of group goals.

[4] For an excellent theoretical analysis of group forces and how they function see Lewin (1951).

As they show, group goals can push production down or up, depending upon the level at which the group sets them. Additional evidence of the influence of the group is shown by the small deviations by members of the group from the goals set by the group. In an experimental study with small groups, Emmy Pepitone (1952) obtained results consistent with the Coch and French findings. She found that both "the quantity and quality of productivity correspond to the degree of responsibility felt to the group."

Results consistent with the experiment of Coch and French have been obtained by the Institute for Social Research in other industrial situations. Thus, Mann (1957) has demonstrated that increased use of group meetings to analyze and act on data dealing with attitudes, perceptions, communication, and motivation improved the job-related attitudes of non-supervisory employees in a number of accounting departments. Mann has also shown that such group meetings can achieve substantial increases in productivity (unpublished). A company with several thousand employees on measured day work achieved a 12 per cent increase in productivity in one year's time. Costs have been reduced in another company (McAnly, 1956; I. A. Rose, 1956).

Experiments by others have also yielded results confirming the general pattern emerging from the research by the Institute. For example, in his experiments and research in textile mills in India, Rice (1958) has obtained substantial evidence of the better results obtained when the work is organized by teams of workers and the social organization of the mill is built on a work-group basis. Bose (1957) reports that results comparable with those obtained by Coch and French were found in an experiment of comparable design.

Chapter 4

COMMUNICATION, INFLUENCE, AND ORGANIZATIONAL PERFORMANCE

Communication is essential to the functioning of an organization. It is viewed widely as one of the most important processes of management. Nevertheless, the communication systems of most companies have serious flaws.

Communication is a complex process involving many dimensions (Hovland, Janis, & Kelley, 1953; Hovland et al., 1957; Hovland & Janis, 1959; Hovland & Rosenberg, 1960). One is the transmission of material from the sender to the target audience. Another is its reception and comprehension. A third is its acceptance or rejection. Frequently the term "communication" is used as though all material which is transmitted is understood and accepted. For example, information placed before employees is assumed to have been "communicated" to them, that is, understood and accepted by them. This may or may not be the case.

Another complicating factor in the process of communication is the diverse nature of the material to be transmitted. There is:

· Cognitive material, such as:
· · information or facts as to the current situation, problems, progress toward goals, etc.
· · ideas, suggestions, experiences
· · knowledge with regard to objectives, policies, and actions
· Motivational and emotional material, such as:
· · emotional climate or atmosphere
· · attitudes and reactions
· · loyalties and hostilities
· · feelings of support, appreciation, or rejection
· · goals and objectives

In view of the complex processes and the varied character of the material, it is not surprising that the communication process often breaks down. In addition, unfavorable attitudes on the part of members of the

44

organization create serious blocks to the transmission and acceptance of information. Studies show, for example, that if pressure from their supervisors for better performance seems unreasonable to the men, it has an adverse effect upon communication, particularly upward communication. The greater the amount of "unreasonable" pressure felt by the men, the greater the difficulty they feel in trying to communicate ideas for improving operations to higher levels of management ($r = 0.73$). Similarly, "unreasonable" pressure for better performance from the supervisor is associated with great reluctance by the men to take complaints or grievances to their superiors (Figure 4-1).

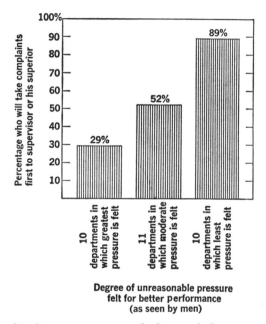

Fig. 4-1. Relationship between extent to which men feel unreasonable pressure for better performance and the extent to which they will take complaints and grievances first to their supervisor or his superior.

Hostility, fear, distrust, and similar attitudes tend not only to reduce the flow and acceptance of relevant information, but also to evoke motives to distort communications both upward and downward. Distrust and lack of confidence lead members of an organization at all levels in the hierarchy to "play it close to the chest," to share a minimum of information with others, and to look with suspicion at the information passed on by others. Distrust leads to communication failures. Reciprocal confidence and trust on the part of the members of an organization seems necessary if the communication process is to function effectively. For example, in a study of communication between scientists in a large organization, Mellinger (1956) found that lack of trust was an important factor keeping subordinates from communicating with their superiors.

Need for Upward as Well as Downward Communication

The classical theories of management place primary emphasis on control, chain of command, and the downward flow of orders and influence. There is no corresponding emphasis on adequate and accurate upward communication. Even supervisory training programs focus on downward communication and influence as part of the process of supervising subordinates. Few give attention to helping the supervisor learn how to influence and communicate effectively with his own superior.

The focus of attention on downward communication is illustrated by the problems considered to be the more important by middle and top management. In meetings with management personnel, we have asked them to think of the most important and difficult communication problem they faced during the previous six months. Then we have said, "Did this problem deal with downward, upward, or sideward communication?" About 4 persons out of every 5 reported that the communication problems of greatest concern to them dealt with downward communication. Only about 1 in 10 indicated that their major problem dealt with upward communication. The balance reported that their problems concerned sideward communication, that is, communication with their peers or involved more than one of these dimensions.

Further evidence on the lack of concern with upward communication comes from a report in the May, 1955, *Industrial Bulletin* of the New York State Department of Labor. The results of a survey covering fifty-three "representative industrial" firms showed that while all the companies surveyed displayed interest in getting management's viewpoints across to workers, nearly all seemed less concerned to discover the workers' views. Most managements in the study relied only on the familiar "suggestion box" to get employee opinion. Other companies relied on the "open-door policy" for receiving communications from workers.

The policy that the boss always has his door open sounds fine, but unless a subordinate is about to resign, he is not likely to go through that open door to suggest that his superior is handling the work in ways that are inefficient, is creating unnecessary difficulties for his subordinates, or is unfair or unreasonable. Moreover, the worse the situation, the more difficult it is for a subordinate to communicate these facts to his chief. Most subordinates have learned to study their superior and tell him only what will please him. This "yessing" the boss may misinform him, but it keeps the subordinate out of hot water and may result in his being rewarded. Even on "important things about the job," subordinates feel much less free to discuss these matters with their boss than the boss realizes. Data dealing with this are shown in Table 4-1.

TABLE 4-1

EXTENT TO WHICH SUBORDINATES FEEL FREE
TO DISCUSS IMPORTANT THINGS ABOUT THE JOB WITH SUPERIORS
AS SEEN BY SUPERIORS AND SUBORDINATES

	Top staff says about foremen	Foremen say about themselves	Foremen say about the men	Men say about themselves
Feel very free to discuss important things about the job with my superior	90%	67%	85%	51%
Feel fairly free....................	10	23	15	29
Not very free	..	10	..	14
Not at all free.....................	..	..	..	6

Upward communication, therefore, is at least as inadequate as downward communication and probably is less accurate because of the selective filtering of information which subordinates feed to their superiors. In view of the influence of upward communication on management's awareness of problems existing in the organization and on the information or misinformation used in making decisions, the inadequacy in upward communication is probably more serious than the deficiencies in downward communication.

One comparison of the accuracy of upward and downward communication is shown in Figure 4-2 (Institute for Social Research, 1951). These data are from a large manufacturing company where time standards have been set for a substantial proportion of the jobs. The method of payment, however, does not involve piece rates. A day rate is used. Actual productivity is expressed as a percentage of each time standard. Expected production is, of course, 100 per cent of each time standard. In Figure 4-2, each vertical line shows the answers from the foremen whose work groups produce the percentage of standard shown at the bottom of the line. Similarly, these vertical lines show the answers of the workers whose actual production is shown at the bottom of the line. The horizontal lines show the answers to the questions for the different groups as designated. Thus, the top line at the left side of the chart shows what the foremen feel to be the production level that management expects. Low-producing foremen (67 per cent of standard and below) feel management expects about 97 per cent. Foremen whose work groups produce at 82 per cent or above feel that management expects about 100 per cent of standard.

The next line from the top on the left, the line of dashes, shows what the men believe the foremen feel is a reasonable production figure. The low-producing men believe that the foremen expect about 95 per cent, while the high producers believe foremen expect about 100 per cent.

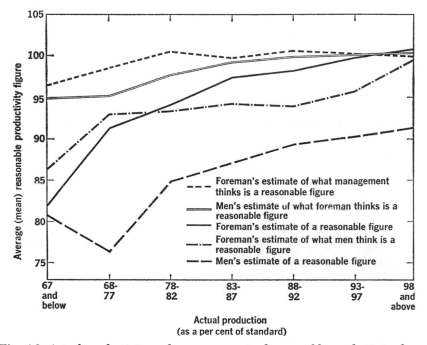

Fig. 4-2. Actual productivity and average perceived reasonable productivity figure.

The solid line shows what the foremen, themselves, believe is a reasonable production figure. It varies from 82 per cent for foremen whose workers produce "67 per cent and below" to 100 per cent for the high-producing foremen. The line with a long dash and one dot shows what the foremen believe the men feel is a reasonable production figure. The bottom line shows what the men, themselves, believe is reasonable production.

Even a cursory examination of the results in Figure 4-2 shows that there is a serious discrepancy between what the foremen think is reasonable production and how the men feel about it. Even more serious, the foremen do not realize how different these views are. Moreover, the men whose production falls below 93 per cent believe that the differences between their views and their foreman's views as to what is reasonable are greater than actually is the case. They magnify the conflict.

All this occurs in a situation involving several thousand men who have close personal contact every day, often with discussion of performance in relation to standards. Every morning each foreman receives a report of what per cent of standard his work group did the previous day and what per cent of standard each man individually did the preceding day. The foreman has the responsibility of reporting to each man his productivity for the previous day and discussing with those men whose productivity was less than 100 per cent how to get production up to standard.

In spite of this close personal contact and frequent discussion of the topic, both men and supervisors are seriously misinformed, on the average, as to the views held by the others. Moreover, the supervisors tend to have a larger error than do the men in their estimates of the views held by the other.

Another conclusion supported by the data in Figure 4-2 is that the higher the productivity, the greater the accuracy of perceptions. (Good communication and high performance go together.) Evidence bearing on the same point is presented in Figure 4-3. These data from another study show that the ease of transmitting ideas upward is associated with departmental effectiveness. Supervisors in the less effective departments report much greater difficulty in getting ideas to higher management than do supervisors in the more effective departments. The measures of departmental effectiveness are based on ratings by higher levels of management and correlate highly with the level of departmental productivity.

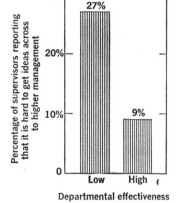

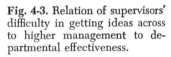

Fig. 4-3. Relation of supervisors' difficulty in getting ideas across to higher management to departmental effectiveness.

Evidence of the inaccuracy of other kinds of upward communication is shown in Table 4-2. These results were obtained by asking workers, "Different people want different things out of their jobs. What are the things you yourself feel are *most important* in a job?" The data in Table 4-2 show the frequency of choice when each worker's first three preferences from the ten items are used. The foremen were asked to indicate how they thought their subordinates felt and to answer the question as to what they, themselves, felt were the most important things in a job. General foremen similarly were asked to indicate how their foremen felt about these items and how they, themselves, felt.

The items in Table 4-2 are grouped in terms of economic and human-satisfaction variables, and not in the order in which they were asked. As will be observed, superiors consistently overestimate the importance their subordinates attach to economic factors and underestimate the importance to them of the human variables. Thus, with regard to "high

TABLE 4-2

WHAT SUBORDINATES WANT IN A JOB COMPARED WITH THEIR SUPERIORS' ESTIMATES *

	As men	As foremen		As general foremen	
	Rated the variables for themselves	Estimated men would rate the variables	Rated the variables for themselves	Estimated foremen would rate the variables	Rated the variables for themselves
Economic variables:					
Steady work and steady wages............	61%	79%	62%	86%	52%
High wages	28	61	17	58	11
Pensions and other old-age-security benefits	13	17	12	29	15
Not having to work too hard.............	13	30	4	25	2
Human-satisfaction variables:					
Getting along well with the people I work with........................	36%	17%	39%	22%	43%
Getting along well with my supervisor.....	28	14	28	15	24
Good chance to turn out good-quality work	16	11	18	13	27
Good chance to do interesting work.......	22	12	38	14	43
Other variables:					
Good chance for promotion..............	25%	23%	42%	24%	47%
Good physical working conditions.........	21	19	18	4	11
Total	†	†	†	†	†
Number of cases................	2,499	196	196	45	45

* From Robert L. Kahn, *Human relations on the shop floor.* In E. M. Hugh-Jones (Ed.), *Human relations and modern management.* Amsterdam: North-Holland Publishing Co., 1958.

† Percentages total over 100 because they include three rankings for each person.

wages," 61 per cent of the foremen estimate that their subordinates will rate it of great importance but only 28 per cent of the men actually do so. Similarly, 58 per cent of the general foremen expect their foremen to attach great importance to this item but only 17 per cent of the foremen conform to these expectations.

It is likely that, for a variety of reasons, these data (Table 4-2) understate the importance of economic motivation. (Economic motives clearly are important forces in working situations. They may not, however, always be used in the most effective manner. For example, paying money for overtime work is inefficient when it encourages low rather than high productivity during regular working hours.) The important point for this discussion of the data in Table 4-2, however, is the extent to which the foreman and the general foreman are in error in estimating how their subordinates see a situation.

In contrast to their estimates on the economic items, the superiors consistently underestimate the importance to their subordinates of those dimensions of the job which deal with such human factors as "getting along well with the people I work with," "getting along well with my supervisor," and "good chance to turn out good-quality work." Among workers, for example, 36 per cent rated "getting along well with the people I work with" of great importance, but only 17 per cent of the foremen estimated that their subordinates would consider this item one of the three most important. The general foremen displayed similar errors in estimating the importance of these items to foremen.

Further appreciation of the magnitude of the error in the superiors' estimates is obtained from another kind of analysis. If the items are ranked in the order of importance as viewed by the men (column 1 in Table 4-2) and if the same is done for the foremen's rating of the items *for themselves* (column 3 in Table 4-2), the correspondence in the rankings is fairly marked ($r = +0.76$). But if the items as ranked by the men's responses are compared with the items as ranked by the foremen's estimates of the men's responses, there is virtually no relationship between the rankings. The general foremen and the foremen are seriously misinformed as to the motivations of their subordinates. They would both be far more accurate in their estimates if they assumed that the values and goals of their subordinates were substantially the same as their own.

Other evidence reflecting the inaccuracy and inadequacy of upward communication is presented in Figure 4-4 (Hamann, 1956). Superiors seriously underestimate the extent to which their subordinates feel that their boss understands their problems. It is striking that foremen and general foremen feel that they understand the problems of their subordinates well, but each level feels that its own boss does not understand the problems of his subordinates.

In Tables 4-3 and 4-4 further data are presented showing the marked discrepancies between the perceptions held by superiors and subordinates as to how well the communication processes are being carried out.

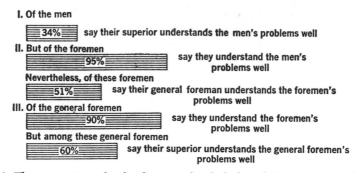

I. Of the men

34% say their superior understands the men's problems well

II. But of the foremen

95% say they understand the men's problems well

Nevertheless, of these foremen

51% say their general foreman understands the foremen's problems well

III. Of the general foremen

90% say they understand the foremen's problems well

But among these general foremen

60% say their superior understands the general foremen's problems well

Fig. 4-4. The proportion of subordinates who feel that their superior understands their problems well compared with the proportion of superiors who feel that they understand the problems of their subordinates well.

TABLE 4-3 *

EXTENT TO WHICH SUPERIORS AND SUBORDINATES AGREE
AS TO WHETHER SUPERIORS TELL SUBORDINATES IN ADVANCE ABOUT CHANGES

	Top staff says as to own behavior	Foremen say about top staff's behavior	Foremen say as to own behavior	Men say about foremen's behavior
Always tell subordinates in advance about changes which will affect them or their work	70% ⎫	27% ⎫	40% ⎫	22% ⎫
Nearly always tell subordinates	30 ⎭ 100%	36 ⎭ 63%	52 ⎭ 92%	25 ⎭ 47%
More often than not tell..	..	18	2	13
Occasionally tell	..	15	5	28
Seldom tell	..	4	1	12

* Data from unpublished studies by Floyd C. Mann of power plants in a public utility.

Superior-Subordinate Communication

A number of recent studies are providing disturbing evidence that communication between managers and supervisors is seriously deficient on such important matters as what a subordinate understands his job to be. The data show that superiors fail to make clear to subordinates precisely

TABLE 4-4 *

EXTENT TO WHICH SUPERIORS AND SUBORDINATES AGREE
AS TO WHETHER SUPERIORS USE SUBORDINATES' IDEAS AND OPINIONS
IN THE SOLUTION OF JOB PROBLEMS

	Top staff says as to own behavior	Foremen say about top staff's behavior	Foremen say as to own behavior	Men say about foremen's behavior
Always or almost always get subordinates' ideas	70%	52%	73%	16%
Often get subordinates' ideas....	25	17	23	23
Sometimes or seldom get subordinates' ideas	5	31	4	61

* Data from unpublished studies by Floyd C. Mann of power plants in a public utility.

what the job is and what is expected of them. Moreover, subordinates do not tell the superior about the obstacles and problems they encounter in doing the job. The discrepancies are as great here as are the other differences in perceptions between superiors and subordinates which we have already examined (Browne & Neitzel, 1952; Evans, 1957).

The results obtained in a study conducted by Maier and his associates (Maier, Hooven, Hoffman, & Read) illustrate the character and magnitude of these discrepancies. Superior-subordinate pairs were interviewed to discover how each member of the pair saw the job of the subordinate. The superiors were chosen from five companies and held positions at the high-middle-management level. Each superior chose one subordinate to make his superior-subordinate pair. The results show large gaps in understanding. The superiors thought the ability to plan or organize and to solve problems were important parts of the subordinate's job. The subordinates did not think so. Their responsibility, they felt, was to execute the decisions and plans of their superiors.

There was almost total lack of understanding between subordinates and superiors concerning "job obstacles" encountered by subordinates. The research team concluded that subordinates fail to tell superiors about their problems, or superiors fail to listen, or subordinates are wrong in their estimates of what the obstacles are (Foundation for Research on Human Behavior, 1960a).

Contributing further to these breakdowns in communications is the unwillingness of subordinates to bring their problems to the man who has the major control over their destiny in the organization. His influence upon their promotions and their future in the company is so great that they cannot afford to let him see their weaknesses. They will share their successes with the boss, but not their failures. A study was made of the effects of separating evaluation from training and coaching by assigning different persons to each role.

A significant increase occurred in the frequency and extent to which subordinates took problems and failures to a superior who served as a trainer but who made no evaluations of them and their performance (Ross, 1957).

In the communication process, action speaks louder than words. Supervisors in a large utility were asked, "On what basis do you judge your standing with your immediate superior?" Figure 4-5 shows the answers.

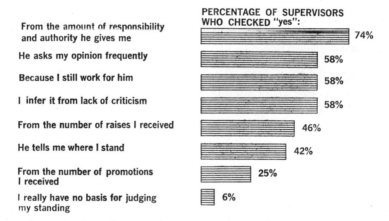

Fig. 4-5. "On what basis do you judge your standing with your immediate superior?"

The supervisors determine how they stand with the boss, not by what he tells them, but by what he does: the extent to which he gives them responsibility and authority, asks their opinions, and gets raises and promotions for them (Mann & Dent, 1954a).

As we have seen, the high-producing managers have more favorable attitudes and better communication in their units than do the low-producing managers. They also use group methods of supervision more often than do the low-producing managers (Chapter 3). These results would suggest that the more favorable the peer-group loyalty in a work group, the better the communication should be. This hypothesis was tested by using the data shown in Figure 4-2. The work groups in that analysis were put into four separate clusters. Those with most favorable peer-group loyalty were put in the first, those with next to the most favorable attitudes in the next, and so on to the work groups with the least favorable attitudes, which were put in the last cluster. The data, when analyzed in this manner, showed that the more favorable the peer-group loyalty, the more accurate the communication and the less the errors of perception. The foremen and men in the cluster with the most favorable peer-group loyalty were more accurate in their estimates of what each thought the other felt to be a reasonable productivity goal. The foremen and men in the cluster with the poorest work-group loyalty were least accurate in estimating what the other felt to be a reasonable figure.

This analysis confirmed the impression that one of the ways the high-producing managers are achieving better communication and more accurate perceptions is by building greater peer-group loyalty. The results also show that the greater the peer-group loyalty, the greater is the agreement between the foremen and the men as to what constitutes a reasonable figure or standard.

The finding that communication is better in work groups with high group loyalty is supported also by the research on small groups. These data show that the more cohesive the group, the greater is the motivation to communicate fully (Cartwright & Zander, 1960).

Influence and Performance

The ability to exercise influence in an organization depends in part upon the effectiveness of its communication processes. It is not surprising, consequently, to find that influence shows a relationship to performance comparable with that shown by communication. These results are given in Figure 4-6.

The data in this chart are from a company which operates nationally and performs a service operation. These data are from 31 geographically separated departments, varying in size from about 15 to 50 employees, which perform essentially the same operations and for which extensive and excellent productivity and cost figures are available continuously. In Figure 4-6, the 10 high-producing departments are the top one-third of the 31 departments in performance; the 10 low-producing are the bottom one-third of these departments. The data were obtained by asking the men, "In general, how much say or influence do you feel each of the following groups has on what goes on in your department?" The choices were, "Little or no influence," "Some," "Quite a bit," "A great deal of influence," "A very great deal of influence," and the question was asked with regard to: "Higher management of company," "The top management in your plant (city)," "Your department manager," "The men in your department."

As the solid lines in Figure 4-6 show, the men in the high-producing departments, in contrast with the men in the low, feel that more influence is exercised at every hierarchical level. They perceive the amount of influence exerted by each level in the organization, including theirs, to be greater than do men in the low-producing departments.

Data obtained from the department managers yield a pattern of relationships similar to that shown in Figure 4-6. The differences, however, are slightly less. Moreover, the managers see themselves as having more influence than any other hierarchical level as to what goes on in the department.

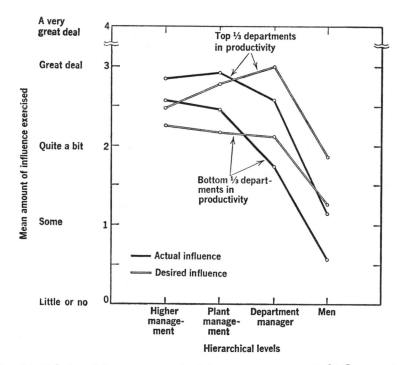

Fig. 4-6. Relation of department productivity to average amount of influence actually exercised by various hierarchical levels and to average amount of desired influence (as seen by nonsupervisory employees).

As might be expected from results previously examined, the greater the amount of unreasonable pressure the men feel from their superiors for better performance, the less influence they see their department manager exercising as to what "goes on in the department" (Figure 4-7). Unreasonable pressure, from the point of view of the men, evidently decreases, rather than increases, the amount of influence exerted by the department head.

The results in Figure 4-6, like so much of the data in this and previous chapters, raise some serious questions about widely held managerial concepts. The prevailing view is that authority and responsibility are lodged in the president of the organization and that he delegates appropriate amounts of responsibility and authority to his subordinates and holds them accountable for results. His subordinates, in turn, delegate appropriate amounts of responsibility and authority to their subordinates, and so on down the line organization. According to this view, managers at the same level performing the same function should receive the same amount of responsibility and authority. Another widely held view is that there is a

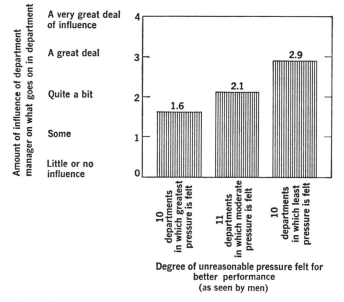

Fig. 4-7. Relationship between extent to which men feel unreasonable pressure for better performance and the amount of influence which they see their manager as being able to exert over operations in their department.

fixed quantity of influence in a company or plant. Consequently, if subordinates are permitted to exercise more influence as to what goes on in the organization, the superiors have correspondingly less. The pie, so to speak, is thought to be just so big, and if some people are given more, others must have less.

Although these views hold elements of truth, they are not by any means the whole story. The actual amount of authority exercised by a manager may be quite different from the amount delegated to him. On the average, the managers of the low-producing departments should have the same amount of authority delegated to them as have the managers of the high-producing departments. But in actual fact, as seen by them and as seen by the men, the managers in the high-producing departments have much more influence than do the managers in the low-producing departments.

The "influence pie" is seen as being bigger in the high-performing departments than in the low.

The data in Figure 4-6 suggest that the amount of influence exercised by the department manager on what goes on in his department depends not only upon the amount of authority delegated to him, but also upon the managerial and motivational principles and practices he uses. Evidently, the manager's leadership methods and skills, including the extent to which he builds his men into a well-knit, loyal group with efficient communication, as well as the capacity to exert influence upward, affect the amount of authority the manager really has. The managers in the high-producing departments build a different kind of management system, a better one, than the system used by the low-producing managers. This better management system, while giving the men more influence, also gives the high-producing managers more influence. The high-producing managers have actually increased the size of the "influence pie" by means of the leadership processes which they use.

The double lines in Figure 4-6 reflect the amount of influence the men want each of the different hierarchical levels to exercise. These data were obtained by asking the same question in the same way but with the words "should have" substituted for "has." Thus, the question became, "In general, how much say or influence do you feel each of the following groups *should have* on what goes on in your department?" As the double lines show, the men in both the high- and low-producing departments feel that the higher levels of management—"higher management" and "plant management"—should have less influence than is now the case, and lower levels in the organization should have appreciably more influence. The results show, moreover, that the men in these two groups of departments do not want the same absolute amount of influence. The amount of increased influence felt desirable is *relatively* about the same in the two groups. These results suggest that as the size of the "influence pie" is increased, the people involved in the better, more effective form of organization recognize that the amount of influence can be further increased with benefit to all.

Conclusions

The research findings summarized in this and the two preceding chapters show that the high-producing managers, much more often than the low-producing managers, have built the personnel in their units or departments into highly effective organizations. These operations are characterized by favorable, cooperative attitudes and high levels of job satisfaction on the part of the members of the organization.

Although the research findings show that this general pattern is *more often* characteristic of the operations of the high-producing managers than the low, the results do *not* show that *all* high-producing managers adhere to this pattern. Technically competent, job-centered, insensitive, and tough management can achieve relatively high productivity. The evidence clearly indicates that if this kind of supervision is coupled with the use of tight controls on the part of the line organization, impressive productivity can be achieved. Members of units whose supervisors use these high-pressure methods, however, are more likely to be among those which have the least favorable attitudes toward their work and their supervisors and are likely to display excessive waste, scrap loss, and turnover. In general, these are the work groups which show the greatest hostility and resentment toward management, the least confidence and trust in their supervisors, the largest number of grievances that go to arbitration, and the greatest frequency of slowdowns, work stoppages, and similar difficulties.

It is important also to recognize that the research findings summarized in these chapters do *not* support the conclusion that *every* organization in which there are high levels of confidence and trust, favorable attitudes, and high levels of job satisfaction will be highly productive. Even though a manager may have built his department into an organization with these qualities, his department will not achieve high productivity unless his leadership and the decision-making processes used by the organization result in the establishment of high performance goals by the members for themselves. High performance goals as well as favorable attitudes must be present if an organization is to achieve a high degree of productivity.

The behavior of the high-producing managers, in drawing upon more motivational forces and using them so that they yield favorable attitudes, points to a fundamental deficiency in the traditional theories of management. These theories are based on an inadequate motivational assumption. They assume that people work only or primarily for economic returns.[1] More specifically, these theories assume that buying a man's time gives the employer control of the subordinate's behavior. Management textbooks emphasize authority and control as the foundation of administration. They either take for granted the power to control or they hold that "the relationship of employer and employee in an enterprise is a contractual obligation entailing the right to command and the duty to obey" (Millett, 1954; O'Donnell, 1952).

---

[1] The gross inadequacy of this assumption with regard to the behavior of people as consumers has been amply demonstrated. See, for example, Katona (1951; 1960) or Lawrence Klein, George Katona, John Lansing, and James Morgan, *Contributions of survey methods to economics,* New York: Columbia University Press, 1954. Evidence that work yields important satisfactions in addition to economic returns is presented in Kahn (1958), Morse & Weiss (1955), and Weiss & Kahn (1960).

The high-producing managers and supervisors know from their experience that the motivational assumptions underlying both the traditional management theories and most of the practices of their own companies are inadequate. These managers, as we have seen, supervise in such a way as to harness important and powerful noneconomic as well as economic motives. High-producing managers appear to recognize also that there is much of value in present procedures and methods and strive to use these resources fully, but with a different management philosophy and a different set of motivational assumptions. For example, they use such resources as motion study, functionalization, and cost accounting in ways which elicit favorable and cooperative, rather than hostile, attitudes and behavior.

Two Generalizations

Two generalizations emerge from the results which have been examined in this and the two previous chapters:

1. The supervisors and managers in American industry and government who are achieving the highest productivity, lowest costs, least turnover and absence, and the highest levels of employee motivation and satisfaction display, on the average, a different pattern of leadership from those managers who are achieving less impressive results. The principles and practices of these high-producing managers are deviating in important ways from those called for by present-day management theories.

2. The high-producing managers, whose deviations from existing theory and practices are creating improved procedures, have not yet integrated their deviant principles into a theory of management. Individually, they are often clearly aware of how a particular practice of theirs differs from generally accepted methods, but the magnitude, importance, and systematic nature of the differences when the total pattern is examined do not appear to be recognized.[2]

[2] A few management theorists, notably Mary Parker Follett (Metcalf & Urwick, 1940), Barnard (1948a; 1948b), and Simon (1947), have anticipated or recognized these changing patterns in management and organization theory and have discussed their nature and application. Others who more recently have pointed to them are Argyris (1957c), Haire (1956; 1959), McGregor (1960), Selznick (1957), and W. F. Whyte (1955).

Chapter 5

THE EFFECT OF MEASUREMENTS
ON MANAGEMENT PRACTICES

The material in Chapters 2, 3, and 4 raises a perplexing question. The data reported present a consistent pattern and lead to the same general conclusions. If this pattern is so consistent, why is it that the majority of supervisors, managers, and top company officers have not arrived at these same conclusions based on their own experience?

The answer lies in the inadequacy of the measurement processes used by most companies. These processes leave large gaps in the amount and kind of information available to company executives. Virtually all companies regularly secure measurements dealing with end results, such as production, sales, profits, and percentages of net earnings to sales. The accounting procedures reflect fairly well the level of inventories, the investment in plant and equipment and the condition of plant and equipment. Most companies have a fair amount of information about the market and their share of it. Some companies have continuous information as to customer reactions to their products and to competing products.

Much less attention is given, however, to another class of variables which significantly influence the end results. These variables, seriously neglected in present measurements, reflect the current condition of the internal state of the organization: its loyalty, skills, motivations, and capacity for effective interaction, communication, and decision-making. For easy reference these variables will be called *intervening* variables. In a few companies, experimental programs are now under way to develop measurements of these intervening variables so that the quality and performance capacity of its human organization will be revealed.

The present practice of watching closely only the level of performance of the end-result variables such as production, sales, costs, and earnings is leading to faulty conclusions as to what kinds of management and leadership yield the best results. What often confuses the situation is that pressure-oriented, threatening supervision can achieve impressive short-run results, particularly when coupled with high technical competence.

61

There is a clear-cut evidence that for a period of at least one year, super-vision which increases the direct pressure for productivity can achieve, typically, significant increases in production if the operations are highly functionalized and if standard operating procedures have been estab-lished. Such increases, however, are obtained at a substantial and serious cost to the organization. (Direct pressure for increased performance does not seem to yield even short-run improvement in jobs, such as conducting research, which have not been or cannot be highly functionalized and standardized.)

An Experimental Study

The deceptive effect of increased supervisory pressure was made clear by an experimental study conducted by the Institute for Social Research in a large corporation (Morse & Reimer, 1956). The study covered 500 clerical employees in four parallel divisions. Each division was organized in the same way, used the same technology, did exactly the same kind of work, and had employees of comparable aptitudes.

Productivity in all four of the divisions depended on the number of clerks involved. The work was something like a billing operation, with loads which varied and peaked from time to time. At any one time, there was a given volume of work which had to be processed as it came along. Since it was impossible to change the volume, the only way in which productivity could be increased was to change the size of the work group.

The four divisions were assigned to two experimental programs on a random basis. Each program was assigned, at random, a division his-torically high in productivity and a division historically below average in productivity. To make sure that the experiment was not slanted in favor of either experimental program, no attempt was made to place a division in the program which would best fit the habitual methods of supervision used by its manager, assistant managers, supervisors, and assistant super-visors. (We now feel that this actually penalized the participative pro-gram, for in the light of subsequent findings and conclusions, such as those reported in Chapter 7, it has become evident that the best way to test the full potentiality of a particular experimental program is to use managers and supervisors whose habitual pattern of supervision fits that program.)

The experiment with these clerical divisions lasted for one year. Beforehand, several months were devoted to planning. There was also a training period for supervisory and managerial staffs lasting for approxi-mately six months. Productivity was measured continuously and computed weekly throughout the year. Employee and supervisory attitudes, percep-tions, motivations, and related variables were measured just before and just after the experimental year. Observations of supervisory behavior and employee responses were also made throughout the experiment.

In two of the four divisions, an attempt was made to change the supervision so that the decision levels were pushed down. More general supervision of the clerks and their supervisors was introduced. At each hierarchical level, supervisors had greater freedom of action within stated policy. In addition, the managers, assistant managers, supervisors, and assistant supervisors of these two divisions were trained in group methods of leadership.[1] They were given training in leadership and membership skills in group processes and also participated in experiences designed to increase the individual's sensitivity to the reactions of others. During the experimental year, the managers and supervisors endeavored to involve subordinates in decisions related to the work and to achieve a relatively high level of participation in all activities and decisions except those having to do with compensation and matters related to it. Experimental changes in these two divisions will be labeled the "participative program."

In the other two divisions, by contrast, a program, which will be labeled the "hierarchically controlled program," called for an increase in the closeness of supervision and a movement upward in the level at which decisions were made. These changes were accomplished by a further extension of the scientific management approach. For example, one of the major changes was to have the jobs timed by the methods department and to have standard times computed. This showed that these divisions were overstaffed except for peak loads by about 30 per cent. The general manager then ordered the managers of these two divisions to cut staff by 25 per cent. This was to be done by transfers and by not replacing the persons who left; no one was to be dismissed.

As much time was devoted to the training of managers and supervisors in this program as occurred in the participative program. In the hierarchically controlled program, however, the training was focused on company policies, on information about the company, and on making clear that managers and supervisors were expected to carry out well the instructions given them.

As a check on how effectively the experimental changes were carried out in the two programs, measurements were obtained for each division as to where decisions were made. One set of measurements was taken before the experimental year started, and the second set was obtained after the completion of the year. The attempts to change the level at which decisions were made were successful. In the hierarchically controlled program a significant shift upward occurred; by contrast, a significant shift downward occurred in the levels at which decisions were made

[1] To this end, liberal use was made of methods developed by the National Training Laboratories (1953).

in the participative program. Also, in the participative program there was an increase in the extent to which employees were involved in decisions affecting them and in the frequency with which decisions were made in work groups.

Changes in Productivity

Figure 5-1 shows the changes in salary costs per unit of work, which reflect the changes in productivity of the divisions. As will be observed, the hierarchically controlled program increased productivity by 25 per

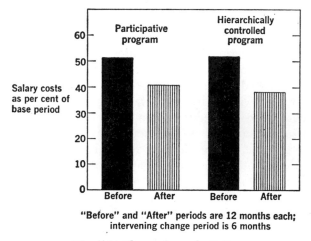

"Before" and "After" periods are 12 months each; intervening change period is 6 months

Fig. 5-1. Change in productivity.

cent. This was a result of the direct orders from the general manager to reduce staff by that amount. Direct pressure produced a substantial increase in production.

A significant increase in productivity (20 per cent) was also achieved in the participative program, but this was not so great an increase as in the hierarchically controlled program. In the participative program, the clerks, themselves, took part in the decision to reduce the size of the work group. (They were aware, of course, that productivity increases were sought by management in making these experiments.) One division in the participative program increased its productivity by about the same amount as each of the two divisions in the hierarchically controlled program. The other participative division, which historically had been the poorest of all the divisions, did not do so well and increased productivity by only about 15 per cent.

Any management having these results available to them would reasonably conclude that the hierarchically controlled program is superior to the participative. They would then adopt the hierarchically controlled program of management and would discontinue all participative forms of management. This is a common pattern of action pursued by many managements today (McMurry, 1958).

The only data normally available to management are of the kind we have just examined in Figure 5-1, namely, data on productivity, earnings, and costs. But let us see how the results of this experiment look when we add to our available information a whole new class of measurements, namely, those dealing with some of the intervening variables.

Changes in the Intervening Variables

Although both programs achieved increases in productivity, they yielded significantly different results in other respects. The productivity increases in the hierarchically controlled program were accompanied by shifts in an *adverse* direction in such factors as loyalty, attitudes, interest, and involvement in the work. Just the opposite was true in the participative program. For example, Figure 5-2 shows that when more general

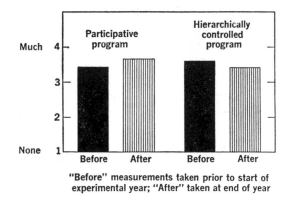

"Before" measurements taken prior to start of experimental year; "After" taken at end of year

Fig. 5-2. Employees' feeling of responsibility to see that work gets done.

supervision and increased participation were provided, the employees' feeling of responsibility to see that the work got done increased. Observations showed that when the supervisor was away, the employees kept on working. In the hierarchically controlled program, however, the feeling of responsibility decreased and when the supervisor was absent the work tended to stop.

Another measurement of the extent to which an employee feels involved in his work is his attitude toward workers who are high producers. The changes in attitudes toward the high producer by the employees in the two programs are shown in Figure 5-3. Here, again, there was a statistically significant shift in opposite directions. In the participative program, the attitudes became more favorable and there was less pressure to restrict production. In the hierarchically controlled program, attitudes became less favorable and there was more pressure to restrict production.

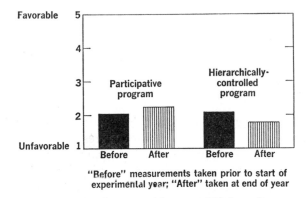

"Before" measurements taken prior to start of experimental year; "After" taken at end of year

Fig. 5-3. Employee attitudes toward high producer.

As Figure 5-4 shows, the employees in the participative program at the end of the year felt that their manager and assistant manager were "closer to them" than at the beginning of the year. The opposite was true

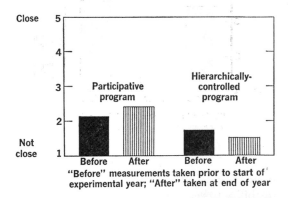

"Before" measurements taken prior to start of experimental year; "After" taken at end of year

Fig. 5-4. How close manager and assistant manager are felt to be to employees.

in the hierarchically controlled program. Moreover, as Figure 5-5 shows, employees in the participative program felt that their superiors were more likely to "pull" for them, or for the company and them, and not be solely interested in the company, while in the hierarchically controlled program, the opposite trend occurred.

As might be expected from these trends, a marked shift in opposite directions showed up during the year in the employees' attitudes toward their superiors and their feeling of satisfaction with them. The data in Figure 5-6 illustrate the shifts which occurred. These data show the changes in employees' feelings as to how well their superiors communicated upward and influenced management on matters which concerned

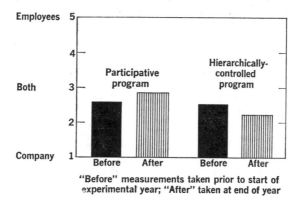

Fig. 5-5. Extent to which superiors "pull" for company or employees.

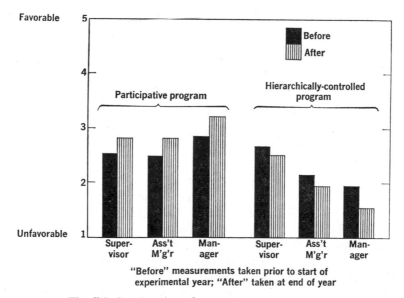

Fig. 5-6. Satisfaction with superiors as representatives.

them. Once again, the participative program showed up better than the hierarchically controlled program. One significant aspect of the changes in attitude in the hierarchically controlled program was that the employees felt at the end of the year that their superiors were relying more on rank and authority to get the work done than was the case at the beginning of the year. "Pulling rank" tends to become self-defeating in the long run because of the hostilities and counterpressures it evokes.

Deterioration under the hierarchically controlled program showed up in other ways. For instance, turnover increased. Employees began to quit because of what they felt to be excessive pressure for production. Toward the end of the experimental year, when evidence of this began to appear in the exit interviews, the company felt it desirable to lessen the pressure somewhat. We do not know what happened to the quality of the work since, unfortunately, this variable was not measured.

These additional findings based on measurements of some of the intervening variables throw quite different light on the results of this large-scale field experiment.

Unfortunately, it was not possible to conduct the participative and hierarchically controlled programs for more than one year because of changes in the over-all operations of the company. The significant trends in opposite directions which occurred in these two programs, as shown by the measurements of the intervening variables, are, however, the trends which would be expected in the light of the studies cited in Chapters 2 to 4. The attitudes, loyalties, and motivations which improved the most in the participative program and deteriorated the most in the hierarchically controlled program are those which these studies have consistently shown to be most closely related *in the long run* to employee motivation and productivity. The results shown in Chapters 2 to 4 are those found *on the average* in organizations; i.e., they represent the stable, long-run condition. This fact indicates that turnover and the adverse attitudes created by the hierarchically controlled program tend typically to affect productivity adversely over a long period of time.

Apparently, the hierarchically controlled program, at the end of one year, was in a state of unstable equilibrium. Although productivity was then high, forces were being created, as the measures of the intervening variables and turnover indicated, which subsequently would adversely affect the high level of productivity. Good people were leaving the organization because of feeling "too much pressure on them to produce." Hostility toward high producers and toward supervision, decreased confidence and trust in management, these and similar attitudes were being developed. Such attitudes create counterforces to management's pressure for high productivity. These developments would gradually cause the productivity level to become lower.

We do not know, as yet, how much time beyond the one year involved in this experiment is required for the typical situation to stabilize and achieve the kinds of patterns shown in Chapters 2 to 4. We know from other experiments in progress that changes in the intervening variables often anticipate changes in the end-result variables by one to two years.

This holds true both for changes which involve improvement and for adverse changes. Further research is under way to obtain more adequate data on these relationships. (Scattered evidence from a variety of sources including case studies suggests to the author that stability is achieved in about two to four years.) The results in Chapters 2 to 4 which reflect the typical, long-range situation, however, give every reason to believe that had the clerical experiment been continued for another year or two, productivity and quality of work would have continued to increase in the participative program, while in the hierarchically controlled program productivity and quality of work would have declined as a result of the hostility, resentment, and turnover evoked by the program.

Managers' Interpretation of Measurements

In the light of these data, let us look at the situation which virtually all supervisors and managers face today. The only measurements provided them are measurements of such end-result variables as productivity and costs. With only this information available and knowing that they are being appraised in terms of it, what conclusions are managers likely to draw as to the kind of leadership they should use to achieve the level of performance expected by higher management? In considering the answer to this question, it is important to keep in mind that these managers usually experience rewards and promotions for achieving high production and low costs over the short run rather than the long run. Moreover, since many managers are transferred after about two years, their attention is focused primarily on short-run results. Given these conditions, the answer is clear. If we look *only* at the productivity and cost data in the clerical experiment (Figure 5-1), the hierarchically controlled pattern of leadership is superior, at least for a period of one year.

The great majority of managers in charge of low-producing units and a substantial proportion of managers who achieve moderately good results have reached this conclusion and have adopted an authoritarian style of leadership.

In using this method of leadership, managers may be worried from time to time by seeing the absence and turnover in their units become greater than they wish. And they may be concerned by the high scrap loss in their departments and the excessive attention to inspection and quality control required for their units. They may also be disturbed by the resentment and hostility displayed by subordinates, and they may be perplexed by the higher rates of grievances, slowdowns, and similar disturbances in their units. All such developments as these may lead them to ease up from time to time on the tight controls and the threatening pressure for production. They may attribute the difficulties and hostility which they encounter to perverse human nature or the unreasonable hostility of labor leaders. But they would have little objective evidence to persuade them that their present leadership practices are inefficient and inadequate. This would be especially true in situations where their own bosses shared their views as to what leadership principles achieve the best results (Harris, 1952).

The findings of the large-scale field experiment with clerical employees help answer the question as to why the results reported in the preceding chapters are not generally recognized and applied by the management of companies and governmental agencies. Until measurements of the causal, intervening, and end-result variables are routinely obtained on each operating subdivision and systematically analyzed to discover trends and interrelations, it is highly unlikely that a company's management will recognize the research findings presented in Chapters 2 to 4 as being typical of its own experience. Moreover, most managements are not likely to accept and apply these conclusions until their own experience leads them to it.

For this reason, if managers are to make the best use of their experience, they need measurements which will paint for them a full and accurate picture of their experience. This will not happen until the measurements which companies obtain routinely are far more extensive and complete than is now the case.

An organization's need for accurate measurements increases as it increases in size, as its investment in plant and equipment increases, and as it uses more effective but more complex forms of social organization. Crude impressions become less accurate and more out of touch with reality as size increases. Moreover, the cost of inadequate and erroneous decisions becomes greater as the organization becomes larger and the investment greater.

The clerical experiment and the subsequent discussion of the relationships between the different kinds of variables help to clarify an important research finding. The different variables such as the intervening and end-result variables need not necessarily change in the same direction (e.g., favorable) at the same time. For example, in the participative program of the clerical experiment, attitudes became more favorable while productivity was increasing. In the hierarchically controlled program, however, the opposite pattern occurred: *attitudes became less favorable while productivity was increasing.*

These results help to illustrate the point that widely different trends can occur among the intervening and end-result variables, depending upon the character of the causal variables. Hierarchically controlled patterns of supervision yield different trends and relationships than do participative patterns.

A second aspect of this general finding is that, at any one point in time, each of the different variables may or may not display corresponding degrees of favorableness. Thus, production may be reasonably high for a time even though relatively unfavorable attitudes exist; or at a given point in time, high productivity can be acompanied by favorable attitudes toward job-related matters; or, at certain times, there may be no relationship at all between level of productivity and the degree of favorableness of employee attitudes. To assume, as is often done, that there is or should be a simple correspondence in the relationships between the intervening and end-result variables is unwarranted. The interrelationships are much more complex than this assumption implies.

Liquidating the Investment in the Human Organization

Let us examine some additional reasons for measuring, periodically, all the significant variables. As was demonstrated in the hierarchically controlled program of the experiment with clerical workers, putting pressure to increase production on a well-established organization engaged in work for which performance standards can be set can yield substantial and immediate increases in productivity. *This increase is obtained, however, at a cost to the human assets of the organization.* In the company we studied, for example, the cost was clear: hostilities increased, there was greater reliance upon authority, loyalties declined, motivation to produce decreased while motivation to restrict production increased, and turnover increased. In other words, the quality of the human organization deteriorated as a functioning social system devoted to achieving the institution's objectives.

It costs money to hire competent personnel, to train them, and to build them into a smoothly and efficiently functioning organization. Virtually all companies today ignore these costs in their accounting and in their decisions as to the relative efficiency of different systems of management. This was true of the company in which the clerical experiment was conducted. If that company had had accounting procedures showing the investment in the human organization, it would have seen that in the two divisions in the *hierarchically controlled* program the value of the human organization to the company was significantly less at the end of the experimental year than at the beginning. In other words, it would have been evident that some of the increased productivity was gained actually by liquidating part of the company's investment in the human organization. The increase in productivity should have been charged with this cost.

On the other hand, had the company's accounting records reflected the value of the company's investment in the human organization in the two divisions in the *participative* program, the management of the company would have seen a different picture. The research data revealed that the value of this investment increased during the year. The management of the two divisions had been of such a character as to advance the productive capacity of the organization as a functioning social system: loyalties had increased, hostilities had decreased, communication was improved, decisions were better since they were based on more accurate and adequate information, and production goals and motivations to produce were increasing. Measurements of these intervening variables showed a significant improvement in these two divisions.

Unfortunately, the accounting operation of this company did not have data on the human costs and investments to make proper charges and credits to the divisions involved. If the changes in productivity levels and costs had been appropriately charged with the liquidation of human assets, on the one hand, and credited with the increased human assets on the other, the financial results achieved by the two experimental programs even during the first year would have been appreciably different.

Financial Rewards for Liquidating Investments

Companies are very careful not to let managers of decentralized plants show spurious profits and earnings by juggling inventory or by failing to maintain plant and equipment. Their accounting procedures measure and report regularly on inventory and on the condition of plant and equipment. "Earnings" achieved by liquidating the assets represented in the human organization are just as spurious as those achieved by liquidating the investment in plant. Yet under present management practices, companies are encouraging their managers, by the facts used in deciding about promotions and by the formulas used to compensate them, to press unduly for immediate production, cost reduction, and similar goals, and thereby to profit personally by reducing the value of the company's investment in the human organization. Other contributing factors are job evaluations focused on the immediate contribution to earnings and profits and measurement of only the end results, which permit the liquidation to occur without the company fully realizing it.

Let us look, for example, at a series of events which often take place in a department or plant engaged in an operation where performance standards and production schedules can be set. A man is put in charge of such a plant or department knowing that he will be favorably judged and rewarded if his department achieves a high level of production. He puts a good deal of pressure on his subordinates and pushes production up. Measurement of the end-result variables indicates that he is a "fine manager." In a year or two his reputation earns him a promotion to another department, where he repeats the performance. In the meantime, hostilities have been developing in his subordinates and those below them in the organization. Just about the time that he moves on, the results of his unreasonable pressure begin to show up in decreased loyalty in the organization, lack of motivation to do a job, turnover, slowdowns, and scrap loss. The new manager reaps the fruits of the promoted manager's behavior and gains the reputation of being a "poor manager," for almost as soon as he takes over, things begin to fall apart. Sometimes the department is so relieved at getting rid of the pressure-oriented manager that they are willing to give the new manager the benefit of the doubt. Even then, however, there is usually deep-seated distrust and hostility, which handicaps him and requires years of organization rebuilding to overcome.

A solution to this undesirable sequence of events is the introduction of adequate periodic measurements of the intervening variables to reveal the current character and quality of the human organization. Estimates or impressions as to the state of these variables usually prove to be seriously inaccurate, as the research findings in Chapters 2 to 4 indicate. For example, the estimates of superiors as to the expectations, perceptions, attitudes, and motivations of their subordinates usually display appreciable errors. Not only is judgment alone inaccurate, but it tends to be most inaccurate in those situations which are unsatisfactory or deteriorating.

Consumers' good will and confidence in the company, in its products, and in its service are often lost in the same way as are investments in the company's human organization. By reducing the quality of the product with low-cost, shoddy output, a manager of a decentralized operation can substantially increase current earnings. When this is done, however, the net income shown on the company books would be spurious and would actually represent a substantial liquidation of the investment made by the company in developing consumer confidence and acceptance. Therefore periodic measurements of consumer perceptions, attitudes, and acceptance should be made, not only for the usual purposes, such as to provide direction in product development and to guide advertising and marketing, but also to protect the company's investment in consumer good will.

Inadequate Measurements—Erroneous Decisions

Working from seriously inadequate measurements, the different levels of management today are expected to guide and change the causal variables—including their own behavior—so as to maintain the end-result variables at the desired levels. As all operating people know, this is extremely difficult. First of all, there usually is a substantial time lag between changes in the causal variable and the resulting changes in the end-result variables. Moreover, this time lag is likely to be different for different changes in the causal variables. This makes it difficult, if not impossible, except in the case of extreme fluctuations, for anyone to be confident of the cause-and-effect relationships between changes in the causal variables (supervisory behavior, for example) and resulting changes in the end-result variables (production, cost, and earnings). This is complicated further by the fact that changes in the end-result variables are influenced also by events external to the organization. Unless a manager knows or is able to detect all these relationships, he is not sure what changes should be made in the causal variables to correct an undesirable state of affairs in the end-result variables.

Because they lack adequate measurements, managers and supervisors today unwittingly make mistakes. For example, a supervisor who at present receives information only on the quantity and quality of work turned out may be in serious error when trying to improve quality. If the low quality of the work is due to hostility toward him, any steps he takes to put pressure on his subordinates to improve quality may result in an immediate short-run improvement. But the increase in hostility toward him as a consequence of this pressure is likely to lead to further long-run decreases in quality at every opportunity which the subordinates feel they can safely seize.

For most purposes, it is important that adverse changes in situations be detected as early as possible so that effective steps can be taken before such changes gain enough momentum to produce a serious problem. For this reason, it is distinctly advantageous to obtain periodic measurements of perceptions, attitudes, expectations, motivations, and similar variables. In most situations, these variables change prior to changes in behavior and, as a consequence, can be used as advance indicators of the changes in behavior that are likely to follow.[2]

There is another advantage in obtaining periodic measurements of these variables. They yield valuable information about the *cause* of any adverse trends. These data on causal factors, in turn, indicate the kinds of corrective action most likely to bring about the desired improvement. Adequate periodic measurement of all three kinds of variables, consequently, are needed. The use of these measurements will be discussed at greater length in Chapter 13.

[2] Attitudinal and motivational data have proved valuable in predicting and understanding the behavior of people as consumers (Katona, 1951; Katona, 1960). It is not surprising, therefore, that the evidence which is available similarly indicates that motivational variables will also anticipate changes in the behavior of people in their role as employees.

A Dilemma

Managers of decentralized operations are faced with a dilemma. The compensation formula, which determines their income, often places great weight on the level of earnings of the unit under their supervision. The only measurements regularly available to them and higher levels of management are the traditional measures of inventory, plant and equipment, production, costs, earnings, turnover, absence, etc. They probably will be transferred to another position in about two years; this is especially likely to happen if they do an excellent job in their present position as judged by the measurements they and top management have available.

Many of these managers recognize more or less clearly that they can get increased performance and earnings by direct, threatening pressure on their subordinates and their organization. They also may recognize that such pressure is apt to lead to undesirable turnover—good people leave the operation after taking as much pressure as they feel is warranted—and to other forms of organizational deterioration.

On the other hand, most of these managers know that it takes time and hard work to build and improve an organization and that efforts at improvement are not likely to pay off immediately in increased performance, decreased costs, and increased earnings. They know that building favorable attitudes, group and institutional loyalty, interpersonal and group skills, good communication, confidence and trust, and high performance goals is a difficult and time-consuming job, even though it results in an organization that achieves and maintains impressive performance.

Each of them has a choice: should he put on the pressure for production and earnings and forget all about organizational building and maintenance, thereby achieving substantial personal earnings and the reputation of being a highly productive manager, or should he seek to build an effective organization in terms of communication, motivation, etc., even though his immediate earnings and productivity record will not be as good? If his experience shows that the odds are against his staying in his present job for more than two or three years, he is apt to appreciate that he will probably not be adversely affected by any of the resentments, hostilities, and turnover he creates through hierarchical pressure. Similarly, he also is aware that if his organization needs building and he devotes appreciable energy and resources to this task, he will not reap much of the benefits of this improvement in the organization.

Faced with this dilemma, some managers choose to be pressure artists and make handsome incomes for themselves irrespective of the damage done to the organization. Ironically, these managers often achieve a reputation with their top management of being outstandingly able managers. Other managers, because of a deep loyalty to their companies, or for other reasons, pursue courses of action of greater benefit to their companies, even if not for themselves.

In a sense, the top management of virtually every company faces a similar choice. A company president can pursue either course of action or some middle ground. The immediate earnings of the company, as well as his bonuses, will reflect the particular course of action he chooses. But over the longer run, the loyalties or hostilities of the employees at every hierarchical level will similarly reflect the management practices used.

These situations, in which managers and company officers are not only permitted to dissipate company assets but are rewarded for doing so, clearly need to be changed. The compensation processes of the organization should reward behavior which helps to implement its objectives and penalize managerial behavior which destroys the organization's assets. The measurement processes, consequently, must be able to show, in a sensitive manner, what is happening at all times with regard to causal variables such as management philosophy and supervisory behavior; intervening variables such as attitudes, expectations, and motivational forces; and end-result variables such as production, cost, and earnings.

Until adequate measurements of the kind proposed are regularly obtained, managers and presidents will continue to be confronted by serious dilemmas. Moreover, confusion as to the underlying causes of many developments, both favorable and unfavorable, will still reign.

Chapter 6

SOME GENERAL TRENDS

The significance of the management system being developed by the highest producing managers can be put in proper perspective by an examination of some general trends in American business with regard to organization and management theory. In considering the points made in this chapter and the conclusions drawn, it will be important to keep in mind that we are dealing in broad generalizations to which there are many specific exceptions. There is much evidence to indicate, however, that the description of the forest is valid, even though many of the trees are not, perhaps, where they should be.

As background, it will be useful to consider some over-all patterns displayed by the research findings. Let us start first by looking further at the relationship between the productivity of workers and their attitudes toward all aspects of their jobs, including supervision. An important fact about these relationships is that they vary with the kind of work performed.

In general, there is only a slight relationship between the attitudes of workers toward all aspects of their job and their productivity in the following situations: (1) machine-paced and assembly-line work, and (2) highly functionalized work in which the job has been broken down into simple, repetitive tasks of short duration and for which standardized procedures have been established. Standards which specify the amount of work each worker is to produce have usually been set for these jobs. Workers doing this kind of job may or may not be on incentive pay (piece rates), and they are usually under a fair amount of direct, hierarchical pressure to produce at the specified standard. This kind of work is found typically in manufacturing, as, for example, in producing automobiles and electrical appliances. It may also be found in highly routine clerical work. In order to refer easily to this kind of machine-paced or highly functionalized task, it will be called a "repetitive" job.

A different pattern of relationships exists between job-related attitudes and productivity for work which cannot be highly functionalized and for which time standards cannot be set. Here, a positive relationship, or correlation, exists between the productivity of workers and their attitudes toward all aspects of the work, including supervision. This positive correlation is usually moderately high; i.e., there is a noticeable tendency for favorable attitudes to be associated with high productivity. This is the kind of work done by people engaged in such tasks as research, engineering, and selling "ordinary" life insurance.[1] For easy reference this kind of job will be called "varied" work.

To manage these two broadly different kinds of work—repetitive and varied—different styles of leadership and management have tended to develop. Two major factors appear to be responsible. Differences in the relationship between attitudes and productivity in the two types of work appear to be one cause. The other factor in the case of both types of work is the absence of measurements of such intervening variables as communication, motivation, and attitudes.

The Pattern for Varied Work

Able, sensitive managers in charge of units doing varied work learn that favorable attitudes are associated with better job performance. They use this knowledge to find and apply improved managerial principles and practices. They seem to be guided by the fact that any new practice or principle must give promise of improving *both* attitudes and productivity. They rapidly sense any unfavorable shift in attitudes among their subordinates and promptly change or stop the activity responsible for this undesirable shift. They avoid practices which may, for a time, increase productivity but which adversely affect attitudes and ultimately will adversely affect productivity. Thus they avoid putting greater hierarchical pressure on workers to increase production. As a consequence, in such work as research, life insurance selling, and other varied work, there is a tendency to make appreciably less use of many of the methods and techniques of scientific management than occurs with repetitive work. The greater sensitivity of the more able managers to the reactions and attitudes of their subordinates leads them, therefore, to achieve improved performance in the case of varied work primarily through using principles and practices which yield more favorable attitudes, higher motivation, better communication, and better decisions.

This does not mean that the kind of work where positive correlations exist between attitudes and performance cannot benefit from the application of scientific management principles. Such work has benefited to some

---

[1] "Ordinary" life insurance is used in the technical sense, i.e., policies of $1,000 or more, usually paid quarterly, semiannually, or annually.

extent and could benefit substantially more. To obtain the full benefit from applying scientific management principles to this kind of work, however, the methods of applying these principles and techniques need to be consistent with the managerial and motivational philosophy of those high-producing managers who have achieved highly favorable attitudes among their supervisors and workers. This, as we shall see, calls for a different approach to the problem than has characteristically been the case.

Low-producing managers in charge of units doing varied work seem to have less sensitivity than do the high-producing managers and fail to recognize that favorable attitudes and better performance tend to go together. As a consequence, they are not guided by both the attitudes and production of their men, but rely largely on production and cost data in their efforts to find better practices and principles of managing. Since these managers tend to ignore attitudes, they introduce and adhere to many practices which adversely affect attitudes. Subsequently, productivity is also affected unfavorably. They may then modify the practice which is adversely affecting production. In making these changes, however, they do so more slowly than do the high-producing managers, and their over-all performance suffers.

The general pattern for varied work, therefore, tends to be as follows:

· There is a fairly wide range between the best and poorest managers in the character of the managerial principles and practices used.
· There is a correspondingly wide range between the best and poorest managers in the variety and magnitude of the motivational forces which are effectively harnessed.
· There is, similarly, a wide range in the productivity, costs, and over-all performance achieved between the best and poorest managers.
· There tend to be relatively high levels of favorable attitudes among the employees in the more productive units and less favorable attitudes among employees in the less productive units.
· There tends to be less than optimum use of some of the tools and resources of scientific management, such as functionalization and organization of the work.

The Pattern for Repetitive Work

An entirely different situation exists for repetitive work—work which is machine-paced or is highly functionalized and for which specific ways of doing each job have been established and time standards have usually been set. There tends to be a relatively low correlation in this kind of work between the attitudes of the workers and their productivity. The magnitude and direction of this relationship also may vary from time to time. In some assembly-line operations, for example, the workers may dislike the job but produce at a relatively high level (Walker & Guest, 1952). In some situations, for substantial periods of time, there may be a tendency for workers who are more productive to have somewhat less favorable attitudes than those who are less productive. This may occur because of hierarchical pressure for increased productivity. Such pressure achieves higher performance, but it also yields less favorable attitudes. This was demonstrated by the hierarchical program in the experiment with clerical workers. In other instances or at other times, there may be a tendency for those who have more favorable attitudes toward their work, company, and boss to be somewhat more productive than those who have less favorable attitudes. In general, for machine-paced or highly functionalized jobs there tends to be, on the average and over the long run, a low positive relationship between the attitudes of the workers and their productivity.

These correlations are low primarily because the range in both performance and attitudes is much less than with varied work. Attitudes rarely become highly favorable because of pressure for production. There are also important factors restricting the range in perfomance, which we shall examine in the next few paragraphs. The restricted range in both attitudes and performance limits correspondingly the size of the observed correlations between these variables.

Although there is a long-range tendency in repetitive work for favorable attitudes and greater productivity to go together, the pattern of relationships varies so much in the short run that even the most sensitive managers lack clear-cut evidence of the existence of such a pattern. As a consequence, managers in charge of repetitive work come to realize that in their efforts to evaluate their own leadership performance and to discover better managerial principles and practices, they need to rely largely on productivity, cost, and earning data to guide them. They are not able, as are the more successful managers in charge of varied work, to be guided primarily by attitudes in seeking better ways to do their jobs. Under these circumstances, managers are stimulated to make increasing use of those principles and procedures which organize the work more specifically and more tightly. When productivity and cost measurements alone are used as a guide, the trends usually discourage participation and the development of increased cooperative motivation, for the reasons made evident by the clerical experiment.

The kinds of principles and procedures which for repetitive work yield improved results rapidly in terms of output and costs are, of course, those which provide more specific organization of the work and tighter standards as to expected output. When a manager uses these principles, which are the principles and practices called for by the classical theories of management, he sees rapid improvement in those performance results revealed by the measurements used. This means, of course, that under these conditions, managers necessarily will move toward making more extensive and intensive use of "scientific" and other classical theories of management, both with regard to their techniques and their philosophy. The reason for this trend is made clear by such research findings as those obtained in the hierarchically controlled program in the experiment with clerical workers.

In companies where the work, predominantly, is highly functionalized and where the intervening variables are not measured, there are, therefore, strong forces pushing all levels of management toward greater and greater use of those principles which organize jobs more precisely and establish tighter hierarchical controls. Decisions are made at higher rather than lower levels in the organization, and the entire pattern characteristic of greater hierarchical pressure for increased production and earnings tends to occur.

The intensive use of this form of management while increasing performance restricts the variability between workers and between departments. Highly specific performance standards act as stabilizing influences upon employee behavior. These standards tend to push the less able employee to produce at the specified rate, or some arbitrary proportion of it which is acceptable to the worker, the union, and the foreman. These same standards—or acceptable quotas—act as ceilings on the performance of the more able workers and hold their production to that level. As a consequence, there tends to be much less variability in performance among workers or units in highly functionalized and standardized operations than occurs with varied work. Moreover, for repetitive work and for the reasons which we have been examining, there tends to be far less variation in the management principles and practices used than is the case with varied work. Scientific management and related management systems are quite specific with regard to the management principles and practices to be used. Consequently, both with regard to performance and with regard to managerial principles and practices, there is much less range or variability for repetitive work than for varied.

Whenever scientific management and related management systems are used skillfully in situations involving repetitive work, production is usually reasonably high, but as in the case of the hierarchically controlled program, the attitudes of employees may be relatively unfavorable. Under these circumstances quality and waste may become a problem and, depending upon the labor market, absence and turnover may become excessively high. Slowdowns, grievances, and similar developments may also occur.

The Job-organization and the Cooperative-motivation Systems

For the reasons which we have been considering in this chapter, two systems of management with different emphases have developed side by side in American business. One system has evolved in the industries and companies where repetitive work predominates; the other, in situations where varied work prevails. The management system for repetitive work, as we have seen, is a highly refined model. Jobs are well organized, waste motion and inefficient activities are at a minimum, standards have been set on a maximum of different jobs, tight budgets and controls are the existing pattern. This system of management relies primarily on the economic motives of buying a man's time and then telling him precisely what to do, how to do it, and at what level to produce. We shall call this the "job-organization" system.

The system of management generally present where varied work prevails tends to use the principles and methods of scientific management and related management principles to a limited degree only. For example, the potential gains from the use of functionalization, better organization of the work, work simplification, and similar procedures have, at most, been only partially realized. High performance in varied jobs tends to be achieved more from enthusiasm and a high level of motivation than from better organization of the job. This system we shall call the "cooperative-motivation" system.[2] As a general rule, the cooperative-motivation system of management taps not only the economic motive, but makes use as well of other powerful motives, such as the ego motives. These additional motives are used in many ways which strengthen and reinforce the motivational forces to achieve the organization's goals and are supplemented by favorable attitudes. The ego motives are often used, however, in less effective rather than more effective ways. This is probably more true of selling than of other varied work. Thus, the ego motives are often used to stimulate competition between members in the organization, as, for example, in sales contests, rather than to increase cooperative efforts to achieve the organization's objectives. As we shall see in subsequent chapters, cooperation among peers yields, on the average, a more successful organization than one in which there is a competitive relation-

---

[2] Continuous-process industries, such as petroleum, soap, and chemicals, where neither repetitive nor varied work prevails, seem to have developed management systems which fall between the cooperative-motivation system and the job-organization system. The management systems of some of these companies resemble the cooperative management system more than the job-organization system. This may be due in part to the importance of the sales activity in the total operation of such companies. It may be due also to the fact that continuous-operation work is more like varied work than it is like repetitive work.

ship. This is true even for situations involving selling (Likert & Willits, 1940).

Both systems of management—the job-organization system and the cooperative-motivation system—can and do yield operations with high performance and low costs, as the remarkable achievement of American industry amply demonstrates. It is equally clear that both systems of management could obtain appreciably better results if the potential power of each were combined with the other. Unfortunately, however, each of these management systems has in it characteristics which block integration so long as the intervening variables are not routinely measured and analyzed.

One important influence preventing their integration arises from the differences in clarity with which each system is seen and stated in management literature. The job-organization system of management is highly developed in its basic theory, in its principles, and in the techniques and methods to be used. The theory and principles of this system grow out of military-organization theory, the important theories of Taylor and his colleagues, and of Church and those who have developed accounting and systems of financial control. These theories have been clearly stated and dominate management literature. They are widely accepted as *the* way to manage an enterprise. Management consulting firms, as a rule, are well versed in these theories and skilled in the application of the techniques and procedures which the job-organization system of management calls for. The historical antecedents of this system of management give it great prestige. In addition, its acceptability has been bolstered by the immediate and impressive improvement in production and reduction in costs achieved in situations where it has been skillfully used. These improvements in results are made evident readily and rapidly by the ease of measuring changes in costs and production in repetitive work.

The situation is quite different for the cooperative-motivation system of management. It has no status as a management system. It has never been described or stated formally as a management theory. Consequently, few of the managers who are using it are fully aware of all its dimensions. The managers most skilled in its use have, as a rule, learned its general character from being "apprenticed" to managers who know how to use it. Even among those managers who are using it successfully, few can give a complete statement of the theory and of its basic principles.

An important reason for its failure to be recognized and stated as a formal management system is the difficulty of obtaining clear-cut evidence of its capacity to bring improvements in productivity and decreases in costs. The improvements achieved from the further application of this cooperative-motivation system of management cannot so readily be demonstrated as can the productivity increases achieved from the further application to repetitive work of the job-organization system. When jobs are reorganized and wasteful motions eliminated, the results in productivity are immediately evident in jobs of a repetitive type. But when better leadership is used and cooperative motivation is increased, there is usually an appreciable delay before improvement in performance occurs. As a consequence, so long as the intervening variables are not periodically measured, such improvement in productivity is not clearly and unquestionably attributed to the cooperative-motivation system of management. An occasional employee-opinion survey does not provide the measurements required. The causal, intervening, and end-result variables all need to be measured regularly, and their interrelationships analyzed in terms of operating units, to reveal clearly trends and their causes.

Trend toward Greater Use of the Job-organization System

In important segments of American industry, there is a trend toward more extended use of the job-organization system of management. The measurement of such end-result variables as production, costs, etc., combined with skillful use of scientific management and related principles and procedures, provides a body of evidence showing that tighter job organization and tighter budgetary and other controls yield improved results. This, of course, is what happened in the hierarchically controlled program in the clerical experiment. Looking at such data, the top management of companies using the job-organization system has impressive evidence before it that the way to achieve further improvement is to make more extended and more skillful use of this system of management. This, of course, is what such top management is doing. More companies are extending and increasing the use of performance measurements and indexes, measured day work, and similar developments. Comparable trends are also occurring in the use of budgets and budgetary controls, with the decisions on budgets often highly centralized. Accompanying these developments are a feeling of increased hierarchical pressure and a growing resentment against it. It is not accidental that the monthly performance report in a large corporation is called the "green hornet," or the "green dragon."

Until the intervening variables such as perceptions, attitudes, expectations, motivations, and the effectiveness of communication are regularly measured and analyzed, the companies using the job-organization system will have no data and little evidence to cause them to question the soundness of the management system which they are now using and to suggest to them the need to modify this management system in any fundamental way.

In very large corporations where repetitive work predominates, the trend toward tighter organization of the job and the extension of standards is occurring largely from the divisional, or decentralized, plant or department level downward. Above these levels, top management has recognized from its own experience that the best results are not achieved by highly centralized decision-making. Although there seems to be a general trend in these companies toward the imposition of tighter budgetary controls on all the divisions, the general organizational pattern is one of decentralization. With the exception of some budgetary limitations and within a framework of general corporate policy, these divisions have considerable autonomy.

The creation of the decentralized divisional structure is one of the important social inventions of this century. It is significant that after organizations reach a certain size, they find that they function better with a decentralized organizational structure. Unfortunately, decentralization usually stops at the plant or divisional level. In companies using decentralization, there is often more centralized control within the decentralized division than existed prior to the occurrence of decentralization.

Even in companies using the cooperative-motivation system of management, conditions do not favor any attempt to combine the best of the cooperative-motivation system and the job-organization system. This can be illustrated by examining the situation of a fairly large, highly successful company, which has a large and effective sales organization. About seven years ago, before we had sufficient research findings to make clear the general pattern presented in this volume, the author was surprised to hear a member of the top management of this company say, "We are not a 'well-managed' company. We don't do any of the things which we are supposed to do." He then told me that virtually all the top management had come up through the sales organization and had been successful members of it. According to his description, the system of management used was predominantly the cooperative-motivation system and not the job-organization system. For example, there was no organization chart, jobs were often not highly functionalized, and employees tended not to be highly and closely controlled. Even in the manufacturing plants of the company, employees did not have to punch in and out on time clocks. The practices and policies of this company's management seem to have been largely determined by its experience in managing its very successful sales organization. This person and, the author believes, the top management of the company generally feel, however, that the company should be much better "organized" and that many more and much tighter controls should exist. The company appears to be moving in this direction, giving up the cooperative-motivation for the job-organization system of management.

Should any company which has been using, primarily, the cooperative-motivation system of management decide to "improve" its management principles and practices, it is likely to obtain help from persons who know the principles and practices of the job-organization system of management. Such specialists will strive to bring about improvements in production and costs by greater specialization in jobs, by eliminating waste motion, defining jobs more precisely, setting time standards, establishing tighter budgetary controls, and introducing a more hierarchically controlled and pressure-oriented system of management. In this development, none of the motivational insights and principles of the cooperative-motivation system of management are used. The power of the cooperative-motivation system is not understood sufficiently well to use the basic motivational concepts of the system in developing and applying job-organization procedures. As a consequence, in this situation, one management system merely replaces the other. The significant gain which could be achieved by combining the best of both systems is not obtained.

The likelihood of a combination of the two systems is further decreased by changes in management personnel. When the job-organization system is introduced into a company which has been using the cooperative-motivation system, it is usually felt that no one presently in the company has the skills required to manage the new method. As a consequence, someone skilled in the job-organization system, but inexperienced in the cooperative-motivation method, is brought in and the new system being introduced is applied in an uncontaminated form.

Appraising the Value and Costs of Management Systems

At present, all the costs which a company incurs because of its particular management system are rarely considered in choosing between alternative systems of management. As we saw in Chapter 5, the costs of building and maintaining an effective human organization are usually ignored in the accounting methods of most companies. Similarly, spurious earnings achieved by liquidating some of the company's investment in the human organization are not charged against the operation and used in evaluating which system of management works best. Other large costs are also neglected. For example, the long and bitter strikes over such questions as local working agreements and the extension of work standards have rarely been charged against the job-organization system of management by companies using that system. Nor has this system been charged with the costs of slowdowns, excessive grievances, and similar developments. Yet the underlying cause of these slowdowns and strikes, which have cost companies, labor, and the public hundreds of millions of dollars and much suffering, appears to be the hostility, resentment, and distrust produced by the motivational forces used in the job-organiza-tion system of management.

When accounting procedures fully charge each system of management with all the costs for which it is responsible, the evidence is likely to indicate that companies should consider seriously the newer system of management proposed in subsequent chapters.

Work Simplification: A Combination of Both Systems

Integration of the two systems has actually occurred in the case of one managerial process, namely, "work simplification." The sensitive insights of Allan Mogensen led him many years ago to change motion study and related industrial engineering procedures into work simplification. Mo-gensen's essential idea is that the power of industrial engineering methods in simplifying tasks and eliminating wasteful activity should be used not by the staff of the industrial engineering department alone, but by all the members of the organization. His view is that the industrial en-gineering department should train supervisors and workers in work-sim-plification methods and give them all the technical assistance and consul-tation they require and seek, but the actual application of the methods is to be done by the workers and supervisors themselves.

As Mogensen says, "Work simplification *always* introduces the human element, it's always designed for foreman and employee participation." Erwin H. Schell, who worked closely with Mogensen and who coined the name "work simplification," feels as Mogensen does: "He [Mogen-sen] used the principles of motion study originally developed by the Gilbreths for structuring a program in which every member of the or-ganization might participate" (Goodwin, 1958, p. 72).

Mogensen finds that the executives of companies with successful work-simplification programs feel that these programs change the attitude of their personnel, that they then work as cooperative teams and not as a collection of "little kingdoms." This creation of cooperative teamwork is seen by many of these executives as more important to their company than the millions of dollars saved through work simplification.

The success of work simplification, on the one hand, and the slow spread of participation to other managerial processes, on the other, raise an important and perplexing question: Why has not the basic philosophy and the general principle of participation upon which work simplification is based spread more rapidly to other processes of management? Mo-gensen feels that it actually has spread to other procedures of manage-ment and to management processes generally in the form of "consultative" management. But consultative management falls far short of the amount of participation which Mogensen insists is necessary in work simplification. In using work simplification, the industrial engineering department does not discuss a problem with employees and then, itself, make the decision. Where work simplification is functioning well, the employees and the foremen are fully involved in making the decision and often make it entirely on their own. In "consultative" management, the higher echelon may discuss a problem with one or all persons on the lower echelon(s), but the decision is often made without any real participation by the lower echelon(s).

The success of work simplification has not resulted in its underlying philosophy being generalized and used as a basic principle of management. There are few, if any, companies which are using a managerial system that applies participation to all management procedures to the extent which Mogensen feels is necessary for the successful operation of work simplification. The forces which have prevented an integration of the two management systems of job organization and cooperative motivation apparently are so strong that even the impressive success of work simplification has only partially overcome them.

The forces preventing this combination are likely to continue until there is a change in the fundamental conditions causing them. Adequate measurements of the causal, intervening, and end-result variables need to be obtained continuously and fully analyzed. When objective measurements clearly reveal the full consequence of alternative courses of managerial action, forces will be created within the organization to move progressively toward combining the best of the job-organization and the cooperative-motivation systems of management and improving the combined system further.

Chapter 7

EFFECTIVE SUPERVISION:
AN ADAPTIVE AND RELATIVE PROCESS [1]

Industry is spending substantial sums on training supervisors and managers in human-relations skills, and yet the results are often disappointing (Fleishman et al., 1955; Foundation for Research on Human Behavior, 1954; Mann, 1957). One of the difficulties appears to be a widespread but erroneous assumption that there are specifically "right" and "wrong" ways to supervise. This leads to the belief in the efficacy of certain prescribed "rules of supervision."

Research findings indicate, however, that the supervisory process is much more complex. Supervisory and leadership practices, effective in some situations, yield unsatisfactory results in others.

One study in which the contradictory patterns of supervision were especially marked was conducted by Pelz (1951; 1952) in a large public utility. Pelz's analysis involved several hundred supervisors and several thousand nonsupervisory employees. He found that for most supervisory practices there was only a slight relationship between the behavior of the supervisor, as reported by the supervisor, and the attitudes and morale of the subordinates. For a number of supervisory practices, there were no statistically significant relationships between the behavior of the supervisors and the reactions of their subordinates. When such population variables as size of work groups, kind of work, and length of service were held constant, there was an increase in the number of relationships that were statistically significant between supervisory behavior and subordinate response, but many of these relationships were negative, or the opposite of those expected. Pelz found, for example, that "giving honest and sincere recognition for a job well done" to a particular group of workers had a significant, negative relationship with morale; i.e., those supervisors who reported giving the most recognition were in charge of work groups who had the lowest morale. These particular groups con-

[1] This chapter is a revised version of the author's article, Effective supervision: an adaptive and relative process, *Personnel Psychol.*, Autumn, 1958.

sisted of white-collar employees who were over forty years of age with high school education or less. Katz, Maccoby, and Morse (1950) in an earlier study found similar though less marked discrepancies between supervisory behavior presumed to be "good" and the responses of subordinates.

W. F. Whyte (1955) cites a study by Dalton in which workers who shared the same management and the same first-level supervision responded quite differently to a piece-rate system. Some workers responded by severely restricting production. Others, but fewer, were "rate busters." Most of the workers fell between the two groups in their behavior with regard to productivity.

In a review of studies done on leadership in various fields, Jenkins (1947) finds that

The situation does not appear to be a particularly happy one with regard to the deriving of general principles or of setting up a systematic theory of leadership from the available information. A few statements may be set forth, however, that appear to hold for the findings of a number of the investigations reviewed, this list should be thought of as a series of hypotheses, for further investgation.

His first statement is as follows:

Leadership is specific to the particular situation under investigation. Who becomes the leader of a given group engaging in a particular activity and what the leadership characteristics are in a given case are a function of the specific situation including the measuring instruments employed. Related to this conclusion is the general finding of wide variations in the characteristics of individuals who become leaders in similar situations, and even greater divergence in leadership behavior in different situations.

One common interpretation of the existence of discrepanies between supervisory behavior and employee response is that there are no basic principles or practices of supervision which will consistently yield the best results in terms of the criteria previously suggested. If certain supervisory acts, such as giving honest and sincere recognition for a job well done, sometimes fail to yield a favorable response from subordinates, the failure is cited as evidence that there can be no basic principles of supervision which are generally applicable and should be consistently practiced.

This interpretation is both right and wrong. It is right in emphasizing that no simple set of specific supervisory practices, as such, will always yield the best results. It is wrong in suggesting that it is not possible to derive generalizations or principles which are applicable to any situation.

There is extensive evidence, as we have seen, that a given supervisory act may not produce the same kind of result with different subordinates or in different situations. There appear to be several reasons for this. It will be useful to examine some of them and to try to discover the generalizations which they suggest.

Some Reasons for the Inconsistent Responses

One reason for the lack of a consistent pattern between supervisory behavior as reported by the supervisor and the response of subordinates is the discrepancy that exists at times between what a supervisor says he does and his actual behavior. Often a supervisor may not be aware of this discrepancy and may actually believe he is doing what he reports. There is evidence that some supervisory training programs increase this discrepancy. They seem to change the verbal response of a supervisor more than they change his actual supervisory behavior (Foundation for Research on Human Behavior, 1954). At times, this discrepancy can be substantial, as shown by the data in Figure 7-1, which were collected by

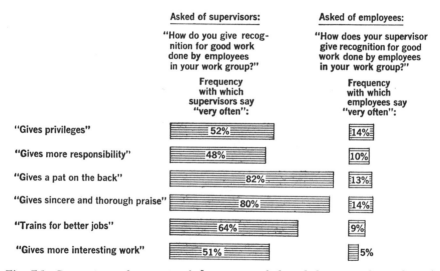

Fig. 7-1. Comparison of supervisors' description of their behavior with employees' description of their experience.

Floyd C. Mann in a study of a large utility. These data show the discrepancies between what supervisors report they do and the way their subordinates see them behaving.

This reason, however, accounts for only part of the contradiction which Pelz and the others have observed. Even when the subordinate's account of the supervisor's behavior is used, substantial discrepancies still exist between supervisory behavior and subordinate response. Different subordinates respond differently to the same supervisory act.

Differences in perception by different employees as to the behavior of their superiors is one cause of the discrepancies. An individual's perceptions depend upon his particular background and previous experience. The findings of the extensive research on social perception (Asch, 1952; Bruner & Tagiuri, 1954; Haire & Grunes, 1950) amply demonstrate that perceptions depend upon past experience.

The expectations, norms, and values of each individual are also important variables affecting his response to the behavior of his superior. These variables are influenced by past experience and also by social factors present both in work and community situations. The importance of social factors upon reactions and behavior at work was an important conclusion drawn from the research of Mayo, et al. (Roethlisberger and Dickson, 1939). Several subsequent studies have yielded results which support and extend this conclusion. These studies also demonstrate that differences in expectations, norms, and values lead to different behavior in response to the same supervisory act.

Whyte and Dalton, for example, in the study mentioned previously (Whyte, 1955), point to the importance of a subordinate's life history and his value system in influencing his expectations and his response to the behavior of his superior. They present evidence to show that in their study the difference in behavior on the part of the "restricters" and of the "rate busters" was due to a basic difference in underlying values between the two groups. These differences in values are felt by Whyte to be due to differences in home background and social environment. The "restricters" were sons of unskilled industrial workers and grew up in large cities. Whyte states that "they had been active in boys' gangs. Such activity tends to build loyalty to one's own group and opposition to authority—whether from parents or management." The "rate busters," on the other hand, came largely from farms or small towns "where they lived under close supervision of parental authority and had little time or opportunity to develop gang activities and the accompanying loyalty to the gang."

Tannenbaum (1954) reports results of a study done in conjunction with the experiment with clerical workers described in Chapter 5. He found that the subordinate's response to the behavior of his peers and superiors was influenced by the personality predisposition of the subordinate. Workers whose predisposition reflected a desire to participate in decisions affecting them responded favorably to an increase in participation. The orientation of about one-sixth of the employees involved in the participative program of the experiment, however, was toward dependent rather than participative behavior, and these workers reacted adversely to the sudden substantial increase in participation in decisions about their work.

Using measures of the extent to which nonsupervisory employees felt they participated in decisions related to their work, Vroom (1960c) found that this psychological participation was related both to attitudes toward the job and to performance. Further analyses revealed that workers who were more authoritarian responded less favorably to participation while those who had great "need for independence" reacted more favorably. This study provides additional evidence that an individual's response to an act by his supervisor will be conditioned by the individual's personality, interpersonal skills, and expectations.

French, Israel, and Aas (1960) in a recent study in Norway obtained similar results. They demonstrated that the response of workers to participating in decisions related to their work was influenced significantly by whether the worker felt that the participation was "legitimate." French defines legitimacy of participation as the extent to which "it is considered right and proper by the parties involved." Workers who felt that their participation in the decision in which they were involved was legitimate responded significantly more favorably to the experience than did workers who felt that their participation was not legitimate.

These findings are supported also by a number of other studies which have indicated that the response of the subordinate depends upon the relationship between what the subordinate experiences and what he expects. Baumgartel (1956), for example, found that scientists' attitudes toward their chiefs were markedly influenced by whether the laboratory chief did or did not conform to the role subordinates expected and desired of him. Jacobson (1951) found a similar pattern among auto workers. The attitudes of the worker toward both his foreman and his shop steward were influenced by the extent to which each conformed to the role expected of him by the workers.

The kinds of supervisory behavior which are appropriate and responded to favorably by subordinates vary not only with the past experiences and values of the subordinates but also vary with the traditions of the working situation, such as office, plant, and sales departments. Thus, the kind of work a person is doing and the kind of working environment in which he finds himself are important factors influencing expectations and reactions.

Another social variable affecting the response of subordinates to a supervisory act is the personality of the supervisor. Some supervisors, for example, are more outgoing and extroverted, others quieter and more reserved. Subordinates come to expect the supervisor to behave in a manner consistent with his personality. Supervisory acts and the ways of expressing one's self which are appropriate for one kind of supervisor may be quite inappropriate for another. When a supervisor behaves in ways which do not fit his personality, his behavior is apt to communicate to his subordinates something quite different from what the supervisor intends.

Subordinates usually view such behavior with suspicion and distrust (Likert & Willits, 1940).

In the study mentioned previously, Pelz (1951; 1952) found another important reason involving expectations which helps to account for the lack of predicted relationships between a supervisor's behavior and the response of his subordinates. Pelz showed that the amount of influence which a supervisor felt he had with his own superior affected the response of his subordinates to his supervisory acts. When supervisors who had above-average influence with their own boss followed procedures which are generally considered to be "good" supervisory behavior, their subordinates tended to react favorably; when supervisors who were below average in the amount of influence they had with their superiors practiced these same desirable supervisory procedures, they usually failed to obtain a favorable reaction, and not infrequently obtained an adverse reaction, from their subordinates.

Pelz interprets his findings to mean that the amount of influence which a supervisor has with his own superior is a "conditioning variable" which affects the results the supervisor will achieve from his supervisory behavior. To function effectively, a supervisor must have sufficient influence with his own superior to be able to affect the superior's decisions when required. Subordinates expect their supervisors to be able to exercise influence upward in dealing with problems on the job and in handling problems which affect them and their well-being. Moreover, the activity and commitments of supervisors frequently increase subordinates' expectations that action will be forthcoming with regard to supplies, equipment, safety and working conditions, pay, promotions, shift assignments, etc. As Pelz's analysis shows, when a supervisor cannot meet these expectations, workers are likely to react unfavorably.

French, Israel, and Aas (1960) also use the concept of conditioning variables to account for differences observed in the effectiveness of participation. They found that the variables "legitimacy" and "relevance" influenced the results foremen obtained when using participation. French holds that these and similar conditioning variables, such as the importance of the problem to the subordinate, will influence the reaction of subordinates to the use of participation by the superior.

The Importance of Background Differences

As the studies which have been cited demonstrate, there are many reasons which help to account for the fact that different subordinates may react quite differently to any particular supervisory act. The supervisory act alone does not determine the subordinate's response. *The subordinate's reaction to the supervisor's behavior always depends upon the relation-*

ship between the supervisory act as perceived by the subordinate and the expectations, values, and interpersonal skills of the subordinate. This generalization appears to be valid for every level in a hierarchical organization and for all kinds of organizations: industrial, governmental, military, and voluntary. It is, of course, consistent with Lewin's field theory (1951) and is supported by research in social psychology, which has demonstrated the importance of intervening variables and interactional effects.

It can be concluded, therefore, that the response of a subordinate to any supervisory act (or to any interaction with the other members of an organization) will depend upon:

1. The perception by the subordinate of the supervisory act or interaction (i.e., how the subordinate sees and interprets the experience)

2. The relationship between these perceptions and the expectations, values, and interpersonal skills of the subordinate

Both of these variables are influenced by the subordinate's background, past experience, values, and culturally conditioned sets.

The generalizations stated in the preceding paragraphs are just as valid when "supervisor" is substiuted for "subordinate," and conversely. Thus, the response of a superior to any act of a subordinate will depend upon (1) the perception by the superior of the subordinate's act, and (2) the relationship between this perception and the expectations, values, and interpersonal skills of the superior. The outcome of each interaction is clearly influenced by the past experience and environment of those persons involved in the interaction.

A General Conclusion

Supervision is, therefore, always a relative process. To be effective and to communicate as intended, a leader must always adapt his behavior to take into account the expectations, values, and interpersonal skills of those with whom he is interacting. This applies to all his relationships with other persons: his superiors, his peers, and his subordinates. This general conclusion is, of course, valid not only for relationships between supervisors and others, but for relationships between salesman and customer, teacher and student, or any other interaction between persons.

There can be no specific rules of supervision which will work well in all situations. Broad principles can be applied to the processes of supervision and furnish valuable guides to behavior (R. Likert, 1955b; R. Likert, 1956a). These principles, however, must be applied always in a manner that takes fully into account the characteristics of the specific situation and of the people involved. Sensitivity to the values and expectations of others is an important dimension of effective supervision.

Measurements of the intervening variables can be of great assistance. They can reveal the expectations, values, and perceptions of the persons with whom each supervisor interacts. Supervisors can be guided by this information and adapt their behavior accordingly as they deal with their subordinates. Moreover, in order to create the conditions for effective supervision, organizations must establish an atmosphere and the circumstances which enable and even encourage every supervisor to deal with the people he encounters in ways which fit their values and their expectations.

The general conclusion stated above does not narrow the range of application of important principles of supervision. On the contrary, it immeasurably broadens them, as we shall see in the next chapter.

Chapter 8

AN INTEGRATING PRINCIPLE
AND AN OVERVIEW

The managers whose performance is impressive appear to be fashioning a better system of management. At the end of Chapter 4 two generalizations were stated based on the available research findings:

· The supervisors and managers in American industry and government who are achieving the highest productivity, lowest costs, least turnover and absence, and the highest levels of employee motivation and satisfaction display, on the average, a different pattern of leadership from those managers who are achieving less impressive results. The principles and practices of these high-producing managers are deviating in important ways from those called for by present-day management theories.
· The high-producing managers whose deviations from existing theory and practice are creating improved procedures have not yet integrated their deviant principles into a theory of management. Individually, they are often clearly aware of how a particular practice of theirs differs from generally accepted methods, but the magnitude, importance, and systematic nature of the differences when the total pattern is examined do not appear to be recognized.

Based upon the principles and practices of the managers who are achieving the best results, a newer theory of organization and management can be stated. An attempt will be made in this chapter to present briefly some of the over-all characteristics of such a theory and to formulate a general integrating principle which can be useful in attempts to apply it.

There is no doubt that further research and experimental testing of the theory in pilot operations will yield evidence pointing to modifications of many aspects of the newer theory suggested in this volume. Consequently, in reading this and subsequent chapters it will be well not to quarrel with the specific aspects of the newer theory as presented. These specifics are intended as stimulants for discussion and as encouragement for experimental field tests of the theory. It will be more profitable to seek to understand the newer theory's general basic character and, whenever a specific aspect or derivation appears to be in error, to formulate more valid derivations and propositions.

Research findings indicate that the general pattern of operations of the highest-producing managers tends to differ from that of the managers of mediocre and low-producing units by more often showing the following characteristics:

· A preponderance of favorable attitudes on the part of each member of the organization toward all the other members, toward superiors, toward the work, toward the organization—toward all aspects of the job. These favorable attitudes toward others reflect a high level of mutual confidence and trust throughout the organization. The favorable attitudes toward the organization and the work are not those of easy complacency, but are the attitudes of identification with the organization and its objectives and a high sense of involvement in achieving them. As a consequence, the performance goals are high and dissatisfaction may occur whenever achievement falls short of the goals set.

· This highly motivated, cooperative orientation toward the organization and its objectives is achieved by harnessing effectively all the major motivational forces which can exercise significant influence in an organizational setting and which, potentially, can be accompanied by cooperative and favorable attitudes. Reliance is not placed solely or fundamentally on the economic motive of buying a man's time and using control and authority as the organizing and coordinating principle of the organization. On the contrary, the following motives are all used fully and in such a way that they function in a cumulative and reinforcing manner and yield favorable attitudes:

· · The ego motives. These are referred to throughout this volume as the desire to achieve and maintain a sense of personal worth and importance. This desire manifests itself in many forms, depending upon the norms and values of the persons and groups involved. Thus, it is responsible for such motivational forces as the desire for growth and significant achievement in terms of one's own values and goals, i.e., self-fulfillment, as well as the desire for status, recognition, approval, acceptance, and power and the desire to undertake significant and important tasks.

· · The security motives.

· · Curiosity, creativity, and the desire for new experiences.

· · The economic motives.

By tapping all the motives which yield favorable and cooperative attitudes, maximum motivation oriented toward realizing the organization's goals as well as the needs of each member of the organization is achieved. The substantial decrements in motivational forces which occur when powerful motives are pulling in opposite directions are thereby avoided. These conflicting forces exist, of course, when hostile and resentful attitudes are present.

· The organization consists of a tightly knit, effectively functioning social system. This social system is made up of interlocking work groups with a high degree of group loyalty among the members and favorable attitudes and trust between superiors and subordinates. Sensitivity to others and relatively high levels of skill in personal interaction and the functioning of groups are also present. These skills permit effective participation in decisions on common problems. Participation is used, for example, to establish organizational objectives which are a satisfactory integration of the needs and desires of all members of the organization and of persons functionally related to it. High levels of reciprocal influence occur, and high levels of total coordinated influence are achieved in the organization. Communication is efficient and effective. There is a flow from one part of the organization to another of all the relevant information important for each decision and action. The leadership in the organization has developed what might well be called a highly effective social system for interaction and mutual influence.

· Measurements of organizational performance are used primarily for self-guidance rather than for superimposed control. To tap the motives which bring cooperative and favorable rather than hostile attitudes, participation and involvement in decisions is a habitual part of the leadership processes. This kind of decision-making, of course, calls for the full sharing of available measurements and information. Moreover, as it becomes evident in the decision-making process that additional information or measurements are needed, steps are taken to obtain them.

In achieving operations which are more often characterized by the above pattern of highly cooperative, well-coordinated activity, the highest producing managers use all the technical resources of the classical theories of management, such as time-and-motion study, budgeting, and financial controls. They use these resources at least as completely as do the low-producing managers, but in quite different ways. This difference in use arises from the differences in the motives which the high-producing, in contrast to the low-producing, managers believe are important in influencing human behavior.

The low-producing managers, in keeping with traditional practice, feel that the way to motivate and direct behavior is to exercise control through authority. Jobs are organized, methods are prescribed, standards are set, performance goals and budgets are established. Compliance with them is sought through the use of hierarchical and economic pressures.

The highest-producing managers feel, generally, that this manner of functioning does not produce the best results, that the resentment created by direct exercise of authority tends to limit its effectiveness. They have learned that better results can be achieved when a different motivational process is employed. As suggested above, they strive to use all those major motives which have the potentiality of yielding favorable and cooperative attitudes in such a way that favorable attitudes are, in fact, elicited and the motivational forces are mutually reinforcing. Motivational forces stemming from the economic motive are not then blunted by such other motivations as group goals which restrict the quantity or quality of output. The full strength of all economic, ego, and other motives is generated and put to use.

Widespread use of participation is one of the more important approaches employed by the high-producing managers in their efforts to get full benefit from the technical resources of the classical theories of management coupled with high levels of reinforcing motivation. This use of participation applies to all aspects of the job and work, as, for example, in setting work goals and budgets, controlling costs, organizing the work, etc.

In these and comparable ways, the high-producing managers make full use of the technical resources of the classical theories of management. They use these resources in such a manner, however, that favorable and cooperative attitudes are created and all members of the organization endeavor to pull concertedly toward commonly accepted goals which they have helped to establish.

This brief description of the pattern of management which is more often characteristic of the high-producing than of the low-producing managers points to what appears to be a critical difference. The high-producing managers have developed their organizations into highly coordinated, highly motivated, cooperative social systems. Under their leadership, the different motivational forces in each member of the organization have coalesced into a strong force aimed at accomplishing the mutually established objectives of the organization. This general pattern of highly motivated, cooperative members seems to be a central characteristic of the newer management system being developed by the highest-producing managers.

How do these high-producing managers build organizations which display this central characteristic? Is there any general approach or underlying principle which they rely upon in building highly motivated organizations? There seems to be, and clues as to the nature of the principle can be obtained by reexamining some of the materials in Chapters 2 to 4. The research findings show, for example, that those supervisors and managers whose pattern of leadership yields consistently favorable attitudes more often think of employees as "human beings rather than just as persons to get the work done." Consistently, in study after study, the data show that treating people as "human beings" rather than as "cogs in a machine" is a variable highly related to the attitudes and motivation of the subordinate at every level in the organization (Figures 2-9 and 2-10).

The superiors who have the most favorable and cooperative attitudes in their work groups display the following characteristics:

· The attitude and behavior of the superior toward the subordinate as a person, *as perceived by the subordinate*, is as follows:
· · He is supportive, friendly, and helpful rather than hostile. He is kind but firm, never threatening, genuinely interested in the well-being of subordinates and endeavors to treat people in a sensitive, considerate way. He is just, if not generous. He endeavors to serve the best interests of his employees as well as of the company.
· · He shows confidence in the integrity, ability, and motivations of subordinates rather than suspicion and distrust.
· · His confidence in subordinates leads him to have high expectations as to their level of performance. With confidence that he will not be disappointed, he expects much, not little. (This, again, is fundamentally a supportive rather than a critical or hostile relationship.)
· · He sees that each subordinate is well trained for his particular job. He endeavors also to help subordinates be promoted by training them for jobs at the next level. This involves giving them relevant experience and coaching whenever the opportunity offers.
· · He coaches and assists employees whose performance is below standard. In the case of a subordinate who is clearly misplaced and unable to do his job satisfactorily, he endeavors to find a position well suited to that employee's abilities and arranges to have the employee transferred to it.
· The behavior of the superior in directing the work is characterized by such activity as:
· · Planning and scheduling the work to be done, training subordinates, supplying them with material and tools, initiating work activity, etc.
· · Providing adequate technical competence, particularly in those situations where the work has not been highly standardized.
· The leader develops his subordinates into a working team with high group loyalty by using participation and the other kinds of group-leadership practices summarized in Chapter 3.

The Integrating Principle

These results and similar data from other studies (Argyris, 1957c; March & Simon, 1958; Viteles, 1953) show that subordinates react favorably to experiences which they feel are supportive and contribute to their sense of importance and personal worth. Similarly, persons react unfavorably to experiences which are threatening and decrease or minimize their sense of dignity and personal worth. These findings are supported also by substantial research on personality development (Argyris, 1957c; Rogers, 1942; Rogers, 1951) and group behavior (Cartwright & Zander, 1960). Each of us wants appreciation, recognition, influence, a feeling of accomplishment, and a feeling that people who are important to us believe in us and respect us. We want to feel that we have a place in the world.

This pattern of reaction appears to be universal and seems to be the basis for the general principle used by the high-producing managers in developing their highly motivated, cooperative organizations. These managers have discovered that the motivational forces acting in each member of an organization are most likely to be cumulative and reinforcing when the interactions between each individual and the others in the organization are of such a character that they convey to the individual a feeling of support and recognition for his importance and worth as a person. These managers, therefore, strive to have the interactions between the members of their organization of such a character that each member of the organization feels confident in his potentialities and believes that his abilities are being well used.

A second factor, however, is also important. As we have seen in Chapter 7, an individual's reaction to any situation is always a function not of the absolute character of the interaction, but of his perception of it. It is how he sees things that counts, not objective reality. Consequently, an individual member of an organization will always interpret an interaction between himself and the organization in terms of his background and culture, his experience and expectations. The pattern of supervision and the language used that might be effective with a railroad's maintenance-of-way crew, for example, would not be suitable in an office full of young women. A subordinate tends also to expect his superior to behave in ways consistent with the personality of the superior. All this means that each of us, as a subordinate or as a peer or as a superior, reacts in terms of his own particular background, experience, and expectations. In order, therefore, to have an interaction viewed as supportive, it is essential that it be of such a character that the individual himself, in the light of his experience and expectations, sees it as supportive. This provides the basis for stating the general principle which the high-producing managers seem to be using and which will be referred to as the *principle of supportive relationships.* This principle, which provides an invaluable guide in any attempt to apply the newer theory of management in a specific plant or organization, can be briefly stated: *The leadership and other processes of the organization must be such as to ensure a maximum probability that in all interactions and all relationships with the organization each member will, in the light of his background, values, and expectations, view the experience as supportive and one which builds and maintains his sense of personal worth and importance.*

The Principle of Supportive Relationships as an Organizing Concept

This general principle provides a fundamental formula for obtaining the full potential of every major motive which can be constructively harnessed in a working situation. There is impressive evidence, for example, that economic motivations will be tapped more effectively when the conditions specified by the principle of supportive relationships are met (Katz & Kahn, 1951; Krulee, 1955). In addition, as motives are used in the ways called for by this general principle, the attitudes accompanying the motives will be favorable and the different motivational forces will be cumulative and reinforcing. Under these circumstances, the full power from each of the available motives will be added to that from the others to yield a maximum of coordinated, enthusiastic effort.

The principle of supportive relationships points to a dimension essential for the success of every organization, namely, that the mission of the organization be seen by its members as genuinely important. To be highly motivated, each member of the organization must feel that the organization's objectives are of significance and that his own particular task contributes in an indispensable manner to the organization's achievement of its objectives. He should see his role as difficult, important, and meaningful. This is necessary if the individual is to achieve and maintain a sense of personal worth and importance. When jobs do not meet this specification they should be reorganized so that they do. This is likely to require the participation of those involved in the work in a manner suggested in subsequent chapters.

The term "supportive" is used frequently in subsequent chapters and also is a key word in the principle of supportive relationships. Experiences, relationships, etc., are considered to be supportive when the individual involved sees the experience (in terms of his values, goals, expectations, and aspirations) as contributing to or maintaining his sense of personal worth and importance.

The principle of supportive relationships contains within it an important clue to its effective use. To apply this general principle, a superior must take into consideration the experience and expectations of each of his subordinates. In determining what these expectations are, he cannot rely solely on his observations and impressions. It helps the superior to try to put himself in his subordinate's shoes and endeavor to see things as the subordinate sees them, but this is not enough. Too often, the superior's estimates are wrong. He needs direct evidence if he is to know how the subordinate views things and to estimate the kinds of behavior and interaction which will be seen by the subordinate as supportive. The superior needs accurate information as to how his behavior is actually seen by the subordinate. Does the subordinate, in fact, perceive the superior's behavior as supportive?

There are two major ways to obtain this evidence. In a complex organization it can be found by the use of measurements of the intervening variables, as suggested in Chapter 5 and discussed at greater length in Chapter 13. It can also be obtained by the development of work-group relationships, which not only facilitate but actually require, as part of the group building and maintenance functions, candid expressions by group members of their perceptions and reactions to the behavior of others (see Chapter 11).

The Central Role of the Work Group

An important theoretical derivation can be made from the principle of supportive relationships. This derivation is based directly on the desire to achieve and maintain a sense of personal worth, which is a central concept of the principle. The most important source of satisfaction for this desire is the response we get from the people we are close to, in whom we are interested, and whose approval and support we are eager to have. The face-to-face groups with whom we spend the bulk of our time are, consequently, the most important to us. Our work group is one in which we spend much of our time and one in which we are particularly eager to achieve and maintain a sense of personal worth. As a consequence, most persons are highly motivated to behave in ways consistent with the goals and values of their work group in order to obtain recognition, support, security, and favorable reactions from this group. It can be concluded, therefore, that *management will make full use of the potential capacities of its human resources only when each person in an organization is a member of one or more effectively functioning work groups that have a high degree of group loyalty, effective skills of interaction, and high performance goals.*

The full significance of this derivation becomes more evident when we examine the research findings that show how groups function when they are well knit and have effective interaction skills. Research shows, for example, that the greater the attraction and loyalty to the group, the more the individual is motivated (1) to accept the goals and decisions of the group; (2) to seek to influence the goals and decisions of the group so that they are consistent with his own experience and his own goals; (3) to communicate fully to the members of the group; (4) to welcome communication and influence attempts from the other members; (5) to behave so as to help implement the goals and decisions that are seen as most important to the group; and (6) to behave in ways calculated to receive support and favorable recognition from members of the group and especially from those who the individual feels are the more powerful and higher-status members (Cartwright & Zander, 1960). Groups which display a high level of member attraction to the group and high levels of the above characteristics will be referred to in this volume as *highly effective groups*. These groups are described more fully in Chapter 11.

As our theoretical derivation has indicated, an organization will function best when its personnel function not as individuals but as members of highly effective work groups with high performance goals. Consequently, management should deliberately endeavor to build these effective groups, linking them into an over-all organization by means of people who hold overlapping group membership (Figure 8-1). The superior in one group is a subordinate in the next group, and so on through the organization. If the work groups at each hierarchical level are well knit and effective, the linking process will be accomplished well. Staff as well as line should be characterized by this pattern of operation.

The dark lines in Figure 8-1 are intended to show that interaction occurs between individuals as well as in groups. The dark lines are omitted at the lowest level in the chart in order to avoid complexity. Interaction between individuals occurs there, of course, just as it does at higher levels in the organization.

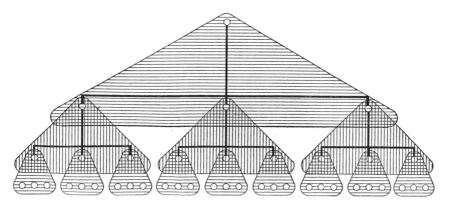

Fig. 8-1. The overlapping group form of organization. Work groups vary in size as circumstances require although shown here as consisting of **four persons**.

In most organizations, there are also various continuing and *ad hoc* committees, committees related to staff functions, etc., which should also become highly effective groups and thereby help further to tie the many parts of the organization together. These links are in addition to the linking provided by the overlapping members in the line organization. Throughout the organization, the supervisory process should develop and strengthen group functioning. This theoretically ideal organizational structure provides the framework for the management system called for by the newer theory.

The Traditional Company Organization

Let us examine the way an organization would function were it to apply this one derivation and establish highly effective groups with high performance goals, instead of adhering to the traditional man-to-man pattern. First, let us look briefly at how the traditional man-to-man pattern usually functions. Figure 8-2 shows the top of an ordinary organiza-

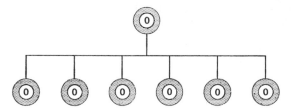

Fig. 8-2. Typical organization chart.

tion chart. Such an organization ordinarily functions on a man-to-man basis as shown in Figure 8-3a. In Figure 8-3a, the president, vice presidents, and others reporting to the president are represented by 0's. The solid lines in Figure 8-3a indicate the boundaries of well-defined areas of responsibility.

The president of such a man-to-man organization has said to us, "I have been made president of this company by the board of directors because they believe I am more intelligent or better trained or have more relevant experience than my fellow managers. Therefore, it is my responsibility to make the top-level decisions." He regularly holds meetings of the people who report to him for purposes of sharing information, but *not* for decision-making.

What happens? The vice president in charge of manufacturing, for example, may go to the president with a problem and a recommendation. Because it involves a model change, the vice president in charge of sales is called in. On the basis of the discussion with the two vice presidents and the recommendations they make, the president arrives at a decision. However, in any organization larger than a few hundred employees, that decision usually will affect other vice presidents and subordinates whose interests were not represented in it. Under the circumstances, they are

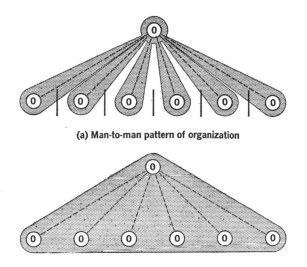

(a) Man-to-man pattern of organization

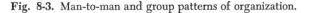

(b) Group pattern of organization

Fig. 8-3. Man-to-man and group patterns of organization.

not likely to accept this decision wholeheartedly nor strive hard to implement it. Instead, they usually begin to plan how they can get decisions from the president which are going to be beneficial to them but not necessarily to sales and manufacturing.

And what happens to the communication process? This president, it will be recalled, holds meetings for the primary purpose of sharing information. But if the manufacturing vice president, for example, has some important facts bearing on an action which he wants the president to approve, does he reveal them at these meetings? No, he does not. He waits until he is alone with the president and can use the information to obtain the decision he seeks. Each vice president is careful to share in these communication meetings only trivial information. The motivational pressures are against sharing anything of importance.

The man-to-man pattern of operation enables a vice president or manager to benefit by keeping as much information as possible to himself. Not only can he obtain decisions from his superior beneficial to himself, but he can use his knowledge secretly to connive with peers or subordinates or to pit one peer or subordinate against the other. In these ways, he often is able to increase his own power and influence. He does this, however, at the expense of the total organization. The distrust and fear created by his behavior adversely affect the amount of influence which the organization can exert in coordinating the activities of its members. Measures of the amount of influence an organization can exert on its members show that distrust of superiors, colleagues, and subordinates adversely affects the amount of influence that can be exercised.

Another serious weakness of the communication process in the man-to-man method of operating is that communications upward are highly filtered and correspondingly inaccurate. Orders and instructions flow down through the organization, at times with some distortion. But when management asks for information on the execution of orders and on difficulties encountered, incomplete and partially inaccurate information is often forthcoming. With these items and with other kinds of communication as well, those below the boss study him carefully to discover what he is interested in, what he approves and disapproves of, and what he wants to hear and does not want to hear. They then tend to feed him the material he wants. It is difficult and often hazardous for an individual subordinate in man-to-man discussion to tell the boss something which he needs to know but which runs counter to the boss's desires, convictions, or prejudices. A subordinate's future in an organization often is influenced appreciably by how well he senses and communicates to his boss material which fits the latter's orientation.

Another characteristic of the man-to-man pattern concerns the point of view from which problems are solved. When a problem is brought to the president, each vice president usually states and discusses the problem from a departmental orientation, despite efforts by the president to deal with it from a company-wide point of view. This operates to the disadvantage of the entire organization. Problems tend to be solved in terms of what is best for a department, not what is best for the company as a whole.

Effect of Competition between Functions

In the man-to-man situation it is clear that sharply defined lines of responsibility are necessary (Figure 8-3a) because of the nature of the promotion process and because the men involved are able people who want promotion.

Now, what are the chances of having one's competence so visible that one moves up in such an organization or receives offers elsewhere? Two factors are important: the magnitude of one's responsibility and the definition of one's functions so as to assure successful performance. For example, if you are head of sales and can get the president to order the manufacturing department to make a product or to price it in such a way that it is highly competitive, that will be to your advantage, even though it imposes excessive difficulties and cost problems on the manufacturing operation.

Each man, in short, is trying to enlarge his area of responsibility, thereby encroaching on the other's territory. He is also trying to get decisions from the president which set easily attained goals for him and enable him to achieve excellent performance. Thus, the sales vice president may get prices set which make his job easy but which put undue pressure on the manufacturing vice president to cut production costs.

One consequence of this struggle for power is that each department or operation has to be staffed for peak loads, and job responsibilities and boundaries have to be precisely defined. No one dares let anybody else take over any part of his activity temporarily for fear that the line of responsibility will be moved over permanently.

The tighter the hierarchical control in an organization, in the sense that decisions are made at the top and orders flow down, the greater tends to be the hostility among subordinates. In autocratic organizations, subordinates bow down to superiors and fight among themselves for power and status. Consequently, the greater the extent to which the president makes the decisions, the greater is the probability that competition, hostility, and conflict will exist between his vice presidents and staff members.

The Group System of Operation

Figure 8-3b represents a company patterned on the group system of organization. One of the presidents we interviewed follows this pattern. He will not permit an organization chart to be drawn because he does not want people to think in terms of man-to-man hierarchy. He wants to build working groups. He holds meetings of his top staff regularly to solve problems and make decisions. Any member of his staff can propose problems for consideration, but each problem is viewed from a company-wide point of view. It is virtually impossible for one department to force a decision beneficial to it but detrimental to other departments if the group, as a whole, makes the decisions.

An effectively functioning group pressing for solutions in the best interest of *all* the members and refusing to accept solutions which unduly favor a particular member or segment of the group is an important characteristic of the group pattern of organization. It also provides the president, or the superior at any level in an organization, with a powerful managerial tool for dealing with special requests or favors from subordinates. Often the subordinate may feel that the request is legitimate even though it may not be in the best interest of the organization. In the man-to-man operation (Figure 8-3a), the chief sometimes finds it difficult to turn down such requests. With the group pattern of operation, however, the superior can suggest that the subordinate submit his proposal to the group at their next staff meeting. If the request is legitimate and in the best interest of the organization, the group will grant the request. If the request is unreasonable, an effectively functioning group can skillfully turn it down by analyzing it in relation to what is best for the entire organization. Subordinates in this situation soon find they cannot get special favors or preferred treatment from the chief. This leads to a tradition that one does not ask for any treatment or decision which is recognized as unfair to one's colleagues.

The capacity of effective groups to press for decisions and action in the best interest of all members can be applied in other ways. An example is provided by the president of a subsidiary of a large corporation. He was younger (age forty-two) than most of his staff and much younger than two of his vice presidents (ages sixty-one and sixty-two). The subsidiary had done quite well under its previous president, but the young president was eager to have it do still better. In his first two years as president, his company showed substantial improvement. He found, however, that the two older vice presidents were not effectively handling their responsibilities. Better results were needed from them if the company was to achieve the record performance which the president and the other vice presidents sought.

The president met the situation by using his regular staff meetings to analyze the company's present position, evaluate its potential, and decide on goals and on the action required to reach them. The president had no need to put pressure on his coasting vice presidents. The other vice presidents did it for him. One vice president, in particular, slightly younger but with more years of experience than the two who were dragging their feet, gently but effectively pushed them to commit themselves to higher performance goals. In the regular staff meetings, progress toward objectives was watched and new short-term goals were set as needed. Using this group process, steady progress was made. The two oldest vice presidents became as much involved and worked as enthusiastically as did the rest of the staff.

Group Decision-making

With the model of organization shown in Figure 8-3b, persons reporting to the president, such as vice presidents for sales, research, and manufacturing, contribute their technical knowledge in the decision-making process. They also make other contributions. One member of the group, for example, may be an imaginative person who comes up rapidly with many stimulating and original ideas. Others, such as the general counsel or the head of research, may make the group do a rigorous job of sifting ideas. In this way, the different contributions required for a competent job of thinking and decision-making are introduced.

In addition, these people become experienced in effective group functioning. They know what leadership involves. If the president grows absorbed in some detail and fails to keep the group focused on the topic for discussion, the members will help by performing appropriate leadership functions, such as asking, "Where are we? What have we decided so far? Why don't we summarize?" (These functions are discussed in Chapter 11.)

There are other advantages to this sort of group action. The motivation is high to communicate accurately all relevant and important information. If any one of these men holds back important facts affecting the company so that he can take it to the president later, the president is likely to ask him why he withheld the information and request him to report it to the group at the next session. The group also is apt to be hard on any member who withholds important information from them. Moreover, the group can get ideas across to the boss that no subordinate dares tell him. As a consequence, there is better communication, which brings a better awareness of problems, and better decision-making than with the man-to-man system.

Another important advantage of effective group action is the high degree of motivation on the part of each member to do his best to implement decisions and to achieve the group goals. Since the goals of the group are arrived at through group decisions, each individual group member tends to have a high level of ego identification with the goals because of his involvement in the decisions.

Finally, there are indications that an organization operating in this way can be staffed for less than peak loads at each point. When one man is overburdened, some of his colleagues can pick up part of the load temporarily. This is possible with group methods of supervision because the struggle for power and status is less. Everybody recognizes his broad area of responsibility and is not alarmed by occasional shifts in one direction or the other. Moreover, he knows that his chances for promotion depend not upon the width of his responsibility but upon his total performance, of which his work in the group is an important part. The group, including the president, comes to know the strengths and weaknesses of each member well as a result of working closely with him.

A few years ago a department of fifteen people in a medium-sized company shifted from a man-to-man pattern of supervision to the group pattern. Each operation under the man-to-man system was staffed to carry adequately the peak loads encountered, but these peaks virtually never occurred for all jobs at the same time. In shifting to group supervision, the department studied how the work was being done. They concluded that seven persons instead of fifteen could carry the load except in emergencies. Gradually, over several months, the persons not needed transferred to other departments and the income of those doing the work was increased 50 per cent. The work is being done well, peak loads are handled, those doing it have more favorable attitudes, and there is less absence and turnover than under the man-to-man system.

Responsibility and Situational Requirements

In every organization there are many basic facts of life which cannot be ignored if the organization is to achieve its objectives. For example, there are often deadlines or minimum financial conditions as to earnings and reserves to be met. These hard, objective realities are the *situational requirements* which impose limitations on the decision-making processes.

The supervisor of every work group must be fully aware of the situational requirements which apply to the operation of his group. In making decisions, he and his group should never lose sight of them. If the group is so divided in opinion that there is not time to reach decisions by consensus which adequately meet these requirements, the superior has the responsibility of making a decision which does meet them. In this event, the superior may be wise to accept the solution preferred by the individuals in the group who will have the major responsibility for implementing the decision, provided, of course, the superior himself feels that the solution is reasonably sound.

Sometimes the differences of opinion exist not between members of the work group, but between the superior and his subordinates. In this event, the superior should participate fully in the discussion and present clearly the evidence which makes him hold another point of view. If after further discussion, the group still prefers a course of action different from that which the chief favors, the superior faces a tough decision. He can overrule the group and take the action he favors. This is likely to affect adversely group loyalties and the capacity of his work group to function well as a group. Or he can go along with the group and accept the decision they prefer. If he overrules the group, the superior usually reduces the amount of work-group loyalty which he has "in the bank." If the costs of a mistake are not too great, he may prefer to accept the group's decision in order to strengthen the group as a group and to provide an opportunity for his group to learn from its mistakes. If the costs of a mistake are likely to be excessive, the superior may feel that he has no choice but to do what his own experience indicates is best. But whatever course of action is taken, *he is responsible and must accept full responsibility for what occurs.*

The "Linking Pin" Function

Figure 8-3 and the preceding discussion have been concerned with the group pattern of organization at the very top of a company. Our theoretical derivation indicates, however, that this pattern is equally applicable at all levels of an organization. If an organization is to apply this system effectively at all organizational levels, an important linking function must be performed.

The concept of the "linking pin" is shown by the arrows in Figure 8-4. The research pointing to the importance of upward influence in an or-

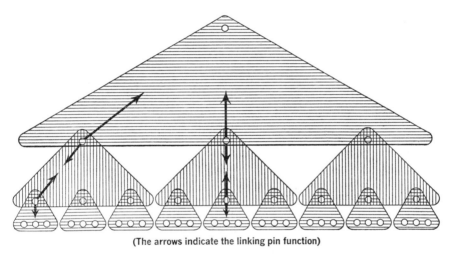

(The arrows indicate the linking pin function)

Fig. 8-4. The linking pin.

ganization has already been described in Chapter 7. The study by Pelz (1951; 1952) showed that there was only a slight relationship between some fifty different measures of supervisory practices and points of view, as reported by the supervisors, and the attitudes and morale of the subordinates. Pelz found that an important variable was responsible for the absence of more marked relationships. This variable proved to be the amount of influence which a supervisor felt he had with his own superior. To function effectively, a supervisor must have sufficient influence with his own superior to be able to affect the superior's decisions. Subordinates expect their supervisors to be able to exercise an influence upward in dealing with problems on the job and in handling problems which affect them and their well-being. As Pelz's analysis shows, when a supervisor cannot exert sufficient influence upward in the hierarchy to handle these problems constructively, an unfavorable reaction to the supervisor and to the organization is likely to occur.

Other research confirms the importance of Pelz's findings and also indicates that the ability to exert an influence upward affects not only morale and motivation but also productivity and performance variables (Katz et al., 1950; Likert & Willits, 1940). Ronken and Lawrence (1952) summarize their findings on this matter as follows:

An additional complication for the foreman was the necessity of learning how to work with new supervisors and a new group of subordinates. When the foreman experienced difficulty in communicating with his superior, he was not able to understand his subordinates' problems or to gain their spontaneous cooperation, and the work suffered. When he felt more confident of his relations upward, he administered his own group with greater skill. During such periods his operators showed considerable initiative in their work, contributed more useful suggestions, and raced with themselves and each other to increase output.

These results demonstrate that *the capacity to exert influence upward is essential if a supervisor (or manager) is to perform his supervisory functions successfully.* To be effective in leading his own work group, a superior must be able to influence his own boss; that is, he needs to be skilled both as a supervisor and as a subordinate. In terms of group functioning, he must be skilled in both leadership and membership functions and roles.

Effective groups with high group loyalty are characterized by efficient and full communication and by the fact that their members respect each other, welcome attempts by the other members to influence them, and are influenced in their thinking and behavior when they believe that the evidence submitted by the other members warrants it. The linking pin function, consequently, will be performed well in an organization when each work group at all the different hierarchical levels above the non-supervisory level is functioning effectively as a group and when every member of each group is performing his functions and roles well. Whenever an individual member of one of these groups fails in his leadership and membership roles (see Chapter 11), the group or groups under him will not be linked into the organization effectively and will fail in the performance of their tasks. When an entire work group ceases to function effectively as a group, the activities and performance of all the work groups below such a group will be correspondingly adversely affected.

The linking pin function requires effective group processes and points to the following:

· An organization will not derive the full benefit from its highly effective groups unless they are linked to the total organization by means of equally effective overlapping groups such as those illustrated in

Figures 8-1 and 8-4. The use of highly effective groups in only one part or in scattered portions of an organization will fail, therefore, to achieve the full potential value of such groups.

· The potential power of the overlapping group form of organization will not be approached until all the groups in the organization are functioning reasonably well. The failure of any group will adversely affect the performance of the total organization.

· The higher an ineffective group is in the hierarchy, the greater is the adverse effect of its failure on the performance of the organization. The linking process is more important at high levels in an organization than at low because the policies and problems dealt with are more important to the total organization and affect more people.

· To help maintain an effective organization, it is desirable for superiors not only to hold group meetings of their own subordinates, but also to have occasional meetings over two hierarchical levels. This enables the superior to observe any breakdown in the linking pin process as performed by the subordinates reporting to him. If in such meetings the subordinates under one of his subordinates are reluctant to talk, never question any procedure or policy, or give other evidence of fear, the superior can conclude that he has a coaching job to do with his own subordinate, who is failing both as a leader and in his performance of the linking pin function. This subordinate needs help in learning how to build his own subordinates into a work group with high group loyalty and with confidence and trust in their supervisor (see Chapters 9 and 11).

· An organization takes a serious risk when it relies on a single linking pin or single linking process to tie the organization together. As will be discussed further in subsequent chapters, an organization is strengthened by having staff groups and *ad hoc* committees provide multiple overlapping groups through which linking functions are performed and the organization bound together.

Organizational Objectives and Goals of Units

The ability of a superior to behave in a supportive manner is circumscribed by the degree of compatibility between the objectives of the organization and the needs of the individuals comprising it. If the objectives of the organization are in basic conflict with the needs and desires of the individual members, it is virtually impossible for the superior to be supportive to subordinates and at the same time serve the objectives of the organization. The principle of supportive relationships, consequently, points to the necessity for an adequate degree of harmony between organizational objectives and the needs and desires of its individual members.

This conclusion is applicable to every kind of organization: industrial, governmental, or voluntary. A business organization, if it is to function well, needs to have objectives which represent a satisfactory integration of the needs and desires of all the major segments involved: its shareowners, its suppliers, its consumers, its employees (including all levels of supervisory and nonsupervisory personnel), and its union(s). If governmental agencies are to function effectively, their objectives similarly must be a satisfactory integration of the needs and desires of all the different segments involved in their activities: employees, citizens, and legislators.

Neither the needs and desires of individuals nor the objectives of organizations are stable and unchanging. The desires of individuals grow and change as people interact with other people. Similarly, the objectives of organizations must change continuously to meet the requirements of changed technologies, changed conditions, and the changes in needs and desires of those involved in the organization or served by it. The interaction process of the organization must be capable of dealing effectively with these requirements for continuous change.

In every healthy organization there is, consequently, an unending process of examining and modifying individual goals and organizational objectives as well as consideration of the methods for achieving them. The newer theory specifies that:

· The objectives of the entire organization and of its component parts must be in satisfactory harmony with the relevant needs and desires of the great majority, if not all, of the members of the organization and of the persons served by it.
· The goals and assignments of each member of the organization must be established in such a way that he is highly motivated to achieve them.
· The methods and procedures used by the organization and its subunits to achieve the agreed-upon objectives must be developed and adopted in such a way that the members are highly motivated to use these methods to their maximum potentiality.
· The members of the organization and the persons related to it must feel that the reward system of the organization—salaries, wages, bonuses, dividends, interest payments—yields them equitable compensation for their efforts and contributions.

The overlapping group form of organization offers a structure which, in conjunction with a high level of group interactional skills, is particularly effective in performing the processes necessary to meet these requirements.

Constructive Use of Conflict

An organization operating under the newer theory is not free from conflict. Conflict and differences of opinion always exist in a healthy, virile organization, for it is usually from such differences that new and better objectives and methods emerge. Differences are essential to progress, but bitter, unresolved differences can immobilize an organization. The central problem, consequently, becomes not how to reduce or eliminate conflict, but how to deal constructively with it. Effective organizations have extraordinary capacity to handle conflict. Their success is due to three very important characteristics:

1. They possess the machinery to deal constructively with conflict. They have an organizational structure which facilitates constructive interaction between individuals and between work groups.

2. The personnel of the organization is skilled in the processes of effective interaction and mutual influence. (Skills in group leadership and membership roles and in group building and maintenance functions are discussed in Chapter 11.)

3. There is high confidence and trust among the members of the organization in each other, high loyalty to the work group and to the organization, and high motivation to achieve the organization's objectives. Confidence, loyalty, and cooperative motivation produce earnest, sincere, and determined efforts to find solutions to conflict. There is greater motivation to find a constructive solution than to maintain an irreconcilable conflict. The solutions reached are often highly creative and represent a far better solution than any initially proposed by the conflicting interests (Metcalf & Urwick, 1940).

The discussion in this chapter has deliberately focused on and emphasized the group aspects of organization and management. This has been done to make clear some of the major differences between the classical and the newer theories of management. It should also sharpen the awareness of the kind of changes needed to start applying the newer theory.

Any organization which bases its operation on this theory will necessarily make use of individual counseling and coaching by superiors of subordinates. There is need in every situation for a balanced use of both procedures, individual and group. Here, as with other aspects of supervision, the balance which will be most appropriate and work best will depend upon the experience, expectations, and skills of the people involved.

Tests of the Newer Theory

The validity of the newer theory of management and of its derivations can be tested in two ways. Tests can be applied experimentally in pilot plants to see whether the newer system significantly improves all aspects of performance: productivity, quality, costs, employee satisfaction, etc. Although it will take several years to know the results, this kind of test is now under way.

The second kind of test is an examination of the extent to which the methods and procedures called for by the theory, or by the derivations based on the theory, are associated with above-average performance in the current operations of companies. The results of this kind of test do not require waiting for the outcome of an experimental application of the theory, but can be examined now. Several tests of this latter kind have recently been made. These were based on data which have been collected during the past few years. The results indicate, as we shall see in Chapter 9, that the newer theory, skillfully used, will produce an organization with impressive performance characteristics.

Chapter 9

SOME EMPIRICAL TESTS
OF THE NEWER THEORY

Data collected in a study conducted in 1955 by the Institute for Social Research provided the material for one test of the newer theory.[1] This test was based on the concept that departments or units whose structure and operation more nearly correspond to the pattern called for by this theory should, if the theory is valid, achieve better results than units which have less similarity to the pattern. The data were collected in 31 geographically separated departments in a company which operates nationally. These departments perform essentially the same operations, and for each there are extensive and excellent productivity and cost figures available continuously. The departments vary in size from about 15 to over 50 employees.

A single score was computed for the manager in charge of each of the 31 departments. These scores are based on seven items in a questionnaire given to managers by the research group. The measurements represent a crude approximation of the extent to which the manager has a supportive attitude toward his men and the extent to which he believes in using group methods of supervision. As we saw in Chapter 8, these are important dimensions of the newer theory. These scores, labeled for convenient reference "attitude toward men," are based on the managers' answers to the questionnaires and reflect their concept of their job. Their actual behavior, in some instances, may not be fully in accord with the point of view they expressed.

The relationships between the attitude-toward-men scores of the managers and the productivity of the department are shown in Figure 9-1. In this figure, each small circle represents a department. The location of each circle in Figure 9-1 shows the productivity of the department, plotted in relation to the vertical axis, and the manager's attitude-toward-men score, along the horizontal axis. As these data show, those managers

[1] This study was conducted by Stanley E. Seashore, Basil Georgopoulos, and Arnold Tannenbaum.

119

who have a favorable attitude-toward-men score achieve significantly higher performance than those managers who have an unfavorable score. Managers who have a supportive attitude toward their men and endeavor to build them into well-knit groups obtain appreciably higher productivity than managers who have a threatening attitude and rely more on man-to-man patterns of supervision. (The correlation coefficient is +0.64.)

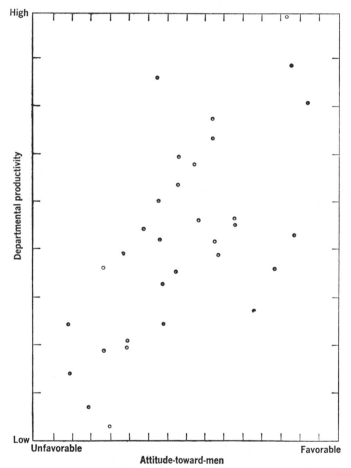

Fig. 9-1. Relationship of attitude-toward-men score of manager to department's productivity.

In addition to the productivity, there are other differences between departments which have supportive managers and those whose managers are less supportive. In those departments in which the manager has an above-average attitude-toward-men score, in contrast to departments in which the manager has a below-average score, the men more often displayed the following reactions:

· In response to the question, "How do you feel about the amount of responsibility you have in your job?" the men in those departments whose managers have above-average attitude-toward-men scores more often want more responsibility. The men in the departments whose managers are not supportive—as shown by their below-average attitude-toward-men score—want less responsibility (Figure 9-2).

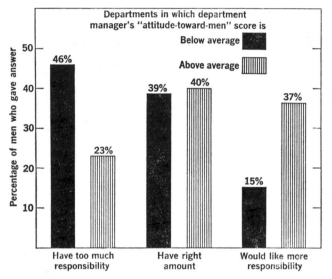

Fig. 9-2. Relation of attitude-toward-men score of department manager to men's reactions to: "How do you feel about the amount of responsibility you have in your job?"

· On the question, "How do you feel about the way your particular job or route was assigned to you?" the men in departments whose managers score above average on the attitude-toward-men scale are appreciably more satisfied than the men in the other departments. (Completely Satisfied = 42 per cent versus 26 per cent; Dissatisfied = 22 per cent versus 40 per cent.)

· Similarly, the men in the departments whose managers are above average on the attitude-toward-men scores are more satisfied with the recognition they have received for their own work than are the men in the other departments. (Completely or Very Satisfied = 46 per cent versus 28 per cent; Dissatisfied = 7 per cent versus 17 per cent.)

· The men in departments whose managers are above average on the attitude-toward-men score more often feel that what their supervisor expects of them is about right. The men in the other departments more often feel that the supervisor expects too much of them. (About Right = 55 per cent versus 28 per cent; Far Too Much = 10 per cent versus 23 per cent.)

· The men in the departments whose managers score above average more often take complaints first to their supervisor or department head. (68 per cent versus 35 per cent.)

· The men in the departments whose managers score above average feel that there is less tension between employees and supervisors (Figure 9-3).

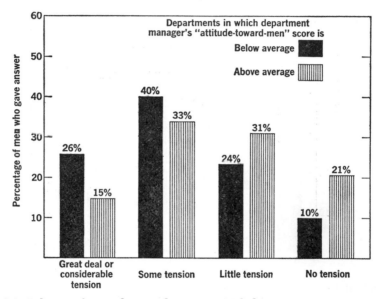

Fig. 9-3. Relation of attitude-toward-men score of department manager to men's reaction to: "On the whole, would you say that in your department there is any tension or conflict between employees and supervisors?"

Test of the Theory by the Group-meeting Method

Two additional but related tests of the validity of the newer theory were made using data from these same 31 departments. These more extensive tests used data obtained from the men as well as the managers to classify the departments.

One of these tests involved classifying the 31 departments on the basis of the extent to which the manager and the men agree that there are worthwhile group discussions involving the supervisors and the men. In the other test, the departments were classified on the basis of the amount of loyalty to the work group expressed by the men. The measurements used included loyalty to the other men, to the supervisors, and to the manager.

Data on the usefulness of group meetings were obtained through the following questions. The managers were asked:

"Are there any *group meetings* [2] in which the nonsupervisory people in your department can discuss things with the supervisors? (Check one.)

_____ Yes, and they are always worthwhile.
_____ Yes, and they are usually worthwhile.
_____ Yes, but usually nothing much is accomplished.
_____ Yes, but they are just a waste of time.
_____ No, we never have such group meetings."

The men were asked a parallel question:

"Are there any group meetings in which the people you work with can discuss things with the supervisors? (Check one.)"

The five alternatives in the manager's questionnaire were also used here. The responses to these questions were employed to classify the departments into the following groups, or clusters:

Cluster A included the 10 departments in which the managers said that meetings were held and that they were always or usually worthwhile and where the men were in substantial agreement with the managers as to the value of the meetings.

Cluster B included all departments, a total of 7, in which the managers stated that group meetings were never held.

Cluster C consisted of 14 departments in which managers said that meetings were held and that they were always or usually worthwhile but the men disagreed with their managers as to the value of these meetings. The men felt that "nothing much was accomplished" or that the meetings were "just a waste of time." Included also in this cluster are two other departments in which both the manager and men agreed that the group meetings held accomplished nothing much or were a waste of time.

The newer theory would predict that Cluster A should show somewhat better results than the other two clusters on all such variables as production, communication, coordination and the exercise of influence, the degree of confidence and trust, mental health and the level of anxiety and stress, attitudes toward supervision, and employee satisfaction.

The poorest results would be expected, theoretically, in Cluster C because meetings called to no purpose imply a disregard for the value of men's time and ideas. This violates the principle of supportive relationships. It is generally ego-deflating. In keeping with the findings reported in Chapter 3 from another study using the same question, the results show that it is better to hold no group meetings at all than to conduct meetings seen by the men as "double talk" and accomplishing nothing.

The term "group meetings" is not confined to formal meetings. The responses of the managers and men to the question showed that informal discussions and sessions at the place of work were often what they meant.

[2] Italics as in the questionnaire.

Apparently the formality of the group meeting is not the significant dimension. The important dimension is the willingness of the manager in formal or informal settings to discuss problems fully with the men, to be genuinely interested in their ideas, and to endeavor to make good use of their ideas, experience, and recommendations. In order to refer easily to this first method of classification, it will be called the "group-meeting method."

The extent to which the three clusters of departments display performance and operating characteristics which correspond with the theoretical pattern will be examined after the second method for classifying the departments into clusters has been described.

The Group-loyalty Test of the Theory

The second approach to arranging the departments in clusters involved classifying them on the basis of level of total work-group loyalty. This second method will be called the "group-loyalty method." Loyalty to the work group includes not only loyalty to the peer members of the group, but loyalty to the superior, as well as loyalty from the superior. The 31 departments were divided into four clusters based on these concepts. Cluster 1, the high cluster, includes all departments which met all the following conditions:

· Falls in the top one-third of departments in its mean peer-group-loyalty scores. (Peer-group loyalty is loyalty among the workers toward one another irrespective of their attitude toward their superior. It was measured by nine questions dealing with attitudes of the men toward one another, their pride in their work group, and their sense of belonging to the group.)
· The mean of the men's attitude toward their immediate supervisor is above the median for the 31 departments.
· The mean of the men's attitude toward their manager is above the median for the 31 departments.
· The manager's attitude-toward-men score (see page 119) is above the median of the 31 departments.

This high cluster includes all departments which have high peer-group-loyalty scores and which are above average (median) in the men's attitudes toward their immediate supervisor and toward their department manager and where the manager is above average (median) in his attitude toward the men as measured by the manager's attitude-toward-men score. This cluster of seven stations is characterized, consequently, by high peer-group loyalty and relatively favorable attitudes on the part of the men toward management and on the part of the manager toward the men.

In Cluster 2, the middle cluster, 10 of the 11 departments met the following conditions:

· Falls in the bottom two-thirds of the departments in the departments' mean peer-group-loyalty score and above the median in one or more of the other three measurements, namely:
· · The men's mean score on attitude toward their immediate supervisor
· · The men's mean score on attitude toward their manager
· · The manager's attitude-toward-men score

The eleventh department is slightly above the median on peer-group loyalty and slightly below the median on the other three measurements.

Cluster 3, the low cluster, also includes 11 units. This cluster consists of departments which were *below* the median on *all* the following:

· Men's mean score on peer-group loyalty
· Men's mean score on attitude toward their immediate supervisor
· Men's mean score on attitude toward their manager

With regard to the manager's attitude-toward-men score, the situation is mixed. On this variable 7 of the 11 departments fall below the median of all departments. In the other 4 departments, the managers fall above the median on the attitude-toward-men score but the men feel that neither their supervisors nor their managers display the supportive behavior claimed by the manager.

Cluster 4, the supplementary low cluster, consists of only 2 departments. In these, there is high peer-group loyalty coupled with the least favorable attitudes toward supervision and management and with managers who have distinctly unfavorable attitude-toward-men scores. These two departments are characterized, consequently, by strong peer-group loyalty among the nonsupervisory employees coupled with hostility between the men and their supervisors and managers.

If the theory presented in Chapter 8 is valid, the four clusters just described should show important differences in operating characteristics and behavior. Cluster 1, the high cluster, consists of departments which appear to be operating more on an overlapping group pattern than a man-to-man pattern. There is greater group loyalty, including loyalty toward the supervisor and manager. Moreover, the managers of these departments have more favorable attitudes toward their subordinates and there appears to be a more supportive atmosphere. This is reflected in the higher attitude-toward-men scores of these managers.

Since the departments in Cluster 1 come closest to meeting the pattern of the theoretical ideal, this, more than the other clusters, should come closest to displaying the pattern of operating characteristics of the ideal model. The other three clusters should, of course, if the theory is valid, show results which fall into a pattern corresponding with the criteria used in grouping them. Cluster 2, usually, should show results less favorable than Cluster 1 but better than Clusters 3 and 4. Cluster 4 would be expected on most variables to show the least favorable results.

Both methods of classifying the departments should, theoretically, yield clusters which differ significantly in their operating characteristics and performance. The high, or effective, cluster of each approach should display operating characteristics more in accord with the ideal pattern than do the poor clusters. Thus, for example, the high, or favorable, clusters (Cluster A and Cluster 1) of departments would be expected to display to a greater extent than the other clusters of departments the following:

· Fuller, more candid communication throughout the organization—upward, downward, and between peers.
· Higher levels of influence and interaction, including greater amounts of influence by subordinates upon superiors as well as greater influence by superiors upon subordinates. There should also be more influence by the men upon their own colleagues; that is, the better quality of these departments as integrated, social organisms should manifest itself in greater coordination. There should be higher levels of total influence and coordination.
· Greater decentralization of the decision-making process, with more decisions made at lower levels. This should be reflected not only in a greater feeling by subordinates that they can exercise influence upon decisions, but also that they have sufficient authority and are sufficiently free to make important decisions affecting their work, such as setting their own work pace.
· Greater acceptance of the goals of the organization and more feeling by the men that they are helping to influence these goals. There should be more favorable attitudes toward the company and a greater feeling that what is expected of them is reasonable even though the group's work goals are higher.
· Higher motivation and evidence of more cumulative and reinforcing motivation and less conflict among motivational forces.
· Better mental health, including less anxiety, nervousness, stress, and conflict between personnel and more confidence, self-assurance, and self-respect.
· Higher productivity.

The Relation of Group Meetings and Group Loyalty to Productivity

When the average productivity of the departments in the different clusters is examined, the results conform to expectations. These results for the two different ways of clustering the departments are shown in Figure 9-4 for the first approach— the group-meeting method—and in Figure 9-5 for the second approach—the group-loyalty method. As the figures show, both approaches yield clusters which show substantial differences in productivity, and these differences correspond to the the theoretical predictions.

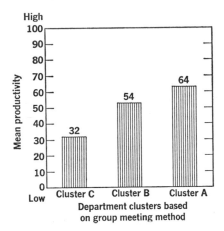

Cluster 4, as would be predicted from the newer theory, is particularly low in productivity. This cluster consists of the two departments in which there is high group loyalty among the workers but relatively hostile and unfavorable attitudes toward their supervisors

Fig. 9-4. Productivity of the different clusters of departments (clusters based on group-meeting method).

and department manager. In these departments, consequently, powerful group forces are oriented against the goals of management and the productivity is very low.

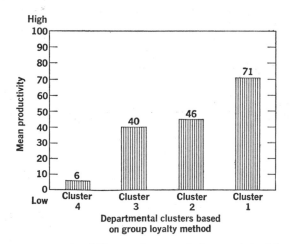

Fig. 9-5. Productivity of the different clusters of departments (clusters based on group-loyalty method).

When the ratings of top management as to the relative effectiveness of the departments are used, results similar to those found for productivity are obtained. This is not surprising since management takes productivity very much into consideration in making its effectiveness ratings.

The two different approaches to classifying the departments—the group-meeting method and the group-loyalty method—both yield results, as we have just seen in Figures 9-4 and 9-5, which conform to predictions made by the newer theory. On other variables, in addition to productivity, the two methods of analysis yield quite comparable findings. The results of only one approach, the group-loyalty method, consequently, will be examined. Occasionally, the results from the group-meeting method will be mentioned. The *group-loyalty* clusters, Clusters 1 to 4, showed, as a rule, slightly larger differences between the high and low clusters than were found between the *group-meeting* clusters, Clusters A to C.

With this general orientation, let us examine the data to see the extent to which the pattern of research results is consistent with the theoretical expectations.

The Relation of Group Loyalty to Communication

The communication process should, in general, be best in the high cluster and poorest in the low clusters. As the data in Figures 9-6 and 9-7

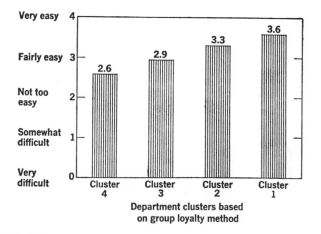

Fig. 9-6. Men's feeling as to ease of feeding ideas upward in the different clusters of departments.

show, this turns out to be the case. Moreover, on several other measurements of the effectiveness of communication, in addition to those in Figures 9-6 and 9-7, the results were as anticipated. Except for Cluster 4, which is discussed below, all the differences are in the expected direction;

that is, for every available measurement of communication, the high cluster of the group-loyalty method shows better communication than the middle cluster; the low cluster, Cluster 3, displays the poorest communication. Communication upward, downward, and between peers appears to be best in those departments which fall in the high cluster on this group-loyalty analysis and poorest in the low cluster.

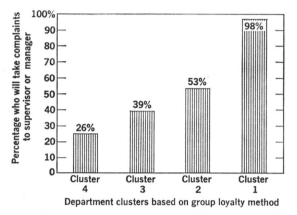

Fig. 9-7. Extent to which men in the different clusters of departments will take complaints first to supervisor or department manager.

The two departments in Cluster 4, the very low cluster, which have high group loyalty among the men but relatively high hostility between management and the men, should show, as they do, somewhat better communication than Cluster 3 on all the variables except the ability to feed ideas upward. The *high peer-group loyalty* facilitates communication among the men. But the break between men and management, reflected in the relatively hostile attitudes between management and men, makes it difficult from the men's point of view for them to feed ideas upward (Figure 9-6). Measures of the sensitivity of the managers to the reactions of the men show that the managers of these two departments are well aware of the men's unfavorable attitudes but apparently are pursuing deliberately a tough, pressure-oriented pattern of supervision on the assumption that it will yield the best results.

As Figure 9-7 shows, there are very large differences between the four clusters with regard to the proportion of men in the departments who will take complaints first to their supervisor or manager. In Cluster 1, which is high in total group loyalty, 98 per cent say they will do so; in Cluster 2, the middle cluster, 53 per cent say they will do so; but among the departments in Clusters 3 and 4 the percentage drops to 39 and 27. Evidently there are substantial barriers in the latter two clusters which block upward communication both of ideas and complaints.

The effect of group loyalty and group meetings upon the efficiency of communication throughout the organization is both marked and important. Not only do the results support the newer theory, but they add evidence beyond that presented in Chapters 2 to 4 that the man-to-man pattern of organization does not achieve the levels of efficient communication required by the complex, highly interdependent human organization made necessary by our present-day technologies. The research findings indicate that the achievement of satisfactory efficiency in the communication process requires a relatively high level of effective group functioning in every work group in the organization. Whenever a work group is ineffective, communication at and through that point in the organization breaks down.

Related to the results examined in Figure 9-7 are the findings shown in Figure 9-8. As would be predicted from the newer theory, the men in

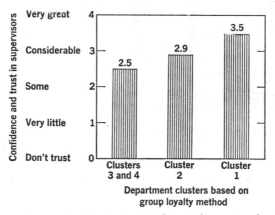

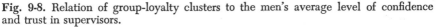

Fig. 9-8. Relation of group-loyalty clusters to the men's average level of confidence and trust in supervisors.

Cluster 1 have significantly more confidence and trust in their supervisors than do the men in the two other clusters. (Clusters 3 and 4 were combined since their scores were the same.) The men in the high departments not only are more willing to take complaints to their superiors than are the men in the low departments, but as Figure 9-8 shows, the men in the departments with high total group loyalty have more confidence and trust in their supervisors than do the men in the low departments. Again the results conform to the relationships which the theory proposed in Chapter 8 would predict.

The Relation of Group Loyalty to Influence

The newer theory places emphasis not only upon efficient communication, but also upon an organizational structure and processes through which influence can be effectively exercised. Theoretically, the overlapping group form of organization should be more effective both with regard to the influence processes and with regard to communication. The analyses just examined show that this form of organization is, in fact, more effective with regard to communication. We should expect similar results with regard to the influence processes.

Measures of the amount of influence exerted were obtained, it will be recalled, by asking the men, "In general, how much say or influence do you feel each of the following groups has on what goes on in your department?" The choices were, "Little or no influence," "Some," "Quite a bit," "A great deal of influence," "A very great deal of influence," and the question was asked with regard to: "Higher management of company," "The top management in your plant (city)," "Your department manager," "The men in your department." The same question was asked also of the managers.

The data show that the results conform to the expected pattern. Thus, the men in the high cluster of departments (Cluster 1) feel to an appreciably greater extent than do the men in the low departments, Clusters 3 and 4, that they exercise influence on what goes on in their departments (Figure 9-9). Moreover, the men in the high cluster, Cluster 1, feel to a greater extent than do the men in the other departments that their mana-

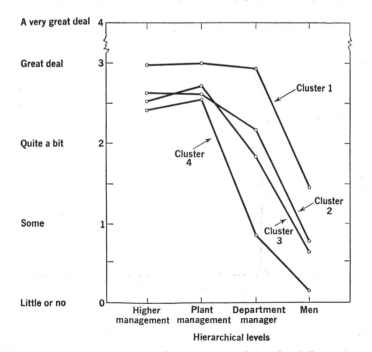

Fig. 9-9. The average amount of influence exercised by the different hierarchical levels as seen by the men in the different clusters of departments (clusters based on group-loyalty method).

gers exercise appreciable influence on what goes on in their departments. In addition, these men feel that higher management levels exercise more influence on their departments than do the men in the other clusters. The men in Cluster 1, in fact, see every level of the organization exercising more influence on what goes on in the department than do the men in the other departments. They see themselves exercising more influence, and they see a greater total amount of influence. (There is an appreciably greater area under the Cluster 1 curve in Figure 9-9.) *There is more reciprocal influence and more coordination in the high cluster departments than in the other departments.*

In the two departments in Cluster 4, there is a very low level of coordination and influence. These are departments, it will be recalled, in which there is high loyalty among the men coupled with relatively hostile attitudes between supervision and the workers. In this situation where there is hostility both on the part of the men toward management and conversely, the capacity of management to exercise influence and achieve effective coordination is affected adversely.

Figure 9-10 presents the curves showing the amount of influence which the men feel each level in the company *should* have on what goes on in

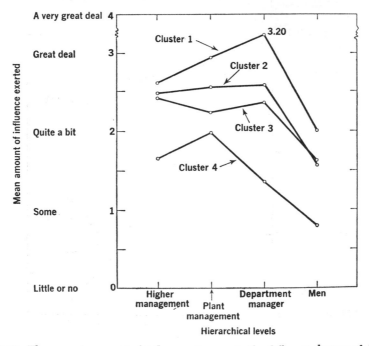

Fig. 9-10. The average amount of influence the men in the different clusters of departments feel that the different hierarchical levels should have (clusters based on group loyalty method).

the department. These data were obtained by asking the same questions on influence but with the words "should have" substituted for "has." A comparison of Figures 9-9 and 9-10 shows that, for each cluster, the men want the department manager and the men to have more influence than the men feel these levels now have. Moreover, the men in each cluster desire higher levels of management to have somewhat less influence than the men now feel is the case.

Other measures of the amount of influence which the men feel that they have confirm the pattern revealed in Figure 9-9. The men in Cluster 1 feel to a greater extent than do the men in the other departments that they are exercising influence. This is the case for such variables as the extent to which the men feel that (1) they had some say in getting their present job assignment, (2) they have influence on their manager, and (3) they have influence on the other men in their departments. On all these variables, Cluster 1 was highest, Cluster 2 next, and Cluster 4, lowest.

When the managers' estimates of the situation are used, the same pattern of results is obtained. The managers in Cluster 1 see both themselves and the men exercising more influence than do the managers of the low clusters, Clusters 3 and 4. Because of the small number of managers involved, these differences are not statistically significant. The results correspond, however, to the men's estimates of the situation.

Results comparable with those based on the group-loyalty method were obtained with the group-meeting method. It makes no difference which method is used for classifying the departments—both methods yield the same pattern of results. In those departments where there are effective group meetings or high total group loyalty—loyalty which includes the men and supervision—management has appreciably more influence than does the management in the other clusters of departments. In all the different departments, the nominal authority may be the same, but as the data show, the actual capacity to exercise influence and achieve greater coordination and better results is quite different. Greater total amounts of influence to achieve coordination exist in those situations where the overlapping group form of organization is present and being used effectively, i.e., where there is high peer-group loyalty coupled with favorable attitudes between management and workers. These results on influence indicate that greater actual authority occurs in those situations in which the organizational structure and management principles used most nearly approach the conditions called for by the newer management theory.

Before proceeding with a consideration of other dimensions in which work groups with high group loyalty differ from those with low, it will be well to look at conclusions which emerge from all the data on communication and influence. These two processes are essential to management.

They are performed better by the high-producing than low-producing managers, as the data in Chapter 4 showed. We have just examined analyses indicating that the high-producing managers achieve better communication and greater influence than the low, by the effective use of group meetings and by building favorable attitudes and greater group loyalty.

The conclusions drawn with regard to the principles and methods used by these better managers are supported by other research of a widely different character. The experiments on small groups show that groups with high group loyalty are particularly effective with regard to communication and the exercise of influence.

Other research on buying behavior and voting behavior shows that groups with which the individual identifies, to which he is attracted, and in which he spends an appreciable amount of his time exercise substantial influence on his behavior (Campbell, Converse, Miller, & Stokes, 1960; Campbell, Gurin, & Miller, 1954; Cartwright, 1949; Cartwright, 1951; Converse, 1958; Foundation for Research on Human Behavior, 1959a; Katz & Lazarsfeld, 1955; R. Likert, 1953b; Lionberger & Coughenour, 1957). Even though the mass media reach large numbers of people, their effectiveness in communication and influence is less potent than the face-to-face group. Groups with high group loyalty are an unusually effective communication and influence medium.

The Relation of Group Loyalty to Pressure, Tension, and Conflict

The higher productivity achieved by the high cluster departments (Cluster 1) is obtained with less sense of pressure, less tension, and less conflict and with greater employee satisfaction than occurs in the departments in the other clusters. Thus, for example, the men in the low clusters (Clusters 3 and 4) differ from the men in the high cluster (Cluster 1) in the extent to which they:

· Feel that their immediate supervisor and department manager expect them to do far too much
· Feel pressure for performance over and above what they think is reasonable
· Feel free to set their own work pace

The results of the group-loyalty method are shown in Figures 9-11 and 9-12. The data demonstrate that the higher productivity of the departments in Cluster 1 is achieved with less sense of pressure and with a greater feeling of freedom in doing the work. Moreover, this higher productivity is achieved with no greater feeling of working hard on the part of the men.

In view of the results shown in Figures 9-11 and 9-12, it is not surprising to find that the men in the departments in Cluster 1 feel that there is less tension and conflict in the organization than do the men in Clusters

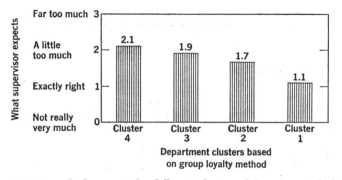

Fig. 9-11. Extent to which men in the different clusters of departments feel that their immediate supervisor expects them to do too much.

2 to 4. Figure 9-13 shows the extent to which the men in the different clusters feel that there is tension or conflict between the men and their supervisors. Comparable patterns of relationships, as seen by the men, exist also for the amount of tension and conflict between the men and

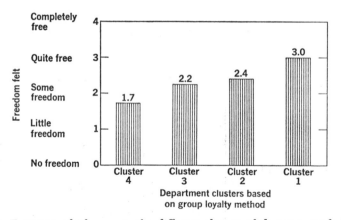

Fig. 9-12. Extent to which men in the different clusters of departments feel free to set their own pace.

higher management and between supervisors and higher management. The men in the departments in Clusters 3 and 4 see much more tension and conflict.

In addition to feeling that there is less tension and conflict between people in the organization, the men in Cluster 1 are much less likely to feel that their immediate supervisor is nervous and worried than the men in Clusters 2 to 4 (Figure 9-14).

Along with higher productivity, less pressure, and less tension and conflict, the men in Cluster 1, in contrast to the men in Clusters 2 to 4, are

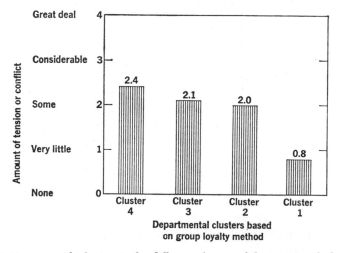

Fig. 9-13. Extent to which men in the different clusters of departments feel that there is tension or conflict between the men and supervisors.

more satisfied with the recognition they receive for their work, with the amount of responsibility they have, with their wages, and with the company as a place to work.

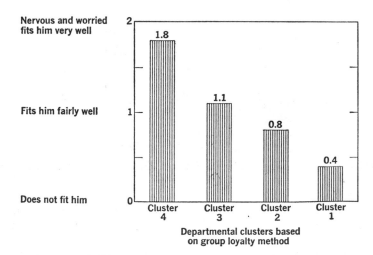

Fig. 9-14. Extent to which men in the different clusters of departments feel that their supervisor is often nervous and worried.

The same pattern of findings as those shown in Figures 9-11 to 9-14 are obtained when the group-meeting method of classification is used.

The preceding analyses yield results consistent with predictions based on the newer theory. Both methods of classifying the departments show that those in the high clusters achieve significantly higher productivity with far less strain, stress, pressure, tension, conflict, and anxiety than do those in the low clusters.

Managerial Behavior and Group Effectiveness

Data are available which shed light on the leadership most likely to achieve impressive performance. From the group-loyalty method of clustering the departments, we can conclude that managers should have supportive attitudes toward their men and should behave so as to create favorable attitudes toward supervision. The data in Chapter 2 describe the kinds of managerial behavior likely to yield favorable attitudes.

The group-meeting method of classifying the departments yields additional evidence. It not only demonstrates that effective group meetings are important; in addition, it reveals some of the ways in which the leadership in Cluster A is felt to be more supportive than is the leadership in the other departments. Thus, for example, the men in Cluster A are less likely than the men in the other clusters to feel that their boss is "quick to criticize," "blames the men," "treats employees as inferiors," "is stubborn," and "looks out for himself first." These results are shown in Figure 9-15.

The men in Cluster A do not think that their supervisors engage in threatening or rejecting behavior. They are more apt than are the men in Clusters B and C to see their supervisor as interested in the welfare of the men (Figure 9-16). They also see their supervisor behaving more supportively in other ways. Thus, they feel more often that their supervisor will "go to bat" for them, and they feel freer to discuss their personal problems with their supervisor. They also see their supervisor as more often asking the men their opinions when a problem comes up involving their work than do the men in Clusters B or C.

As might be expected, the men in Cluster A feel more often than do men in the other clusters that their department manager handles people well.

The results summarized above and illustrated in Figures 9-15 and 9-16 are again consistent with major concepts of the newer theory. The theory calls for behavior by the superior which is seen by the subordinate as supportive. Supportive behavior by the superior includes, of course, patient understanding, unselfishness, concern for the welfare of subordinates on the job and off the job, and a desire to obtain and use the ideas and experience of subordinates. As the preceding results show, the men in the high-cluster departments, much more often than the men in the other departments, see their superiors behaving supportively in these and similar ways.

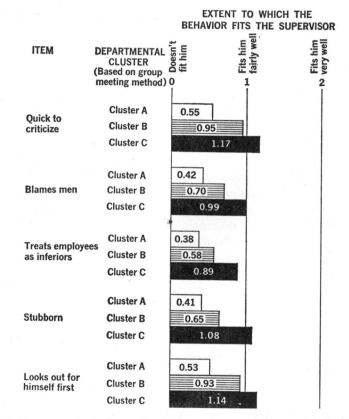

Fig. 9-15. Extent to which men in the different clusters of departments feel that their supervisor is—or is not—supportive (clusters based on group-meeting method).

An important concept of the newer theory, which was elaborated in Chapter 8, is that better results will be obtained when members of an organization are built into effectively functioning groups rather than dealt with on a man-to-man basis. One way to build such groups is to use group meetings to solve operating problems. Support of the newer theory is provided by the results obtained when departments are classified on their use of group meetings. As we have seen in this chapter, the departments in which the manager makes effective use of group meetings are significantly better in productivity, communication, influence, and attitudes and have much less anxiety, stress, and conflict than do the other departments. These data show that skilled use of group meetings, both formal and informal, for dealing with problems can contribute significantly to high performance and better over-all organization.

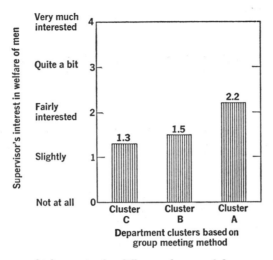

Fig. 9-16. Extent to which men in the different clusters of departments feel that their supervisor is interested in the welfare of the men (clusters based on group-meeting method).

Summary

In this chapter, we have made some tests of the newer theory of management by asking whether relationships, expected if the newer theory is valid, actually exist. Using data collected in 1955, analyses were made to see whether supportive behavior by the superior is associated with better productivity. This was found to be the case (Figure 9-1). Other analyses tested whether units displaying an overlapping group form of organization and containing groups which functioned well as groups would be better in productivity and in all other respects than units which did not use the group pattern of operation. In spite of the fact that quite crude measurements of limited reliability were used to classify the departments into clusters, impressive results emerged. Two different methods of classifying them as to the extent they did or did not use group processes yielded the same results. Departments which gave evidence of making better use of group processes proved to be appreciably better than departments which did not. All the analyses, by clusters, were consistent with expectations based on the newer theory of management and lend support to the theory's validity.

Chapter 10

VOLUNTARY ORGANIZATIONS

The ten-year program of research on leadership and organizational performance, started in 1947 by the Institute for Social Research, included plans for studies of voluntary organizations. These studies seemed important for two reasons. In the first place, it was reasonable to assume that the same general principles of leadership and organization which yield the best results in industry and government would also yield the best results for all other kinds of organizations, including voluntary organizations. The validity of this assumption needed to be tested. Secondly, it seemed probable that research on leadership and organizational principles in voluntary organizations would enrich the insights, broaden the general conclusions and principles emerging from the research in industry and government, and sharpen our understanding of how to apply these principles most effectively.

The studies of voluntary associations undertaken by the Institute for Social Research have yielded some surprising results. It was found that when the economic motive is not present in an organization, the manner in which the other motives function stand out much more clearly. This makes it possible to examine in a stronger light the leadership and management processes which are associated with high levels of performance when motives other than economic are used. A more thorough understanding of the character of such motives is thereby obtained. This knowledge reveals ways in which these motives can be yoked to economic motives to achieve a more effective and unified form of organization.

The studies of voluntary organizations not only revealed the same basic principles of organization and leadership as were found in industry and government, but one of these studies, in particular that of the League of Women Voters of the United States, added important new dimensions and gave new insights into organizational processes.

The following discussion draws heavily on four publications. Two of them (Tannenbaum & Donald, 1957; Tannenbaum, 1958) are original reports of the research. The other two (J. Likert, 1958; J. Likert, 1960) are booklets prepared for the League of Women Voters of the United States and published by them.

In this study, 104 local Leagues were selected so as to be representative of all 1,100 local Leagues in the United States. The method of sampling used yielded an unbiased probability sample. Each local League had a chance of selection proportional to the size of its membership.

A sample of members within these 104 Leagues was then drawn by using current membership lists. Approximately 25 names were randomly drawn in each League, except in some of the larger Leagues, where a larger sample was required. In addition to this sample, all the presidents of the 104 Leagues were included in the study. A supplementary sample of board members of local Leagues was also drawn in order to have enough board members for analysis as a separate group.

All the persons who were included in the cross-section sample and in the two supplementary samples of League presidents and board members were asked to fill out a mailed questionnaire. The high motivation of the members of the League is shown by the very high rate of return of these questionnaires. Thus, for the cross-section sample, 79 per cent returned their questionnaires, 95 per cent of the board members did so, and 100 per cent of the presidents. A total of 2,905 members or officers completed questionnaires. This is the sample used in the following analyses.

To study the relationship between leadership and local League effectiveness, a measure of "effectiveness" was required. Jane Likert (1958, pp. 4–5) describes this measure as follows:

. . . Two independent sources of information were tapped: (1) the judgments of 29 League members most of whom were or had been officers or board members of the national organization. These persons came from many parts of the country and had information and League experience, which in the view of the National office, gave them broad familiarity with the League; (2) the other source used was the research data themselves.

Each of the 29 women who served as judges was asked to rate the effectiveness of each of the sample Leagues. League effectiveness was defined as the extent to which a League accomplishes its goals. The general criteria used by the League in evaluating local Leagues' strengths and weaknesses were presented to guide the raters in their evaluations: size of League in relation to the size of the community, growth of League, the quality and quantity of League materials, the level of participation of members, their interest in League activities and their knowledge about them, success in fund-raising campaigns, and effect on their community. A set of instructions and a standardized form were provided so as to make more comparable the judgments of each of the experts.

The first bit of evidence that the judges had done a good job and that the effectiveness scores were meaningful was a high degree of agreement among the raters as to the relative effectiveness of the sample Leagues (reliability coefficient was 0.82).

To try to determine how valid was their common judgment, effectiveness scores were related to independent criteria. One pragmatic test of League effectiveness would be to give the members a job which has relevance to the League's work and see whether they get it done. If one found that Leagues rated effective did such a job well and Leagues rated less effective did the job less well, we should have independent evidence of the validity of the effectiveness ratings. This was the case. On the basis of the League ratings, it was possible to predict which Leagues would be more likely to return the League survey questionnaires first and which would need prodding to get them in. The less effective Leagues required more prodding.

If the ratings of over-all effectiveness given by the 29 League judges agreed with the specific items which the research data indicate are present in effective Leagues, we should have further confirmation on the soundness of the judgments. There was sufficient agreement to indicate that the effectiveness scores have validity. Members in effective Leagues reported greater membership activity than did those in less effective Leagues. They also reported more often that their Leagues were doing a high caliber job and were having a greater impact on their communities than did the members of the less effective Leagues. Members in effective Leagues also indicated a greater degree of loyalty in the face of community opposition to the organization. In these and in other respects, the research data supported the validity of the effectiveness ratings. While the ratings were based on judgmental and not on objective evidence, they appear to yield an approximate measure of local League effectiveness.

Pressure and Activity

An important factor contributing to the effectiveness of a local League is the strength in its members of the motivational forces to be active in the League. In the more effective Leagues, greater motivational forces to be active in League affairs are generated in both leaders and members. The data show that the more effective the League, the greater is the pressure which both members and leaders feel to participate. Moreover, as might be expected, the more pressure people feel to participate, the more active they are. This relationship is shown in Figure 10-1. As this figure shows, in those Leagues where members feel greater pressure *from some source* to participate, there is a much higher level of member activity on the average than is the case in Leagues where members feel much less pressure to participate.

Although there is a marked, positive relationship between the total pressure to participate felt by the members and the level of membership activity, the data indicate that there are real differences in the results produced by pressure from different sources. Some sources produce a positive effect upon activity, and therefore increase activity, and other sources produce a dampening effect upon activity. In those Leagues in which the members feel that there is pressure from the president or the board to participate, there are substantially lower levels of member ac-

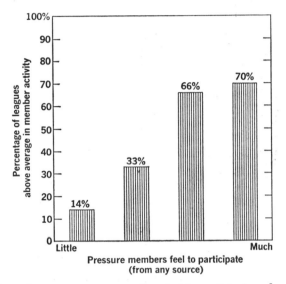

Fig. 10-1. Relation between pressure members feel to participate and member activity.

tivity and the Leagues are substantially less effective than is the case when the pressure comes from other sources. This adverse effect of pressure from the president upon League effectiveness is shown in Figure 10-2.

This figure shows a perplexing relationship. In those situations where no member feels pressure from the president to participate, only 53 per cent of the Leagues are above average in effectiveness. This is in contrast to the situation where less than "10 per cent feel pressure" from the president; in the latter case, 81 per cent of the Leagues are above average in effectiveness. It is probable that the first situation, where no one feels pressure from the president, contains two quite different sets of conditions. The first set may include Leagues whose leadership pattern is fundamentally laissez-faire. There is an absence of leadership, and goals and objectives are vague, confused, or missing; there are few commitments and little pressure to participate from any source—president, board, or members upon members. These Leagues, of course, are likely to be low in effectiveness, and few or none will be above average. The other set of conditions may involve Leagues in which the president and the board have so organized the League that the pressures to participate are coming from other members and unit leaders and not directly from the president or board. A very high proportion of such Leagues is likely to be above average in effectiveness, probably in excess of 81 per cent. The 53 per

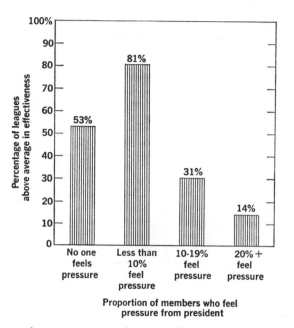

Fig. 10-2. Relation between pressure from president felt by members and League effectiveness.

cent, then, of Leagues above average in effectiveness is probably made up of two groups of Leagues which reflect the two different sets of conditions just described.

Although members react negatively to pressure from the president or from the board (Figure 10-2), nevertheless, they react favorably or positively to pressure from themselves, from other members, and from their unit and discussion leaders. Figure 10-3 is typical of the results obtained. This figure shows the relationship between the pressure members feel from unit or discussion leader and the level of League effectiveness. As will be observed in this figure, as the proportion of membership who feel pressure from a unit or discussion leader increases, the proportion of Leagues above average in effectiveness becomes greater.

The research results indicate that members react favorably to a feeling of pressure to participate if it comes from themselves or from members of their own face-to-face group; i.e., they react favorably to pressure from other members, their discussion leader, and their unit leader. They appear to resent and react unfavorably to pressure from higher levels of leadership, such as the board or president. These League members are behaving much as workers in industry do in accepting the goals and pressures of their own face-to-face group and resisting pressure from other sources, especially pressure from sources higher in the organization.

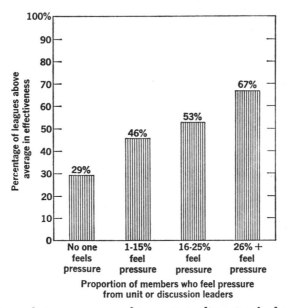

Fig. 10-3. Relation between pressure from unit or discussion leaders and League effectiveness.

It is striking that board members display the same kind of behavior as the members themselves. Board members react positively to pressure from other board members, but react negatively or unfavorably to pressure from the president. In fact, the greater the pressure from the president, the less active the board members tend to be. Moreover, in Leagues in which the board members report a high degree of pressure from the president, the same board members report that they feel very little self-imposed pressure. As a consequence, the more the president becomes a source of pressure within an organization, the less do the board members themselves put pressure on each other or on themselves. The Leagues with active board members are the Leagues in which board members report that they themselves—not their president—are their main source of pressure.

If pressure to participate is to be productive and to lead to greater member activity and to greater League effectiveness, the pressure must come from an "acceptable" source. There appear to be two major sources which are acceptable to both leaders and members and which yield motivational forces directed toward achieving the organization's goals. One source is internal, the pressures which come from one's own commitments, values, and internalized goals. The other source is pressure which arises from the goals and objectives established by the face-to-face group of which the person is a regular member. These goals and objectives, established through participation by the group, become powerful sources of pressure. Each member of the group expects each other member to carry her fair share of the tasks required to realize the goals which the group has established. She also assumes a similar obligation herself. As a consequence, she accepts, as proper, pressure from the other members to perform the functions expected of her and, in turn, puts corresponding pressure on the other members.

The motivational processes just described appear to be equally important and effective at every level in the League. As the research findings which we have examined show, these processes operate at the board level in local Leagues and also at the unit level. So long as persons are members of highly effective face-to-face groups which engage in relevant decision-making, these processes and the resulting motivational forces appear to be important.

Influence and Effectiveness

Research findings dealing with the influence process cast further light on the function of leadership, and especially on the role of the president. League members appear to be consistent in their behavior. Just as they react unfavorably to pressure from the president to participate, they feel that the membership should have appreciably more influence than they now have on matters of concern to the local League.

The question used to obtain data on the amount of influence now exercised is as follows: "In general, how much influence do you think the following groups or persons actually have in determining the policies and actions of your local League?" This question was asked separately for each of the following categories: "Your local president," "Your local board as a group (excluding the president)," "Your local membership as a whole (excluding the board)," "The state board," "The national board." For each of these different persons or groups the following choices of answers could be checked: "No influence," "A little influence," "Some influence," "A great deal of influence," "A very great deal of influence." To obtain evidence on the amount of influence which the membership feels is desirable, the same question was asked with "should" substituted for "actually."

As Figure 10-4 shows, the membership of the League thinks that the membership generally should have appreciably more influence than they now feel is the case. These results take on additional significance when the amount of influence exerted by the membership is related to League effectiveness.

When the results from the question on the amount of influence actually exerted is related to League effectiveness, the data show that presi-

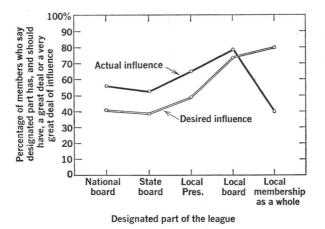

Designated part of the league

Fig. 10-4. The amount of influence members feel that various parts of the League have—and should have—on their local League.

dents in the more effective Leagues have no more influence on the average than do the presidents in the less effective Leagues. This relationship was found to exist when the effect of the size of the local League was removed by statistical methods of analysis (partial correlation). It seemed desirable to remove the effect of League size since both League size and the size of the community have a marked relationship with judged effectiveness.

In contrast to the finding that there is no relationship between the amount of influence exercised by the president and the effectiveness of the League, there is a marked relationship between the amount of influence exercised by the membership in a League, as seen by the members, and League effectiveness. In the more effective Leagues, the members feel that the membership has appreciably more influence than do the members in the less effective Leagues.

The above conclusions concerning the relationship between effectiveness and the amount of influence exercised by the president and the relationship between effectiveness and the amount of influence exercised by the membership are the same irrespective of whether the analyses are based on data from the members or from the board.

Just as there is an appreciable relationship between the level of member influence on local League affairs and League effectiveness, there is a correspondingly marked relationship between the level of member influence in a local League and the level of member activity. This relationship is shown in Figure 10-5.

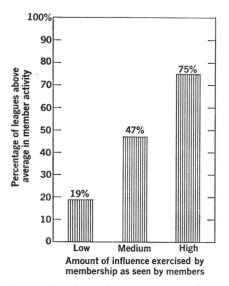

Fig. 10-5. Relation between amount of influence exercised by membership on activities of local League and proportion of Leagues above average in member activity.

The leadership of a local League plays an important role in determining the amount of influence exerted by the membership of the League on League activities. The amount of influence which the members of a local League feel that they actually have is related to the amount of influence which the board members of that League feel the members should have, and both are related to League effectiveness. Board members in the more effective Leagues want the membership to have a high level of influence on policies and activities in the local League to a greater extent than do the board members of the less effective Leagues. In Leagues where the board members want the members to have a high level of influence, the members more often feel that they do have a high level of influence. Conversely, in Leagues where board members feel that the leaders should have a high degree of influence and members should have little influence, the leaders, as seen both by themselves and by the members, are more likely to have a great deal of influence and members very little than is the case in other Leagues. Thus, the amount of influence which leaders feel that the members should have seems to be an important variable in determining the actual amount of influence which the members are able to exert in a particular local League.

For each League, an index can be computed which relates the amount of membership influence, as seen by the members, to the amount of influence exercised by the president, as seen by the members. This ratio, called the member-president influence index, has a marked relation, as would be expected from the preceding results, to League effectiveness. This relationship is shown in Figure 10-6.

As might be expected, the member-president index shows a marked relationship also to the level of activity of members in a local League. This is shown in Figure 10-7. The data are shown separately for large and small Leagues. Small Leagues were defined as those with less than 200 members; large as those with 200 or more members. As will be observed,

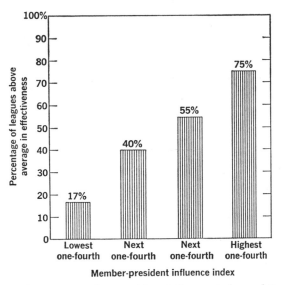

Fig. 10-6. Relation between member-president influence index and League effectiveness.

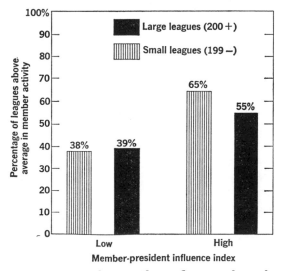

Fig. 10-7. Relation between member-president influence index and member activity.

the relationship between the member-president index and the level of member activity is greater in small Leagues than in large Leagues, but irrespective of size, there is a marked relationship.

The Flow of Information and Effectiveness

In the more effective Leagues, the members not only exercise more influence than they do in the less effective Leagues, but they also feel that they are kept better informed than do the members in the less effective Leagues. They feel that they are kept better informed by all sources of information, namely, by the president, the board members, the national League, the state League, and by other members. Figure 10-8 shows the

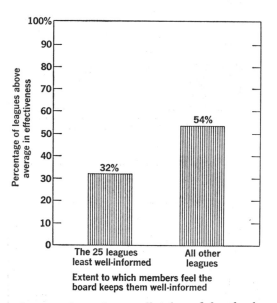

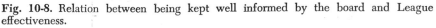

Fig. 10-8. Relation between being kept well informed by the board and League effectiveness.

relationship between being kept well informed by the board and League effectiveness. Relationships of comparable magnitude exist between League effectiveness and being kept informed by the president and by other members. Somewhat less marked relationships exist between League effectiveness and the feeling that the national League and the state League keep one informed.

Relationships comparable with that between League effectiveness and the feeling that one is kept well informed exist also between League effectiveness and the extent to which members feel that each of the following is interested in their ideas: the president, board members, and other members.

This same variable of interest in members' ideas on the part of the president or board members also has a marked relationship to member activity. This is shown in Figure 10-9. As will be observed from an exami-

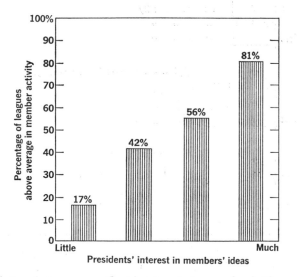

Fig. 10-9. Relation between presidents' interest in members' ideas and member activity.

nation of this figure, among Leagues where the members feel the president has little interest, the proportion of Leagues above average in member activity is 17 per cent. Among those Leagues where the members feel the president has considerable interest or much interest in their ideas, the proportion of Leagues above average in member activity is 81 per cent.

When the results are analyzed in terms of the level of activity of individual members, the findings show the importance of displaying interest in members' ideas on the part of all persons: the local League president, board, and membership. The more a member feels that there is interest in her ideas, the greater is the probability that she will be active. These results are shown in Figure 10-10.

The importance of interest in members' ideas is supported by other results. Thus, in the more effective Leagues, the presidents are felt by board members to understand the views and sentiments of members to a greater extent than is the case of presidents of less effective Leagues.

In view of the close relationship between communication and influence, it is not surprising that interest in ideas of members is associated with the amount of influence which members feel they exert in a local League. There is a close relationship between the interest of board members in the ideas of members and the member-president influence index. A similar

Of all those members who feel that <u>no</u> interest is shown in their ideas by:

Local president	10%	are high in activity
Local board	9%	" " " "
Other members	10%	" " " "

Of all those members who feel that <u>little</u> interest is shown in their ideas by:

Local president	20%	are high in activity
Local board	23%	" " " "
Other members	23%	" " " "

Of all those members who feel that <u>some</u> interest is shown in their ideas by:

Local president	25%	are high in activity
Local board	32%	" " " "
Other members	35%	" " " "

Of all those members who feel that <u>quite a bit</u> or <u>very much</u> interest is shown in their ideas by:

Local president	31%	are high in activity
Local board	35%	" " " "
Other members	37%	" " " "

Fig. 10-10. Relation of member activity to feeling that leaders—or other members—are interested in members' ideas.

relationship exists with regard to the president's interest in members' ideas. This shows that the more the members feel that the president's and board's behavior indicates an interest in their ideas, the greater is the amount of influence which these members feel they are exerting.

These data on influence, on being kept well informed, and on the extent to which others are interested in one's ideas demonstrate that there is a marked relationship between League effectiveness and the extent to which there is within the local League both an efficient flow of information in all directions and the capacity for all persons within the League to exercise relatively high levels of influence upon other members and upon leaders. As we have already observed, these same variables are also related to the level of member activity. Keeping members informed, displaying a genuine interest in their ideas, and enabling them to exert influence are, of course, important applications of the principle of supportive relationships.

The more effective Leagues are aided in achieving their objectives by better communication, better decisions, and greater coordination of the efforts of their members. The influence process is, however, not unidirectional, i.e., from top downward, but involves the exercise of influence in all directions. Members and leaders in the more effective Leagues all feel that they can exert more influence upon each other than is the case in the less effective Leagues. There is correspondingly better-focused coordination of the efforts of leaders and members on achieving the goals of the organization. The effective Leagues have an interaction system which accomplishes appreciably more than do the less effective Leagues.

It is not possible to demonstrate from the results which have been examined the direction of causality; that is, we cannot prove from these data whether conviction by board members that the membership should be able to exert influence contributes to making a local League effective or whether effective Leagues make board members feel that the membership should exert influence. Although these variables are probably somewhat circular in causality in that each contributes causally to the other, the major direction of causality appears to be in the direction of increased League effectiveness when the organizational structure and leadership-membership processes result in members feeling that they are exercising high levels of influence and are being kept well informed and that others, including the leaders, are interested in their ideas. The data suggest that if a member feels that she is exercising influence on what goes on in the League, and if she is kept well informed and others are interested in her ideas, she is more likely to be active and also more likely to behave in ways which make that particular League an effective organization.

Size and Effectiveness

There is another important dimension of the more powerful interaction system which characterizes the operation of the more effective Leagues. This dimension becomes evident when the operations of Leagues are analyzed in relation to their size. There is a tendency for Leagues, as they increase in size, to increase in effectiveness up to a particular point. At a membership size of about 400, that tendency disappears. As a consequence, further increases in size are not accompanied by further increases in effectiveness. There seems to be a relatively sharp point of diminishing return as Leagues exceed a membership of about 300 to 400. As Leagues become greater than 400 in size, their effectiveness per member becomes progressively less (Figure 10-11).

Associated with this decrease in effectiveness per member as Leagues grow in size above a membership of about 400 is a decrease in the proportion of members who are active; that is, as Leagues increase in size, the proportion of members who are active decreases. The opposite is true of the leaders. In the very large Leagues, the leaders, both president and board members, are much more active than are the leaders in Leagues with fewer than 400 members. There is a very marked relationship be-

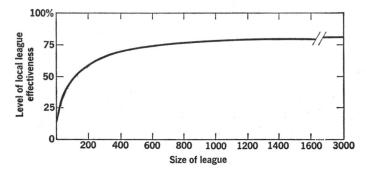

Fig. 10-11. Relation of size of League to League effectiveness.

tween the size of the League and the level of president and board-member activity. This relationship for board members is shown in Figure 10-12. As will be observed, only 7 per cent of the Leagues with less than 100 members are above average in board-member activity. On the other hand, 88 per cent of the Leagues with over 400 members are above average in the activity level of their board members.

As Leagues increase in size, especially as they exceed a membership of about 400, important changes occur in the behavior of the leadership

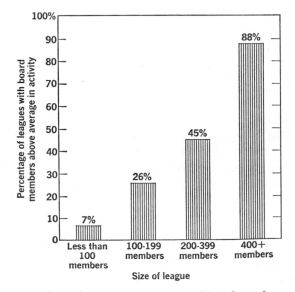

Fig. 10-12. Relation between League size and board-member activity.

and in the interactions which occur within the League. Even though the president and board members are more active in the larger Leagues and spend more time on League affairs, they tend to engage in activity which gives them less intimate, sustained face-to-face contact with the membership than occurs in smaller Leagues. Thus, the presidents of Leagues with a membership of over 400 attend general meetings much more often than do presidents of smaller Leagues. This does not mean that the presidents of smaller Leagues do not go to their general meetings, but apparently the large Leagues have more such general meetings than do the smaller Leagues. At large meetings, the presidents do not have the opportunities afforded by units and committee meetings for full, frank discussion of League affairs with members. (Most units and committees in local Leagues are composed of about fifteen members or less.) In relation to the size of the League, therefore, the presidents of large Leagues appear to have less opportunity for candid personal interaction with a substantial proportion of the membership than is the case in the smaller Leagues.

In the very large Leagues, the president and board members attend as many unit meetings as do the president and board members in smaller Leagues, but since the very large Leagues have many more units than the smaller Leagues, the character of board-member participation in the unit meetings is quite different. In Leagues of 400 or fewer members, it is the general practice to have in each unit a board member as a regular and established member of that unit. In the very large Leagues, however, there are many more units than there are board members. As a consequence, most units will be visited only occasionally by a board member.

If an individual is to function effectively and fully as a group member, she must be in regular attendance at group meetings. This is particularly true for individuals who have a different status in the group than do most of its members. This means, of course, that a board member as a visitor at a unit meeting is not likely to be able to join in the interaction of the group in the same give-and-take manner as she would if she were a full-fledged member of the unit attending regularly. Moreover, the unit is likely to be affected by her presence and be unable to function and communicate in the relaxed, candid manner characteristic of its usual meetings. The full, frank exchange of ideas, suggestions, and criticism needed to achieve a highly effective League is apt to be dampened when a person of high status is present in the group as a visitor and not as a fully accepted member of the group.

In the very large Leagues with membership in excess of 400, the members generally have far fewer opportunities for candid, frank interaction with leaders. They do not have the opportunity for the kind of interaction which the secure, supportive atmosphere of small, effectively functioning groups provide. As a consequence, the entire face-to-face small-group interactional process of local Leagues breaks down as Leagues exceed a membership of about 400.

As Jane Likert (1958, pp. 13–14) reports:

It is not surprising to find, therefore, that relative to their size the very large Leagues have, to an appreciably lesser extent than do the smaller Leagues, those powerful resources for communication and interaction (the small, well-established group) which the research findings show are associated with high member influence and a high degree of member activity. As seen by members, the larger the League:

· The less the president is interested in their ideas.
· The less the board is interested in their ideas.
· The frequency with which the members give information to the president is less.
· The frequency with which the members give information to the board is less.
· The frequency with which the members receive information from the president is less.
· The frequency with which the members receive information from the board is less.
· The less is the influence of members on the president.
· The less is the influence of members on the board.

The larger the League, the more it lacks a social system which uses fully the available woman power. The large Leagues are well aware of this fact and many of them are making great efforts to overcome their special difficulties.

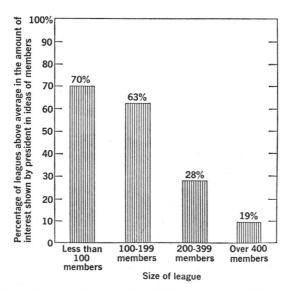

Fig. 10-13. Relation between League size and the proportion of Leagues above average in the amount of interest shown by the president in the ideas of members (as seen by the members).

Figure 10-13 illustrates the character of the relationship between League size and such variables as the interest shown by leaders in the ideas of members.

As might be expected from the results which have been examined, the data show that the more opportunities existing for *face-to-face contact and discussion* between leaders and members, the greater is the amount of influence which the members themselves feel that they have on the policies and activities of their local League. Thus, the greater the number of unit meetings which are attended regularly by the president or the board members, the greater is the amount of influence which members feel that they have on local League affairs. When board members attend "few or very few" meetings, only 38 per cent of such Leagues are above average in member-president influence index. On the other hand, when board members attend "very many" unit meetings, 85 per cent of such Leagues are above average in the member-president influence index.

The Influence of Structure and Size upon Effectiveness

The typical structure of a local League seems to account for the drop in effectiveness per member as Leagues increase in size above a membership of about 400. This structure also appears to be responsible for the changed pattern of relationship between members and leaders as Leagues exceed this size. The usual structure of a local League makes excellent provision for candid, face-to-face interaction in well-established groups for a membership up to about 400. Above that number, it is not possible with the usual structure to have all the members and leaders in well-established groups that are linked together by multiple overlapping groups. As a consequence, as the data show, in the larger Leagues more use is made of general meetings and there is less face-to-face interaction.

The usual structure of a local League is shown schematically in Figure 10-14. This figure is not completely accurate for all Leagues. For example, there may be more than one agenda item at each level and the committee organization may vary from League to League, but the figure presents correctly the general pattern. This structure functions about as follows: Each member of a local League belongs to a "unit." These units, which average about fifteen members, meet regularly. Their sessions are devoted to carrying out the business of the League: studying and discussing "agenda items" which have been established as the program objectives of the League, discussing possible legislative action, discussing the program objectives for the League for the ensuing year, etc. These units are important interactional entities in the local League and provide the opportunities for the information flow and the exercise of influence which we have found to be important for a high degree of League effectiveness.

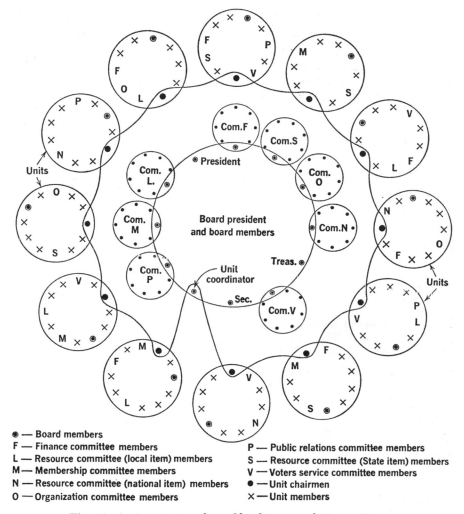

Fig. 10-14. Organization chart of local League of Women Voters.

If the units are to function well, there must be efficient coordination between each unit and the rest of the organization. Each unit needs to be linked to the rest of the organization through persons who are members of a unit and also members of effectively functioning groups which provide overlapping linkage with all the other units. As Figure 10-14 shows, the unit chairmen serve as linking pins that link each of the units to the unit coordinator, who, in turn, links this group of unit chairmen to the board of the local League.

Another linkage occurs as shown in Figure 10-14 by having each board member serve as regular member of each of the units. The findings leading to the newer theory suggest that this probably is a tighter linkage than would occur if the unit chairmen and unit coordinator alone provided the link between the board and the member.

Another linkage is provided by the resource chairmen and members of the resource and other committees who are also members of the different units. Board members are chairmen of most committees. The different resource committees provide each unit with a member who has devoted time and study to one of the agenda items, such as, for example, revision of the city charter. During the time the unit is discussing this problem, the member of the unit who is also a member of the relevant "resource committee" serves as an expert and a source of information. These resource persons through their resource committee and its chairman, who is a board member, serve as additional linking pins, linking the units together via the resource committee and via the board.

Multiple linkage is consequently provided by the overlapping membership in units, committees, and board. This gives the organization alternative paths of communication and interaction. For example, an idea can go from a member to the chairman of the unit, who subsequently meets with other chairmen and the unit coordinator, or to the board member attending the unit or committee, or to a member of the unit (other than the board member) who is also a member of the committee, and via her and the committee chairman to the board. If for any reason one path is blocked, there are other ways for information to flow to and from the board and for influence to be exerted.

The optimum size of units in local Leagues has been found from experience to be about fifteen to twenty persons. This is also true of boards. Similarly, the optimum size of resource committees is usually not more than about fifteen to twenty persons. It becomes increasingly difficult for the unit coordinator or a resource-committee chairman to develop an effectively functioning committee or group when the number of members grows much larger than fifteen or twenty. The experience of local Leagues indicates that as the groups increase in size, there is some decrease in effectiveness per member, and as the groups exceed about twenty, the decrease in effectiveness becomes more marked. From this figure of fifteen to twenty persons as the maximum for efficient unit or committee functioning, one can readily demonstrate that the present structure for local Leagues will work well for a membership of up to about 300 to 400. Thus, if units vary in size between fifteen to twenty and if the committees or board which links such units into an over-all organization also vary in size between fifteen to twenty, then the maximum number of members which the organization can handle effectively will be between 300 and 400 (15 times 20 is 300, and 20 times 20 is 400). If face-to-face interaction in continuing, well-established groups is necessary in a local League for high levels of member activity and effectiveness per member, then with the present organizational structure at about 300 to 400 members, there should start to be a noticeable falling off in League effectiveness.

This, of course, is precisely what the data from the national study of local Leagues show to be the case. As we saw in Figure 10-11, Leagues increase in effectiveness as they increase in size up to about 300 to 400 members. Below this number, the larger the League, the more effective it tends to be. Above this number, the relationship virtually disappears and greater size is not associated with greater effectiveness. The very large Leagues appear to lack an organizational structure which leads to face-to-face interaction in well-established groups linked together by multiple overlapping groups. Since they do not have a structure enabling face-to-face interaction and influence, the very large Leagues lack the kinds of processes leading to high member motivation, a high level of member activity, and high effectiveness per member.

The data on League effectiveness in relation to League size and the results on the changes in the leadership and membership behavior as Leagues increase in size are consistent with the derivation in Chapter 8 as to the superiority of the overlapping group form of organizational structure. The data show that in order to achieve better communication, greater activity, more coordinated activity, and high effectiveness per member, a League requires an organizational structure made up of effective small face-to-face groups linked into a total organization by overlapping groups made up of persons who are performing the linking pin function successfully. This form of organizational structure appears to be necessary if the information, influence, and motivational processes which are necessary for high League effectiveness are to be performed well.

The Interaction System and Effectiveness

As might be expected from the preceding findings, the presidents of the effective Leagues give more attention than do presidents of other Leagues to creating and sustaining the kind of interaction system necessary for League effectiveness:

1. They create for the League an organizational structure which enables it to develop high levels of communication, interaction, and influence. This structure, as we have seen, consists of highly effective groups linked into a tightly knit total organization by persons who are members of more than one group.

2. They help the leaders and members in each group (unit, committee, or board) achieve a high level of interactional skill. This they do by:

· · Helping them to establish in each group the underlying philosophy and values necessary to create a supportive climate which permeates all the activities of the group. This is accomplished through sharing relevant information with them, being interested in their ideas, being willing to be influenced by them, not competing for prestige, and in similar ways behaving so as to show confidence and trust in them and respect for their ability and integrity.

· · Helping them to develop the concepts, skills, and sensitivity to others required for participating in the interactional processes of highly effective groups (see Chapter 11). This can be done by example and, when such help is sought, by coaching and counseling.

· · Aiding each group to develop favorable attitudes and loyalties among the members toward each other, the organization, and its objectives. The favorable attitudes and loyalties help bind the organization together and help maintain the friendly, supportive atmosphere characteristic of a highly effective group.

3. They create a positive value for high performance throughout the organization by such steps as establishing the expectation that everyone will do a "League-like job."

4. They stimulate and encourage the League to set for itself, through the interaction process, objectives which are often difficult but which members and leaders alike feel are urgent, important, and worthwhile.

Chapter 11

THE NATURE OF
HIGHLY EFFECTIVE GROUPS

We concluded in Chapter 8 that the form of organization which will make the greatest use of human capacity consists of highly effective work groups linked together in an overlapping pattern by other similarly effective groups. The highly effective work group is, consequently, an important component of the newer theory of management. It will be important to understand both its nature and its performance characteristics. We shall examine these in this chapter, but first a few words about groups in general.

Although we have stressed the great potential power of the group for building effective organizations, it is important to emphasize that this does *not* say that all groups and all committees are highly effective or are committed to desirable goals. Groups as groups can vary from poor to excellent. They can have desirable values and goals, or their objectives can be most destructive. They can accomplish much that is good, or they can do great harm. There is nothing *implicitly* good or bad, weak or strong, about a group.

The nature of the group determines the character of its impact upon the development of its members. The values of the group, the stability of these values, the group atmosphere, and the nature of the conformity demanded by the group determine whether a group is likely to have a positive or negative impact upon the growth and behavior of its members. If the values of the group are seen by the society as having merit, if the group is stable in its adherence to these values, and if the atmosphere of the group is warm, supportive, and full of understanding, the group's influence on the development of its members will be positive. A hostile atmosphere and socially undesirable or unstable values produce a negative impact upon the members' growth and behavior.

Loyalty to a group produces pressures toward conformity. A group may demand conformity to the idea of supporting, encouraging, and giving recognition for individual creativity, or it may value rigidity of behavior,

162

MEMO

from the desk of Michael P. Dumler:

To

Re

Date

with seriously narrowing and dwarfing consequences. This latter kind of pressure for conformity keeps the members from growing and robs the group of original ideas. Many writers have pointed to these deleterious effects of conformity. They often overlook the capacity of groups to stimulate individual creativeness by placing a high value on imaginative and original contributions by their members. As Pelz's findings, reported in Chapter 2, demonstrate, groups can contribute significantly to creativity by providing the stimulation of diverse points of view within a supportive atmosphere which encourages each individual member to pursue new and unorthodox concepts.

Some business executives are highly critical of groups—or committees— and the inability of committees to accomplish a great deal. Their criticisms are often well warranted. In many instances, committees are wasteful of time and unable to reach decisions. Sometimes the decisions, when reached, are mediocre. Moreover, some members of management at various hierarchical levels use committees as escape mechanisms—as a way to avoid the responsibility for a decision.

The surprising thing about committees is not that many or most are ineffective, but that they accomplish as much as they do when, relatively speaking, we know so little about how to use them. There has been a lack of systematic study of ways to make committees effective. Far more is known about time-and-motion study, cost accounting, and similar aspects of management than is known about groups and group processes. Moreover, in spite of the demonstrated potentiality of groups, far less research is being devoted to learning the role of groups and group processes and how to make the most effective use of them in an organization than to most management practices. We know appreciably less about how to make groups and committees effective than we know about most matters of managing.

We do know that groups can be powerful. The newer theory takes this into account and tries to make constructive use of the group's potential strength for developing and mobilizing human resources.

In this and other chapters the use of the term "group" may give the impression that groups have the capacity to behave in ways other than through the behavior of their members. Thus, such expressions appear as the "group's goals," "the group decides," or the "group motivates." In many instances, these expressions are used to avoid endless repetition of the words, "the members of the group." In other instances, something more is meant. Thus, in speaking of "group values," the intent is to refer to those values which have been established by the group through a group-decision process involving consensus. Once a decision has been reached by consensus, there are strong motivational forces, developed within each individual as a result of his membership in the group and his relationship to the other members, to be guided by that decision. In this sense, the group has goals and values and makes decisions. It has properties which may not be present, as such, in any one individual. A group may be divided in opinion, for example, although this may not be true of any one member. Dorwin Cartwright puts it this way: "The relation between the individual members and the group is analogous to the distinction made in mathematics between the properties of a set of elements and the properties of the elements within a set. Every set is composed of elements, but sets have properties which are not identical with the properties of the elements of the set."

The Highly Effective Work Group

Much of the discussion of groups in this chapter will be in terms of an ideal organizational model which the work groups in an organization can approach as they develop skill in group processes. This model group, of course, is always part of a large organization. The description of its nature and performance characteristics is based on evidence from a variety of sources. Particularly important are the observational and experimental studies of small groups such as those conducted by the Research Center for Group Dynamics (Cartwright & Zander, 1960; Hare et al., 1955; Institute for Social Research, 1956; Institute for Social Research, 1960; Thibaut & Kelley, 1959). Extensive use is made of data from studies of large-scale organizations (see Chapters 2 to 4). Another important source is the material from the National Training Laboratories (Foundation for Research on Human Behavior, 1960d; National Training Laboratories, 1953; National Training Laboratories, 1960; Stock & Thelen, 1958). The NTL has focused on training in sensitivity to the reactions of others and in skills to perform the leadership and membership roles in groups.

In addition to drawing upon the above sources, the description of the ideal model is derived from theory. Some of the statements about the model for which there is little or limited experimental or observational data have been derived directly from the basic drive to achieve and maintain a sense of importance and personal worth. At several points in this chapter and Chapter 12 the author has gone appreciably beyond available specific research findings. The author feels, however, that the generalizations which are emerging based on research in organizations and on small groups, youth, and family life, personality development, consumer behavior, human motivation, and related fields lend strong support to the general theory and the derivations contained in this book.

It has been necessary to go beyond the data in order to spell out at this time in some detail the general pattern of the more complex but more effective form of organization being created by the higher-producing managers. The author hopes that the theory and model proposed will stimulate a substantial increase in basic and developmental research and that they will be tested and sharpened by that research.

The body of knowledge about small groups, while sufficiently large to make possible this description of the ideal model, is still relatively limited. Without question, as the importance of the work group as the basic building block of organizations becomes recognized, there will be a great increase in the research on groups and our knowledge about them. The over-all pattern of the model described here will be improved and clarified by such research. Our understanding of how to develop and use groups effectively will also be greatly advanced.

The following description of the ideal model defines what we mean by a highly effective group. The definition involves reference to several different variables. Each of them can be thought of as a continuum, i.e., as a characteristic which can vary from low to high, from unfavorable to favorable. For example, a group can vary from one in which there is hostility among the members to one in which the attitudes are warm and friendly. The ideal model is at the favorable end of each variable.

The Nature of Highly Effective Work Groups

The highly effective group, as we shall define it, is always conceived as being a part of a larger organization. A substantial proportion of persons in a company are members of more than one work group, especially when both line and staff are considered. As a consequence, in such groups there are always linking functions to be performed and relationships to other groups to be maintained. Our highly effective group is not an isolated entity.

All the persons in a company also belong to groups and organizations outside of the company. For most persons, membership in several groups both within and outside the company is the rule rather than the exception. This means, of course, that no single group, even the highly effective work group, dominates the life of any member. Each member of the organization feels pressures from membership in several different groups and is not influenced solely by loyalty to any one group.

Since the different groups to which a person belongs are apt to have somewhat different and often inconsistent goals and values, corresponding conflicts and pressures are created within him. To minimize these conflicts and tensions, the individual seeks to influence the values and goals of each of the different groups to which he belongs and which are important to him so as to minimize the inconsistencies and conflicts in values and goals. In striving for this reconciliation, he is likely to press for the acceptance of those values most important to him.

The properties and performance characteristics of the ideal highly effective group are as follows:

1. The members are skilled in all the various leadership and membership roles and functions required for interaction between leaders and members and between members and other members.

2. The group has been in existence sufficiently long to have developed a well-established, relaxed working relationship among all its members.

3. The members of the group are attracted to it and are loyal to its members, including the leader.

4. The members and leaders have a high degree of confidence and trust in each other.

5. The values and goals of the group are a satisfactory integration and expression of the relevant values and needs of its members. They have helped shape these values and goals and are satisfied with them.

6. In so far as members of the group are performing linking functions, they endeavor to have the values and goals of the groups which they link in harmony, one with the other.

7. The more important a value seems to the group, the greater the likelihood that the individual member will accept it.

8. The members of the group are highly motivated to abide by the major values and to achieve the important goals of the group. Each member will do all that he reasonably can—and at times all in his power—to help the group achieve its central objectives. He expects every other member to do the same. This high motivation springs, in part, from the basic motive to achieve and maintain a sense of personal worth and importance. Being valued by a group whose values he shares, and deriving a sense of significance and importance from this relationship, leads each member to do this best. He is eager not to let the other members down. He strives hard to do what he believes is expected of him.

9. All the interaction, problem-solving, decision-making activities of the group occur in a supportive atmosphere. Suggestions, comments, ideas, information, criticisms are all offered with a helpful orientation. Similarly, these contributions are received in the same spirit. Respect is shown for the point of view of others both in the way contributions are made and in the way they are received.

There are real and important differences of opinion, but the focus is on arriving at sound solutions and not on exacerbating and aggravating the conflict. Ego forces deriving from the desire to achieve and maintain a sense of personal worth and importance are channeled into constructive efforts. Care is taken not to let these ego forces disrupt important group tasks, such as problem-solving. Thus, for example, a statement of the problem, a condition which any solution must meet, a suggested solution, or an item of relevant fact are all treated as from the group as a whole.

Care is taken so that one statement of the problem is not John's and another Bill's. A suggested solution is not referred to as Tom's and another as Dick's. All the material contributed is treated as *ours:* "One of our proposed solutions is *A,* another is *B.*" In all situations involving actual or potential differences or conflict among the members of the group, procedures are used to separate the ego of each member from his contribution. In this way, ego forces do not stimulate conflict between members. Instead, they are channeled into supporting the activities and efforts of the group.

The group atmosphere is sufficiently supportive for the members to be able to accept readily any criticism which is offered and to make the most constructive use of it. The criticisms may deal with any relevant topic such as operational problems, decisions, supervisory problems, interpersonal relationships, or group processes, but whatever their content, the member feels sufficiently secure in the supportive atmosphere of the group to be able to accept, test, examine, and benefit from the criticism offered. Also, he is able to be frank and candid, irrespective of the content of the discussion: technical, managerial, factual, cognitive, or emotional. The supportive atmosphere of the group, with the feeling of security it provides, contributes to a cooperative relationship between the members. And this cooperation itself contributes to and reinforces the supportive atmosphere.

10. The superior of each work group exerts a major influence in establishing the tone and atmosphere of that work group by his leadership principles and practices. In the highly effective group, consequently, the leader adheres to those principles of leadership which create a supportive atmosphere in the group and a cooperative rather than a competitive relationship among the members. For example, he shares information fully with the group and creates an atmosphere where the members are stimulated to behave similarly.

11. The group is eager to help each member develop to his full potential. It sees, for example, that relevant technical knowledge and training in interpersonal and group skills are made available to each member.

12. Each member accepts willingly and without resentment the goals and expectations that he and his group establish for themselves. The anxieties, fears, and emotional stresses produced by direct pressure for high performance from a boss in a hierarchical situation is not present. Groups seem capable of setting high performance goals for the group as a whole and for each member. These goals are high enough to stimulate each member to do his best, but not so high as to create anxieties or fear of failure. In an effective group, each person can exert sufficient influence on the decisions of the group to prevent the group from setting

unattainable goals for any member while setting high goals for all. The goals are adapted to the member's capacity to perform.

13. The leader and the members believe that each group member can accomplish "the impossible." These expectations stretch each member to the maximum and accelerate his growth. When necessary, the group tempers the expectation level so that the member is not broken by a feeling of failure or rejection.

14. When necessary or advisable, other members of the group will give a member the help he needs to accomplish successfully the goals set for him. Mutual help is a characteristic of highly effective groups.

15. The supportive atmosphere of the highly effective group stimulates creativity. The group does not demand narrow conformity as do the work groups under authoritarian leaders. No one has to "yes the boss," nor is he rewarded for such an attempt. The group attaches high value to new, creative approaches and solutions to its problems and to the problems of the organization of which it is a part. The motivation to be creative is high when one's work group prizes creativity.

16. The group knows the value of "constructive" conformity and knows when to use it and for what purposes. Although it does not permit conformity to affect adversely the creative efforts of its members, it does expect conformity on mechanical and administrative matters to save the time of members and to faciliate the group's activities. The group agrees, for example, on adminstrative forms and procedures, and once they have been established, it expects its members to abide by them until there is good reason to change them.

17. There is strong motivation on the part of each member to communicate fully and frankly to the group all the information which is relevant and of value to the group's activity. This stems directly from the member's desire to be valued by the group and to get the job done. The more important to the group a member feels an item of information to be, the greater is his motivation to communicate it.

18. There is high motivation in the group to use the communication process so that it best serves the interests and goals of the group. Every item which a member feels is important, but which for some reason is being ignored, will be repeated until it receives the attention that it deserves. Members strive also to avoid communicating unimportant information so as not to waste the group's time.

19. Just as there is high motivation to communicate, there is correspondingly strong motivation to receive communications. Each member is genuinely interested in any information on any relevant matter that any member of the group can provide. This information is welcomed and trusted as being honestly and sincerely given. Members do not look

"behind" the information item and attempt to interpret it in ways opposite to its purported intent. This interest of group members in information items and the treatment of such items as valid reinforces the motivation to communicate.

20. In the highly effective group, there are strong motivations to try to influence other members as well as to be receptive to influence by them. This applies to all the group's activities: technical matters, methods, organizational problems, interpersonal relationships, and group processes.

21. The group processes of the highly effective group enable the members to exert more influence on the leader and to communicate far more information to him, including suggestions as to what needs to be done and how he could do his job better, than is possible in a man-to-man relationship. By "tossing the ball" back and forth among its members, a group can communicate information to the leader which no single person on a man-to-man basis dare do. As a consequence, the boss receives all the information that the group possesses to help him perform his job effectively.

22. The ability of the members of a group to influence each other contributes to the flexibility and adaptability of the group. Ideas, goals, and attitudes do not become frozen if members are able to influence each other continuously.

Although the group is eager to examine any new ideas and methods which will help it do its job better and is willing to be influenced by its members, it is not easily shifted or swayed. Any change is undertaken only after rigorous examination of the evidence. This stability in the group's activities is due to the steadying influence of the common goals and values held by the group members.

23. In the highly effective group, individual members feel secure in making decisions which seem appropriate to them because the goals and philosophy of operation are clearly understood by each member and provide him with a solid base for his decisions. This unleashes initiative and pushes decisions down while still maintaining a coordinated and directed effort.

24. The leader of a highly effective group is selected carefully. His leadership ability is so evident that he would probably emerge as a leader in any unstructured situation. To increase the likelihood that persons of high leadership competence are selected, the organization is likely to use peer nominations and related methods in selecting group leaders.

An important aspect of the highly effective group is its extensive use of the principle of supportive relationships. An examination of the above material reveals that virtually every statement involves an application of this principle.

Leadership Functions

Several different characteristics of highly effective groups have been briefly examined. The role of the leader in these groups is, as we have suggested, particularly important. Certain leadership functions can be shared with group members; others can be performed only by the designated leader. In an organization, for example, the leader of a unit is the person who has primary responsibility for linking his work group to the rest of the organization. Other members of the group may help perform the linking function by serving as linking pins in overlapping groups other than that provided by the line organization, but the major linking is necessarily through the line organization. The leader has full responsibility for the group's performance and for seeing that his group meets the demands and expectations placed upon it by the rest of the organization of which it is a part. Other members of the group may share this responsibility at times, but the leader can never avoid full responsibility for the adequate performance of his group.

Although the leader has full responsibility, he does not try to make all the decisions. He develops his group into a unit which, with his participation, makes better decisions than he can make alone. He helps the group develop efficient communication and influence processes which provide it with better information, more technical knowledge, more facts, and more experience for decision-making purposes than the leader alone can marshal.

Through group decision-making each member feels fully identified with each decision and highly motivated to execute it fully. The over-all performance of the group, as a consequence, is even better than the excellent quality of the decisions.

The leader knows that at times decisions must be made rapidly and cannot wait for group processes. He anticipates these emergencies and establishes procedures with his group for handling them so that action can be taken rapidly with group support.

The leader feels primarily responsible for establishing and maintaining at all times a thoroughly supportive atmosphere in the group. He encourages other members to share this responsibility, but never loses sight of the fact that as the leader of a work group which is part of a larger organization his behavior is likely to set the tone.

Although the leader accepts the responsibility associated with his role of leader of a group which is part of a larger organization, he seeks to minimize the influence of his hierarchical position. He is aware that trying to get results by "pulling rank" affects adversely the effectiveness of his group and his relationship to it. Thus, he endeavors to deemphasize status.

He does this in a variety of ways that fit his personality and methods of leading, as for example by:

· Listening well and patiently
· Not being impatient with the progress being made by the group, particularly on difficult problems
· Accepting more blame than may be warranted for any failure or mistake
· Giving the group members ample opportunity to express their thoughts without being constrained by the leader pressing his own views
· Being careful never to impose a decision upon the group
· Putting his contributions often in the form of questions or stating them speculatively
· Arranging for others to help perform leadership functions which enhance their status

The leader strengthens the group and group processes by seeing that all problems *which involve the group* are dealt with by the group. He never handles such problems outside of the group nor with individual members of the group. While the leader is careful to see that all matters which involve and affect the whole group are handled by the whole group, he is equally alert not to undertake in a group-meeting agenda items or tasks which do not concern the group. Matters concerning one individual member and only that member are, of course, handled individually. Matters involving only a subgroup are handled by that subgroup. The total group is kept informed, however, of any subgroup action.

The leader fully reflects and effectively represents the views, goals, values, and decisions of his group in those other groups where he is performing the function of linking his group to the rest of the organization. He brings to the group of which he is the leader the views, goals, and decisions of those other groups. In this way, he provides a linkage whereby communication and the exercise of influence can be performed in both directions.

The leader has adequate competence to handle the technical problems faced by his group, or he sees that access to this technical knowledge is fully provided. This may involve bringing in, as needed, technical or resource persons. Or he may arrange to have technical training given to one or more members of his group so that the group can have available the necessary technical know-how when the group discusses a problem and arrives at a decision.

The leader is what might be called "group-centered," in a sense comparable with the "employee-centered" supervisor described in Chapter 2. He endeavors to build and maintain in his group a keen sense of responsibility for achieving its own goals and meeting its obligations to the larger organization.

The leader helps to provide the group with the stimulation arising from a restless dissatisfaction. He discourages complacency and passive acceptance of the present. He helps the members to become aware of new possibilities, more important values, and more significant goals.

The leader is an important source of enthusiasm for the significance of the mission and goals of the group. He sees that the tasks of the group are important and significant and difficult enough to be challenging.

As an over-all guide to his leadership behavior, the leader understands and uses with sensitivity and skill the principle of supportive relationships.

Many of these leadership functions, such as the linking function, can be performed only by the designated leader. This makes clear the great importance of selecting competent persons for leadership positions.

Roles of Membership and Leadership

In the highly effective group, many functions are performed either by the leader or by the members, depending upon the situation or the requirements of the moment. The leader and members, as part of their roles in the group, establish and maintain an atmosphere and relationships which enable the communication, influence, decision-making, and similar processes of the group to be performed effectively. This means not only creating positive conditions, such as a supportive atmosphere, but also eliminating any negative or blocking factors. Thus, for example, groups sometimes have to deal with members who are insensitive, who are hostile, who talk too much, or who otherwise behave in ways adversely affecting the capacity of the group to function. In handling such a problem, the group makes the member aware of his deficiency, but does this in a sensitive and considerate manner and in a way to assist the member to function more effectively in the group. The members of most ordinary groups stop listening to a member who expresses himself in a fuzzy or confused manner. In a highly effective group, the members feed back their reaction to the person involved with suggestions and assistance on how to make his contributions clear, important, and of the kind to which all will want to listen. Friendly assistance and coaching can help a member overcome excessive talking or help him to learn to think and express himself more clearly.

Benne and Sheats (1948) have prepared a description of the different roles played in well-functioning groups. These roles may at times be performed by one or more group members, at other times by the leader. The list, while prepared on the basis of roles in discussion and problem-solving groups, is useful in considering the functions to be performed in any work group which is part of a larger organization.

The following material is taken from the Benne and Sheats article (pp. 42–45) with slight modifications. Group roles are classified into two broad categories:

1. *Group task roles.* These roles are related to the task which the group is deciding to undertake or has undertaken. They are directly concerned with the group effort in the selection and definition of a common problem and in the solution of that problem.

2. *Group building and maintenance roles.* These roles concern the functioning of the group as a group. They deal with the group's efforts to strengthen, regulate, and perpetuate the group as a group.

Group Task Roles

The following analysis assumes that the task of the group is to select, define, and solve common problems. The roles are identified in relation to functions of facilitation and coordination of group problem-solving activities. Each member may, of course, enact more than one role in any given unit of participation and a wide range of roles in successive participations. Any or all of these roles may be performed, at times, by the group "leader" as well as by various members.

A. *Initiating-contributing:* suggesting or proposing to the group new ideas or a changed way of regarding the group problem or goal. The novelty proposed may take the form of suggestions of a new group goal or a new definition of the problem. It may take the form of a suggested solution or some way of handling a difficulty that the group has encountered. Or it may take the form of a proposed new procedure for the group, a new way of organizing the group for the task ahead.

B. *Information seeking:* asking for clarification of suggestions made in terms of their factual adequacy, for authoritative information and facts pertinent to the problems being discussed.

C. *Opinion seeking:* seeking information not primarily on the facts of the case, but for a clarification of the values pertinent to what the group is undertaking or of values involved in a suggestion made or in alternative suggestions.

D. *Information giving:* offering facts or generalizations which are "authoritative" or involve presenting an experience pertinent to the group problem.

E. *Opinion giving:* stating beliefs or opinions pertinent to a suggestion made or to alternative suggestions. The emphasis is on the proposal of what should become the group's view of pertinent values, not primarily upon relevant facts or information.

F. *Elaborating:* spelling out suggestions in terms of examples or developed meanings, offering a rationale for suggestions previously made, and trying to deduce how an idea or suggestion would work out if adopted by the group.

G. *Coordinating:* showing or clarifying the relationships among various ideas and suggestions, trying to pull ideas and suggestions together or trying to coordinate the activities of various members or sub-groups.

H. *Orienting:* defining the position of the group with respect to its goals by summarizing what has occurred, departures from agreed upon directions or goals are pointed to, or questions are raised about the direction the group discussion is taking.

I. *Evaluating:* subjecting the accomplishment of the group to some standard or set of standards of group functioning in the context of the group task. Thus, it may involve evaluating or questioning the "practicality," the "logic," or the "procedure" of a suggestion or of some unit of group discussion.

J. *Energizing:* prodding the group to action or decision, attempting to stimulate or arouse the group to "greater" activity or to activity of a "higher quality."

K. *Assisting on procedure:* expediting group movement by doing things for the group—performing routine tasks, e.g., distributing materials, or manipulating objects for the group, e.g., rearranging the seating or running the recording machine, etc.

L. *Recording:* writing down suggestions, making a record of group decisions, or writing down the product of discussion. The recorder role is the "group memory."

Group Building and Maintenance Roles

Here the analysis of member-functions is oriented to those activities which build group loyalty and increase the motivation and capacity of the group for candid and effective interaction and problem-solving. One or more members or the leader may perform each of these roles.

A. *Encouraging:* praising, showing interest in, agreeing with, and accepting the contributions of others; indicating warmth and solidarity in one's attitudes toward other group members, listening attentively and seriously to the contributions of group members, giving these contributions full and adequate consideration even though one may not fully agree with them; conveying to the others a feeling that—"that which you are about to say is of importance to me."

B. *Harmonizing:* mediating the differences between other members, attempting to reconcile disagreements, relieving tension in conflict situations through jesting or pouring oil on troubled waters, etc.

C. *Compromising:* operating from within a conflict in which one's ideas or position is involved. In this role one may offer a compromise by yielding status, admitting error, by disciplining oneself to maintain group harmony, or by "coming half-way" in moving along with the group.

D. *Gate-keeping and expediting:* attempting to keep communication channels open by encouraging or facilitating the participation of others or by proposing regulation of the flow of communication.

E. *Setting standards or ideals:* expressing standards for the group or applying standards in evaluating the quality of group processes.

F. *Observing:* keeping records of various aspects of group process and feeding such data with proposed interpretations into the group's evaluation of its own procedures. The contribution of the person performing this role is usually best received or most fittingly received by the group when this particular role has been performed by this person at the request of the group and when the report to the group avoids expressing value judgments, approval, or disapproval.

G. *Following:* going along with the group, more or less passively accepting the ideas of others, serving as an audience in group discussion and decision.

The *group task roles* all deal with the intellectual aspects of the group's work. These roles are performed by members of the group during the problem-solving process, which usually involves such steps as·

1. Defining the problem
2. Listing the conditions or criteria which any satisfactory solution to the problem should meet
3. Listing possible alternative solutions
4. Obtaining the facts which bear on each possible solution
5. Evaluating the suggested solutions in terms of the conditions which a satisfactory solution should meet
6. Eliminating undesirable solutions and selecting the most desirable solution

The *group building and maintenance roles* are, as the label suggests, concerned with the emotional life of the group. These roles deal with the group's attractiveness to its members, its warmth and supportiveness, its motivation and capacity to handle intellectual problems without bias and emotion, and its capacity to function as a "mature" group.

The membership roles proposed by Benne and Sheats, while they are not definitive or complete, nevertheless point to the many complex functions performed in groups and dealt with by leader and members. The members of a highly effective group handle these roles with sensitivity and skill, and they see that the emotional life of the group contributes to the performance of the group's tasks rather than interfering with them.[1]

The highly effective group does not hesitate, for example, to look at and deal with friction between its members. By openly putting such problems on the table and sincerely examining them, they can be dealt with constructively. An effective group does not have values which frown upon criticism or which prevent bringing friction between members into the open. As a consequence, it does not put the lid on these emotional pressures, causing them to simmer below the surface and be a constant source of disruption to the performance of group tasks. The intellectual functions of any group can be performed without bias and disruption only when the internal emotional tensions and conflicts have been removed from the life of the group. Differences in ideas are stimulating and contribute to creativity, but emotional conflict immobilizes a group.

Group building and maintenance functions and group task functions

[1] Although the Benne and Sheat list does not define each category unambiguously, it is useful in helping a group analyze and improve its processes. Another list has been prepared by Bales (1950) which has relatively precise definitions. The Bales list will be of interest to those who wish to do research on group processes or who wish to observe and analyze them systematically.

are interdependent processes. In order to tackle difficult problems, to solve them creatively, and to achieve high performance, a group must be at a high level of group maintenance. Success in task processes, fortunately, also contributes to the maintenance of the group and to its emotional life, including its attraction to members and its supportive atmosphere.

In the midst of struggling with a very difficult task, a group occasionally may be faced with group maintenance problems. At such times, it may be necessary for the group to stop its intellectual activity and in one way or another to look at and deal with the disruptive emotional stresses. After this has been done, the group can then go forward with greater unity and will be more likely to solve its group task constructively.

The leader and the members in the highly effective group know that the building and maintenance of the group as well as the carrying out of tasks need to be done well. They are highly skilled in performing each of the different membership and leadership roles required. Each member feels responsible for assuming whatever role is necessary to keep the group operating in an efficient manner. In performing these required roles, the member may carry them out by himself or in cooperation with other group members. Each exercises initiative as called for by the situation. The group has a high capacity to mobilize fully all the skills and abilities of its members and focus these resources efficiently on the jobs to be done.

The larger the work group, the greater the difficulty in building it into a highly effective group. Seashore (1954) found that group cohesiveness, i.e., attraction of the members to the group, decreased steadily as work groups increased in size. This finding is supported also by other data (Indik, 1961; Revans, 1957).

To facilitate building work groups to high levels of effectiveness it will be desirable, consequently, to keep the groups as small as possible. This requirement, however, must be balanced against other demands on the organization, such as keeping the number of organizational levels to a minimum. This suggests the desirability of running tests and computing the relative efficiencies and costs of different-sized work groups. It is probable also that the optimum size for a group will vary with the kind of work the group is doing.

The highly effective group as described in this chapter, it will be recalled, is an "ideal model." It may sound completely unattainable. This does not appear to be the case. There is impressive evidence supporting the view that this ideal can be approximated, if not fully reached, in actual operations in any organization. This evidence is provided by the highest-producing managers and supervisors in American industry and government. If the measurements of their work groups and the reports of their work-group members are at all accurate, some of these managers have built and are operating work groups strikingly similar to our ideal model.

This chapter started by observing that groups can have constructive or destructive goals and can achieve these goals fully or partially, that there is nothing inherently good or bad about groups. If we reflect on the nature and functional characteristics of the highly effective group, however, some qualification of our initial comments may be warranted. In the highly effective group, the members can and do exercise substantial amounts of influence on the group's values and goals. As a consequence, these goals reflect the long-range as well as the short-range needs, desires, and values of its members. If we assume that the long-range desires and values will reflect, on the average, some of the more important long-range values and goals of the total society, we can draw some inferences about the highly effective group. These groups will, in terms of probability, reflect the constructive values and goals of their society. They are likely to be strong groups seeking "good" goals.

Chapter 12

THE INTERACTION-INFLUENCE
SYSTEM

Every organization is a human enterprise whose success depends upon the coordinated efforts of its members. It has several important characteristics and processes:

· It has a structure.
· It has observational and measurement processes which collect information about the internal state of the organization, the environment in which the organization is functioning, and the relationship of the organization to this environment.
· It has communication processes through which information flows.
· It has decision-making processes.
· It has action resources to carry out decisions, such as the personnel of the organization—skilled and unskilled—and the machinery, equipment, and energy sources used by them.
· It has influence processes.
· It has attitudinal dimensions and motivational characteristics, such as the basic motivational forces it seeks to draw upon in using the efforts of its members and the degree of favorableness or unfavorableness of attitudes and loyalties toward the organization, its component parts, and its members.

These processes are interrelated and interdependent. Their nature is determined by the organizational theory used and the kinds of motivational forces harnessed by the organization. If the motivations used are largely punitive and rely on fear, unfavorable and hostile attitudes are produced. Such an organization must have communication and decision-making processes of a character to cope with hostility, suspicion, and resentment. If, on the other hand, the organizational theory and motivational forces are of a character to yield favorable attitudes and a cooperative orientation on the part of members of the organization, then the communication, decision-making, and control processes can be quite different.

The various processes of an organization, its management theory, and the motivations it taps are highly interdependent and must be consistent and compatible if it is to function even reasonably well.

These interdependent motivations and processes constitute an over-all system which coordinates, integrates, and guides the activities of the organization and all its members. Its quality determines the organization's capacity to achieve effective communication, to make sound decisions, and to motivate, influence, and coordinate the activities of its members. The better the over-all system is and the better it functions, the greater will be the power of the organization to use fully and in a coordinated manner the skills, abilities, and resources of the persons in the organization. For easy reference, this system will be referred to as the *interaction-influence system.*

Decision-making, Influence, and Results

Several times during recent years, meetings of middle and top management have been asked the question: "If a manager permits his subordinates to exercise influence on what goes on in his department, does he have correspondingly less influence?" Quite consistently, these groups felt that the manager would have less influence than he now has if he permitted his subordinates to have more.

This reaction raises an interesting question, since the managers' impressions differ so markedly from research data. The findings, reported in Chapter 4, show that high-producing managers have built an operation in which more influence is exerted by all levels of the organization, including the nonsupervisory, than occurs in units which produce less. These data were obtained in response to the question: "In general, how much say or influence do you feel each of the following groups has on what goes on in your department?" The choices were, "Little or no influence," "Some," "Quite a bit," "A great deal of influence," "A very great deal of influence," and the question was asked with regard to: "Higher management of company," "The top management in your plant (city)," "Your department manager," "The men in your department."

Why is there this discrepancy between the research findings and the belief of top managers that permitting subordinates to exercise an increased amount of influence will reduce the amount that the manager can exert? It may be that the top managers were thinking only of decisions as such. If a manager makes decisions all by himself and therefore has total influence over these decisions, obviously he will have less influence if he shares his influence on decisions with his subordinates.

The question addressed to the members of middle and top management, however, did not ask about the amount of influence exerted on decisions. It focused on "what goes on in his (the manager's) department." It apparently is easy to confuse decision-making with carrying a decision into action. The question asked in the meetings of these top managers goes beyond the decision itself—as did the question asked of the men and managers in the thirty-one departments. "What goes on" deals with action, and action involves both decisions and their implementation. If a manager is to have influence over what goes on in his department, he must have influence not only on the decisions, but also on the motivation and skill with which these decisions are carried out. If his influence stops when the decisions are made and the decisions are poorly executed because of lack of motivation or skill in his subordinates, the manager's influence over what goes on in his department is not very great.

The answers of the men in the thirty-one departments seem to deal with action and reflect the amount of influence exerted both on the decisions and on their implementation. This is reflected clearly in the data reported in Chapter 9. As will be recalled, in the Cluster 4 departments, both the managers and the men are seen as having far less influence than the departments in the other clusters on what goes on in the department. (Cluster 4 includes the departments where the men are loyal to each other but where there is marked hostility between management and the men.) In this situation management may make the decisions but may also have trouble getting the decisions carried out well. The men, on the other hand, are able to exercise little influence on the decisions as such. As a consequence, both the manager and the men have appreciably less influence on the results than is the case in the other departments, especially those in Cluster 1.

In Cluster 1, the men see themselves and their managers as exercising appreciably greater amounts of influence on what goes on than do the men in the other clusters. This was also true of the situation as the managers see it. In Cluster 1, where more favorable attitudes exist and where group methods of supervision are more common than in the other clusters, the decisions are implemented with cooperative motivation and the men are able through group processes to exercise influence on the decisions. Both managers and men, as a consequence, have more influence on what goes on, and there is greater coordinated effort and better performance.

These results indicate that if the question involving the exercise of influence on what goes on in a department deals not only with decisions but also with their implementation, different systems of management yield differing amounts of influence. The highest-producing managers have developed and are using a system of management which gives them —as seen by them and their subordinates—more influence over the activities of their departments than that exercised by less successful managers. As was observed in Chapters 4 and 9, the size of the influence pie, as seen by all, is actually greater.

Interaction-Influence System of Newer Theory

The interaction-influence system called for by the newer theory resembles those built by the highest-producing managers. As described in Chapter 8, the organizational structure consists of highly effective work groups linked together by other such groups. The performance of the linking process is a major function of the work groups which form the line organization. Additional linkage is usually provided by work groups or committees consisting of both line and staff or staff alone. Such work groups can be either relatively permanent, or they can be *ad hoc* groups set up to deal with a particular problem.

The more effective the groups which perform the linking function, the more tightly knit and better coordinated the total organization and the more effective its interaction-influence system. Moreover, the greater the number of different work groups which perform this linking function by providing at least some overlap between work groups, the better the interaction-influence system and the more tightly knit and better coordinated the organization. Multiple linkage provides additional channels through which information can flow and influence can be exerted. These additional linkages also act as sinews binding the organization together and making it stronger and more effective. With the exception of the work groups comprising the line organization, each of the different groups which perform this multiple linking has to have, of course, important tasks in addition to its linking function. There should be no more overlapping work groups than are needed to perform necessary tasks other than the linking process.

The effectiveness of the interaction-influence system of an organization and the capacity of this system to deal with difficult problems depend *Key* upon the effectiveness of the work groups of which the structure consists and upon the extent to which multiple linkage is provided. An organization with an interaction-influence system operating flawlessly under the newer theory of management would consist of highly effective work groups linked together by other highly effective work groups. Based on what we know about such groups, this organization would show, hypothetically at least, the following operating pattern:

- Each member of the organization would be loyal to his own work group, to its leader, and to the organization as a whole.
- The members of each work group would be skilled in their respective roles.

- Every member of the organization would feel that the overlapping groups which link the organization together enable him satisfactorily to exert influence on all parts of the total organization.
- Every member of the organization would feel that the values and goals of his work group amply reflect his own values and needs. He would also feel that the value and objectives of the entire organization adequately reflect the values and needs of all members.
- Every member of the organization would be identified with the objectives of the organization and the goals of his work group and see the accomplishment of them as the best way to meet his own needs and personal goals.
- Every member of the organization would be motivated to behave in ways best calculated to help the organization accomplish its objectives. Cooperative motivation would prevail throughout the organization. Members would press for excellent performance, efficient methods, and low waste.
- Since the pressure for production would come from the members themselves in the form of both individual and group goals, the anxieties associated with pressure from a superior in a hierarchy would be absent.
- All the members of the organization, especially the leaders, would have a high level of accurate sensitivity to the reactions and behavior of other members. This sensitivity would enable the members of the organization to be alert also to the reactions of persons outside the organization but important to it, such as shareholders, customers, and suppliers.
- The communication processes of the organization would be efficient. The high level of motivation among the members of the organization to achieve its objectives fully and with minimum waste would encourage them to see that the communication system was operating well. In keeping with the group maintenance processes of highly effective groups, they would continuously examine and appraise the communication process and take the necessary steps to keep the system itself at maximum efficiency.
- Important information would flow to the points in the organization where the information is relevant for decisions and action. This would apply to such information as that dealing with problems, experience, suggestions, objectives, methods, processes, and technologies. There would not be the serious but neglected problems which now require crises and breakdowns to call them to the attention of that part of the organization able to deal with them. New and important opportunities which exist for the organization would be recognized and urged upon those responsible for action.
- Every member of the organization would be able to exert influence on

the decisions and actions of the organization. The amount of influence which he would be able to exert would depend upon the significance of his ideas and contribution. But everyone would know and feel that his voice would be heard on matters of concern to him.

· The total amount of influence exerted within the organization would be greater than for an organization of comparable size using the more traditional methods of organization.

· Decisions in this model organization would be made with all the relevant information available at the points where the decisions are made. The information used would be accurate and adequate because of the efficiency of the communication processes. Better use than is ordinarily the case would be made of technical information and knowledge. At present, the leader himself must have such knowledge if full use is to be made of it. With highly effective groups, the character of the decision-making process is such that the group uses all the technical and other relevant information already possessed by any member of the group. Moreover, technical information would flow from the other parts of the organization through the linking process to the work group which requires it.

The interaction-influence system just described represents a theoretical ideal. The nearer the system of a particular company approaches this ideal, the better will be the communication, decision-making, and motivation processes of the organization. The further it deviates from the model, the poorer these processes will be. Companies which apply the newer theory can progressively approach this ideal in their operations as they create an overlapping group form of organizational structure and as they build their work groups to higher and higher levels of effectiveness.

Cooperative Working Relationships

An important dimension of an interaction-influence system, on which our model organization would make a good score, is so often overlooked that it has no term to describe it. There are terms for referring to the structure of an organization, such as its organization chart. There are also terms to refer to the positions within the organization. These are referred to as "positions" or "jobs" and when vacant are at times referred to as "openings" or "slots." The work to be done in each position or job is covered by a "job description" or "position guide." The individuals who fill these positions are spoken of as "employees" or "staff members" and sometimes even as "bodies."

The neglected concept deals with the differences in an organization occurring between the time when it is first created and the positions first filled and a later time when it has settled down into a smoothly functioning organization. Even though the best possible structure were established for the new organization and even though it were staffed with the best possible personnel selected by means of the best selection procedures, the performance of the new operation at first would be significantly below its later performance.

To function well a completely new organization has to shake down into a well-knit, smoothly functioning entity. What we shall call *cooperative working relationships* have to be established. Irrespective of the level of interpersonal sensitivities and group skills possessed by its members, each work group in the organization has to develop the confidence and trust, the loyalties and favorable attitudes which characterize a highly effective group. Members must come to know each other well enough to understand the communications coming to them from others. They must know what others mean by their comments and by their day-to-day behavior. Each person must learn his own role and that of every other member to whom he must relate. Common expectations for the group as a whole must be established.

Rotation and changed personnel assignments are valuable and needed for such purposes as developing personnel, stimulating creativity, pumping new blood into old groups, and handling technological changes and organizational growth, but they tend to prevent work groups from becoming highly effective. In order to achieve and maintain a high level of cooperative working relationships, rapid changes in personnel assignments should be avoided in so far as possible.

The adverse effects of necessary changes in personnel assignments can be minimized and the period required to develop a highly effective group shortened by training the people affected in interpersonal sensitivity and skills and in the different roles to be performed. Training should be given also in ways of establishing highly effective work groups in a minimum length of time after rotation.

Every organization can be evaluated in terms of its level of cooperative working relationships. Organizations with an effective interaction-influence system would, of course, receive a high score when measured on this dimension.

Ideal Model and Organizational Structure

The ideal model of an interaction-influence system appears to be useful as an over-all guide in efforts to improve an organization whether it is operating under the classical theories of management or under the newer theory. Thus, it appears both from theory and research findings that the closer the interaction-influence system of an organization approaches a multiple overlapping group form of structure and the more effective the groups, the better are the communication, motivation, and other processes of the organization. In so far as these conditions fail to be met, the various processes appear to be less satisfactory.

The value of the ideal model for analyzing the communication and related processes of an organization can be illustrated by an example or two. In large, multiplant, decentralized corporations, the interaction-influence system often appears to be weakest both in structure and function at the point between corporate headquarters and the heads of the decentralized plants. Usually there is no overlapping group structure at that point, and if there is, it seldom functions well because of the difficulties caused by geographical distance. There are few group meetings, for example. The interaction-influence system is often weak in both structure and function at the point between sales headquarters and regional sales offices and between the latter and the local salesmen. Scattered evidence suggests that it is at precisely these points of weak overlapping group linkage that the communication, influence, and coordination processes break down and cause many corporations serious problems.

The ideal model of the interaction-influence system appears to be a valuable analytical tool to help organizations discover weaknesses. The place to look for breakdowns in the interaction-influence system is at the points where the overlapping group form of structure is absent or functioning poorly. The study of the League of Women Voters provides an example. As reported in Chapter 10, the effectiveness of local Leagues was found to increase with size up to a membership of about 300 to 400 (see Figure 10-11, size-effectiveness curve). Beyond this point, further increase in size did not yield a corresponding increase in effectiveness and the effectiveness per member began to decrease. Up to about 400 members, local Leagues have an organizational structure which makes full use of the overlapping group form of organization and with linking provided by multiple overlapping groups. Above that number, the structure no longer makes adequate provision for each member or leader to be a member of a relatively small group (15 to 20 persons) linked to other groups and the total organization by multiple overlapping small groups. Figure 10-14 shows this organizational structure. As was observed in Chapter 10, with a board of twenty members and units of twenty members each, this organizational structure can handle a maximum of 400. Beyond this number, the structure is inadequate and, as would be predicted, effectiveness per member diminishes.

Line-Staff Relationships

The ideal model of an interaction-influence system appears to have important implications also for line-staff relationships. It is striking that this, also, is a point where the multiple overlapping group form of organization is often absent or, if present, functions poorly. The newer theory with its overlapping group form of organization suggests that a change in thinking about the principles of line-staff relationship could bring important improvements in company operation. The character of these needed changes can be discussed more profitably after an examination of what the concept of hierarchy means under present theories of management in contrast to the concept of organizational levels in the newer theory.

Under the classical theories of management, the authority and responsibility for the operation of the enterprise are lodged in the president. He delegates to his immediate subordinates some of his authority and responsibility and holds them accountable for specified performance. They, in turn, delegate part of their authority and responsibility to their immediate subordinates, and so the delegation proceeds down through the organization. All the authority or influence is seen as coming from the top downward.

Under the newer theory, influence upward and sideward is as much a part of organizational processes as influence downward. Consequently, different levels in the organization should not be thought of in terms of more or less authority but rather as coordinating or linking larger or smaller numbers of work groups. At higher, or more central, levels of the organization, the problems, goals, recommendations, and influence processes of a larger number of units would converge via the overlapping group structure for resolution and integration than would be the case at lower levels. The higher levels would therefore coordinate decisions which influence more people. This does not mean, however, that the higher levels would always exert more influence. Often, one small work group of technical experts would exert more influence on an important decision than would the company president. Similarly, as the experience of companies which use the Scanlon Plan (Lesieur, 1959) have demonstrated, the employees in one department or shop would at times exercise the determining influence in important decisions on products or prices.

What does this concept of structure and authority imply for line-staff relationships in companies operating under present theories of management? The traditional concept that the line has the authority and staff is only advisory is breaking down increasingly as technical processes and other problems become more complex. In many companies today, parts of the staff are exercising more influence than the line because of the great complexity of the technical processes and of the expertness of the staff. This often causes serious friction and conflict. The newer theory would suggest that the way to deal with the problem of line-staff relationships is to have the line build an effective interaction-influence system involving multiple overlapping groups through which communication, decision-making, and influence processes could occur. Staff would also help in building this overlapping group structure with much of the multiple overlapping provided by many staff and staff-line committees and work groups. This interaction-influence system would provide the mechanism to enable the organization to arrive at sound decisions, with all relevant parts of the organization contributing fully from their specialized knowledge and skills. The contributions of line and staff would vary with the problem and with the resources each possessed.

Under this concept of staff-line relationships, the line would not have the sole responsibility and authority to make decisions with staff advice. The line would have the authority and responsibility for building a highly effective interaction-influence system through which the best decisions would be made, with both line and staff contributing.

Appropriate Levels for Decisions

When an organization consists of these linked, overlapping groups, the question arises as to what problems or topics are appropriate agenda for each group level in the organization. We would suggest as a general rule that at each level the problems considered should be those for which the chief of the group has responsibility. Thus, for example, if he is the department head, the problems should be problems of the department and not those of the sections whose heads report to him. The problems of the subordinate, i.e., the section head, are the appropriate agenda for the group of which the subordinate is chief. The agenda items appropriate for consideration by the president and his work group are matters of company-wide concern.

A group can appropriately address itself to the problems of a subordinate member of the group when such a member seeks the advice and counsel of his peers as well as his superior. In a sense, the problem is still that of the superior, namely, obtaining the best advice and assistance for one of his subordinates. If the problem is one which the other subordinates are likely to encounter in one form or another, an analysis of it by the group not only draws fully upon all the resources available within the group for solving it, but benefits all the subordinates as well. It enables them to recognize such problems at early stages, when they are easier to handle.

If the newer theory were put into operation, forces would be created within the interaction-influence system to push decisions to the appropriate level. If a decision were made at too low a level and adversely affected work groups other than those represented or involved in the decision, these groups would insist on being represented through the linking process and would push the decision to the level where their influence would be felt. If decisions were made in the organization at higher levels than warranted, the lower levels in the organization would exercise influence upward to change the level at which the decisions were made. This would also occur if the decisions were too detailed and specific. The members of a work group, functioning as a group, can communicate and exert influence upward far more effectively than they can as individual subordinates in a man-to-man system of management. The interaction-influence system of the newer theory would provide a mechanism for organizational self-correction.

The size of the different work groups in an organization which must be linked together may, of course, vary greatly. For example, a group of specialists, consultants, or scientists may consist of only two or perhaps five or six. For some other kinds of work, the work groups may be quite large—twenty, thirty, or more persons. But irrespective of the size of the work groups, all of them must be linked together in one tightly knit social fabric by the kinds of interaction processes described in this and related chapters.

Building an Effective Interaction-Influence System

Unfortunately, there is not a large body of systematic knowledge nor are there well-developed procedures for dealing with the problem of building the kind of effective interaction-influence system called for by the newer theory. The importance of this problem, like that of building highly effective groups, has been recognized only recently. Some experience and research findings are available, and more will be added steadily as work on this problem proceeds during the next decade.

A few managers in most medium-sized and large organizations are building relatively effective interaction-influence systems in the part of the company for which they are responsible. These managers can be discovered and their principles and procedures learned by obtaining the kinds of measurements needed to judge the quality of the interaction-influence system they use and to recognize the causal factors which determine this quality. These measurements are discussed in the next chapter.

An account of the activities of one or two managers who are building effective interaction-influence systems may suggest how it can be done. A few years ago, a man who had worked with the Institute on a prior experiment became a regional sales manager. He decided to seek high performance by using the participative approach. He instituted regular meetings with his fourteen local sales managers. He and his managers met as a group to tackle common problems and to develop the best solutions to these problems. He also encouraged his local managers to hold regular meetings with their supervisors and salesmen and assisted these managers by observation and coaching to develop skill in running their own meetings.

The regional manager used his regular meetings to train his managers as well as to deal with regional problems. Managers were taught sound methods for solving problems by using these problem-solving processes in the meetings. They learned how to handle interpersonal problems with subordinates by practicing on their peers. They learned to use role-playing by acting out different ways of attacking the problems dealt with in the meetings. In a similar manner, they developed skills in group processes, counseling, and interviewing. They also improved their capacity to understand, analyze, and use the wide variety of available sales and performance data by using these data to develop plans, set objectives, and analyze their own progress. The regional manager conceived of training not as something abstract and separate, but as an integral part of planning, evaluating, and decision-making.

The region has made impressive progress under this manager. When he took over, it was below the top one-fourth of all regions in the company in over-all performance. In two years it was leading the company and is continuing to do so by an increasingly wide margin. Of four local sales managers slated for discharge under the former manager, one was helped to find another job, one is doing well, and two are among the top one-sixth of all the local sales managers in the company in performance.

From the standpoint of traditional sales management, the results are hard to understand. The regional manager has had no experience as a salesman, nor has he been a sales supervisor or a local sales manager. He never presses his managers for sales volume. He is not using sales meetings as pep rallies for "stirring up the boys," nor is he employing the usual sales competition to achieve high motivation. His behavior as a sales manager is highly unorthodox. By conventional standards of sales management, he should not be achieving his outstanding results.

One of the forces at work here is the regional manager's enthusiasm for the job, his expectations that everyone will do his best, and his pride in the performance record already made. His subordinates reflect this enthusiasm and have set high performance goals for themselves and for their region. Then, too, he has developed several processes which make his operation effective. His communication system is efficient—everyone has ready access to all the facts they require. In addition, there is sharing of important facts as decisions are made in staff meetings. Problems are not left to fester, but are raised and dealt with as they occur. The decision-making processes are good. Group methods are used with increasing skill. People participate in decisions affecting them. Managers, supervisors, and salesmen are given help when it is needed. The regional manager, while aware of the importance of selecting able persons and while taking great care in filling managerial and supervisory openings, has achieved his record performance largely with the staff he acquired when he took charge of the region.

In another large company, the president is making skillful use of what might well be called "anticipatory management" to help develop and strengthen the interaction-influence system of his organization. Before a problem occurs or before it becomes serious, he stimulates his organization to think about and devise strategies to cope with it. For example, prior to the time when the impact of the 1957–1958 recession hit his organization, he had already drawn the attention of his upper and middle management to the likelihood of a recession. As probability of a recession became more evident, he and his own work group considered what steps could be taken to minimize the adverse effects of the recession and what to do to keep costs to a minimum. They decided to take the problems to lower levels of management through work-group channels. They put before each management work group the necessity for reducing costs, but emphasized that it be done in ways which would not weaken the organization. As a result of these discussions, the organization made sufficient cuts in costs to stay well below its reduced income. The savings were sufficient to enable the company to make capital expenditures during the recession at favorable prices and thereby to strengthen the company's competitive position in the postrecession period.

The anticipatory-management approach to this problem was quite different from that used in many companies and had a very different effect upon the interaction-influence system and upon the quality of the human organization. Many companies handled the problem of cost reduction in the 1957–1958 recession by an arbitrary across-the-board cut in costs and personnel, which had a demoralizing effect upon its employees. Attitudes became less favorable, confidence and trust decreased, and the sense of individual responsibility for reducing costs and waste in order to maintain the health of the organization generally decreased. The interaction-influence system in these companies was impaired appreciably.

The newer theory and the ideal model of an interaction-influence system point to a central and major function of management. The superior at every level in an organization has a primary responsibility to build an effective interaction-influence system in that part of the organization which his own work group coordinates. The more central the work group, the more important is this task. Its importance is underscored by the research findings which show that organizations can vary substantially in the extent to which they mobilize and coordinate the activities of their members to achieve their goals. If a president wishes to develop an organization which will utilize to the maximum the potential capability of every member of the organization, he must build a highly effective interaction-influence system. This is a difficult but essential task. The next chapter will deal with important resources available to help in this undertaking.

Chapter 13

THE FUNCTION OF MEASUREMENTS

It is difficult, if not impossible, to build and maintain a highly effective interaction-influence system without the guiding information provided by adequate measurements of the causal and intervening variables. It is hard to tell from the production, earnings, and cost data, for example, how well the overlapping group structure of an organization is functioning and how adequate and accurate the communication processes are. Moreover, it is hard to tell from measures of costs and earnings whether particular attempts to improve any operation such as upward communication actually do so and which kinds of changes are bringing the greatest improvement. Measurements are needed which deal with all the important processes of an organization if a highly effective interaction-influence system is to be built and maintained.

Progress in the social sciences in recent years makes it possible to obtain measurements of the intervening variables dealing with the quality and performance capacity of a human organization. Instruments to measure these variables either are available or can be developed by existing methodology. It is possible to measure:

· The extent of member loyalty to an organization and identification with it and its objectives.
· The extent to which members of the organization at all hierarchical levels feel that the organization's objectives are consistent with their own needs and goals and that the achievement of the company's objectives will help them achieve their own.
· The extent to which the goals of units and of individuals are of a character to facilitate the organization's achievement of its objectives.
· The level of motivation among members of the organization with regard to such activities as:
· · Performance, including both quality and quantity of work done.
· · Elimination of waste and reduction of costs.
· · Improving the products.
· · Improving technological processes.

- · Improving the organization and its procedures.
- · The extent to which members of the organization feel that the atmosphere of the organization is supportive and helps maintain each individual's sense of personal worth.
- · The degree of confidence and trust among peers, between the different hierarchical levels, and between the different organizational units. The confidence and trust which the line has in the staff and the staff in the line.
- · The amount and quality of cooperation within each unit of the organization, between units, and between line and staff.
- · The amount of stress and anxiety felt by members of the organization and the sources of stress. The effect of this anxiety upon their health and well-being as revealed by higher rates of absence, accidents, and similar symptoms.
- · The character of the organizational structure: what it is supposed to be and what it is in actual fact, e.g., who reports to whom about what, the number of superiors and subordinates each person has, the extent to which the structure consists of overlapping groups, the amount of multiple overlapping, etc.
- · The character of the decision-making process:
  - · Which individuals and which groups make what decisions?
  - · What facts are used in making these decisions, and how accurate and adequate are these facts?
  - · During the decision-making process and after the decision is made, what motivational forces are created in persons to carry out the decision or to block its execution?
  - · How do members of the organization feel about the decision-making process?
    - · Do they feel that decisions are made at the right level, and by the right people? Is participation adequately used?
    - · Do members feel that their ideas, information, knowledge of processes, and experience are being used?
    - · Do members feel that important problems are recognized and dealt with promptly and well?
    - · Do they feel that the decision-making processes make full use of all the available information relevant to the decision?
- · The level of competence and skill of the different groups in the organization to interact effectively in solving problems and doing other tasks.
  - · The extent to which each work group is functioning as a highly effective group.
- · The efficiency and adequacy of the communication process upward, downward, sideward:

· · The extent to which each subordinate and his superior have the same understanding as to responsibilities, authority, goals, and deadlines.

· · The extent to which each superior is correctly informed as to the expectations, reactions, and perceptions of each of his subordinates, and conversely.

· · The extent to which each superior is correctly informed of the obstacles, problems, and failures his subordinates are encountering in their work; the assistance his subordinates find helpful or of little value and the assistance they wish they could get.

· The efficiency of the influence process in each unit and throughout the organization:

· · The amount of influence that different members of the organization and the different hierarchical levels feel they exercise and the amount of influence others see them actually exercising.

· · The kinds of influence processes used, with what skill and with what effectiveness, by whom, and with what results.

· The extent to which the roles of each of the different members of the organization are clear, unambiguous, and functionally appropriate:

· · The degree to which each member of the organization has a clear understanding of his own job and role in the organization.

· · The extent to which those persons in the organization who must relate to one another have a correct understanding not only of their own role but the roles of those to whom they relate and with whom they interact.

· The level of leadership skills and abilities of supervisors and managers, including their basic philosophy of management and orientation toward the processes of leadership, and their sensitivities and skills in using group methods of supervision.

· The actual behavior of managers and subordinates as revealed through focused observations of them at work during samples of time.

· · Their allocation of time among the different functions which they perform.

· The native ability and the personality traits of the members of the organization. If aptitude scores are obtained as people join the organization, then trends in these scores will show whether the current management is improving the basic quality of the personnel through its hiring practices or is letting the quality deteriorate through unfavorable turnover.

On many of the above variables, it will be important to measure not only how each person sees and feels about the present situation, but what he expects or wishes it to be.

As we shall see in subsequent sections of this chapter, these measurements, regularly obtained, are indispensable to members of an organization in building a highly effective interaction-influence system. For most of the above variables, analyses can be made which will show why the existing conditions occur, what changes or different conditions are likely to yield better results, and how best and most effectively to go about producing changes in the desired direction.

Problems of Measuring and Analyzing the Intervening Variables

The methodologies used and problems encountered in securing accurate measurements, making the suggested analyses, and interpreting the results correctly are a complex subject and might well be the topic of another book. Some common errors of measurement and interpretation will illustrate the complexity of the measurement and analytical processes.

It is commonly assumed, for example, that if persons are asked why they behave as they do, the reasons given are valid statements of the motivational forces at work. This assumption, unfortunately, is incorrect. For example, when people are asked to signify what they would like in a job, their ranking of desirable job characteristics often does not correspond with what they actually want. When the reaction of employees to such factors as promotional opportunities, level of pay, and kind of supervision are compared with over-all job satisfaction, the order of the items as shown by the correlations is often different from the ranking made by the employees. The factors which they place highest in a list are not necessarily the ones which correlations reveal are most important in influencing how they feel about the job.

A related error occurs in the interpretation of data. For example, if employees say that the thing they like best about their job situation is the clean, well-lighted space in which to work, it does not follow that this factor is most important in producing favorable over-all attitudes. It is even possible that those who give this as their first choice have the least favorable over-all attitudes toward the company. Similarly, the items which are reacted to least favorably cannot be interpreted as the variables which are most important in producing unfavorable over-all attitudes.

It is not the level of favorableness or unfavorableness of response to an item which shows the importance of that item in influencing the over-all job attitude. Its importance is revealed by the extent to which it is correlated with the total or over-all job-attitude score. Suppose, for example, that an over-all attitude score were obtained by combining the scores on ten different items dealing with such factors as safety, recreation, working conditions, pay, supervision, and fringe benefits. Suppose, further, that some of these items, such as attitudes toward the recreation facilities, have little or no relationship to the total score; others, such as supervisory behavior, have a marked relationship. In this example, the item most closely related to the over-all job-attitude score would be the most important in influencing the over-all attitude either favorably or unfavorably. An item with little relationship to the total attitude score is of little importance in influencing the over-all attitude irrespective of whether the average response of members to that item is highly favorable or highly unfavorable.

These few examples illustrate some of the common errors of measurement and interpretation. Errors such as these are leading companies to draw incorrect conclusions and to concentrate on variables which may have but slight or symptomatic importance. In some instances, the efforts made by a company to improve a situation actually affect employee reactions and motivations adversely.

The measurement of these variables is a complex process and requires a high level of scientific competence. It cannot be done by an untrained person. Nor can it be done simply by asking people questions that have not been pretested or by handing them a ready-made questionnaire. Accurate measurements of the variables suggested, sound analyses of the data obtained, and correct interpretation of the results require the professional assistance of social scientists with years of training in this methodology. As in accounting, professional assistance is needed in setting up the measurement program and in laying out the analyses to be made. Once the program is launched and experience is obtained in using the results, professional assistance other than occasional consultation may no longer be required.

Relationships among the Causal, Intervening, and End-result Variables

At first glance, the list of variables presented above may seem to deal largely with attitudes. This is not the case. These variables deal with all aspects of the interaction-influence system, as Figure 13-1 and the following discussion will help to demonstrate. The complex interdependence and interrelationships among the variables must be understood if the most effective use of these measurements is to be made. Figure 13-1 [1] depicts in a rough and approximate manner many of the relationships between the causal, intervening, and end-result variables. Thus, as the first broad arrow on the left in Figure 13-1 shows, the causal variables, such as the organizational structure and the behavior of managers and superiors, impinge upon the personalities of the members of the organization. These two—the causal variables and the personalities—in-

---

[1] Figures 13-1 and 13-2 are modifications of a diagram originally prepared by R. L. Kahn and F. C. Mann.

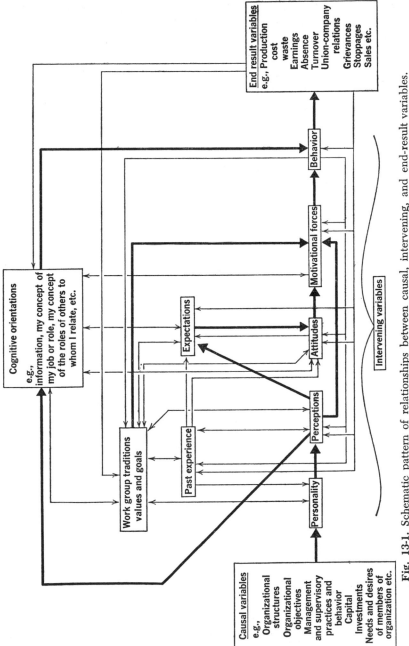

Fig. 13-1. Schematic pattern of relationships between causal, intervening, and end-result variables.

197

teract and determine the perceptions. Thus, each member's perception of the behavior of his superior is determined both by the character of this behavior and by the personality of the member. These perceptions are also influenced, as the thin single-line arrows are intended to show, by such factors as the individual's past experience, his expectations, and the traditions and values of his work group.

The individual's perceptions then lead, as the broad arrows in Figure 13-1 indicate, to cognitive orientations. This refers to dimensions of the individual's intellectual understanding: his concept of his job—what he thinks he is supposed to do and how he is supposed to do it—and his concept of the organization and its objectives.

As the lower broad arrow leading from perceptions is intended to show, perceptions lead directly to motivational forces. Thus, if the individual seeks promotion and perceives that effective participation in his work group is likely to lead to his advancement, he will be motivated to behave accordingly.

The third broad arrow leading from perceptions shows that they also lead to attitudes via a process in which expectations perform a modifying or conditioning function. Attitudes are determined not by perceptions alone, but by the relation of the individual's perceptions to his expectations. This can be illustrated by attitudes toward a new idea. If a member of an organization has an idea which he believes to be creative and important and he expects a very favorable reaction from his work group and others in the organization when he presents it, he will be disappointed and disturbed when it is not enthusiastically received. On the other hand, if he does not think highly of his idea and does not expect it to be given much attention, he will be pleased when it receives even lukewarm reception. Pay increases also show the effect of this phenomenon. If an individual expects a small increase in pay and receives a moderate increase, he is pleased and has a favorable attitude toward his compensation. On the other hand, the same moderate increase would result in an unfavorable attitude were he expecting a large increase. People's reactions to experiencing or not experiencing participation depend similarly upon the expectations they have with regard to it. These situations are examples of the general proposition, discussed in a previous chapter, that an individual's attitudes will depend in each situation upon how well his perceived experience meets or exceeds his expectations.

It is well to keep in mind that the expectations of an individual are shaped by what happens to him. At times, the leadership and the interaction-influence system of an organization alter an individual's expectations in ways which were not intended. For instance, suppose the decision-making processes of an organization in one way or another encourage certain workers or groups of workers to feel that they will be given desirable shifts only. If the decision is made that these workers are to have their share of undesirable assignments, they will have appreciably less favorable attitudes than would have been the case had they been led from the beginning to expect their fair share of such assignments.

Motivational forces, as Figure 13-1 indicates, stem from perceptions directly, from attitudes, and from the values and goals of the individual's work group. It is quite possible for the motivational forces arising from one's attitudes and from one's work group to be in conflict with the motivational forces which come directly from perceptions. This situation, as the data in Chapters 2 to 4 show, is common in many companies today. This occurs, for example, when an individual realizes that he will lose his job or be demoted if he does not step up the quantity (or quality) of his work. He is motivated to behave accordingly, so long as he wishes to keep the job. If, however, he and his colleagues in his work group view such treatment by his superior as threatening and unwarranted, he and they are likely to react with unfavorable attitudes. As a consequence, there will be conflicting motivational forces: the direct motivational force based on his desire not to lose his job will lead him to improve the quantity of his work; the other motivational forces based on his own unfavorable attitudes and on the attitudes and goals of his peers in his work group will cause him to strive, in every way he can safely, to avoid carrying out the behavior desired by the organization. Under these circumstances, the motivational forces stemming from his own attitudes and those of his colleagues tend to decrease the strength of the motivational forces coming directly from his perceptions.

It is also possible for the motivational forces stemming from these three different sources—perceptions, attitudes, and the values and goals of the individual's work group—to be additive and to reinforce each other harmoniously. This will occur when the interaction-influence system of an organization is working well. In such an organization, the compensation system will be seen by its members as rewarding them for behavior that helps implement the organization's goals. The perceptions based on the economic rewards, the goals of each work group, and the attitudes of the members of the organization will all lead to behavior which will improve methods, reduce waste and costs, and increase productivity. All the motivational forces would then be cumulative and reinforcing.

"Behavior" is shown in Figure 13-1 as stemming from both cognitive orientations and motivational forces. This is intended to show that behavior always reflects both the individual's concept of what he is supposed to do (his cognitive orientation) and his will to do it (his motivational forces). It assumes that the individual has the necessary skills.

Behavior, of course, leads, as the figure shows, to such results as production, sales, earnings, etc. These results are reflected in the measurements of such end-result variables as those dealing with production, costs, earnings, and waste. Behavior includes such activities as planning, obtaining tools and materials, working, and cooperating in efforts to do the job most efficiently. Data on these dimensions are readily obtained from interviews and by observations using time samples.

The thin arrows in Figure 13-1 are intended to portray additional patterns and directions of influence. For example, the arrows connecting the box marked "end-result variables" with "behavior," "motivational forces," "attitudes," "expectations," "perceptions," and "work group traditions," etc., show that the results revealed by the measurements of the end-result variables influence all the variables just mentioned. As knowledge of the results become known, they can influence each of the other variables. A line also connects the "end-result variables" box with that marked "past experience" to show that these measurements become past experience and influence the entire process accordingly. "Behavior" is similarly shown as connected to those other variables and for similar reasons.

"Perceptions" are connected by double-headed thin arrows to the boxes labeled "past experience" and "work group traditions." These two-way arrows are intended to show that perceptions both influence these other variables and are also influenced by them. For example, one's past experience helps to determine what one perceives in a situation, but these perceptions become past experience and, consequently, in turn enrich and modify the individual's body of past experience.

The thin arrow connecting "personality" and "work group traditions, values, and goals" also has heads pointing in both directions to show that influence flows in both directions between these variables. Thus, the personalities of the members of a work group help to determine the traditions, values, and goals of the work group. At the same time the traditions, values, and goals of the work group tend progressively, over a period of time, to alter and shape the personalities of the work-group members.

It is important to reemphasize that Figure 13-1 is, at best, only a crude approximation of what actually happens. It can be illustrated in other ways, and many other important variables would have to be added if the entire process were to be fully and accurately represented. For example, the abilities and skills of the members of the organization are not shown, nor is communication as such. Many of the processes involving communication, however, are indicated. Much of the behavior of managers and supervisors, for example, involves communication. Similarly, much of what flows along the wide as well as the narrow arrows in the figure also involves communication.

A modification of Figure 13-1 can be drawn to help illustrate the use and values of obtaining measurements of the intervening variables. This is Figure 13-2. If the only data which the work groups in an organization

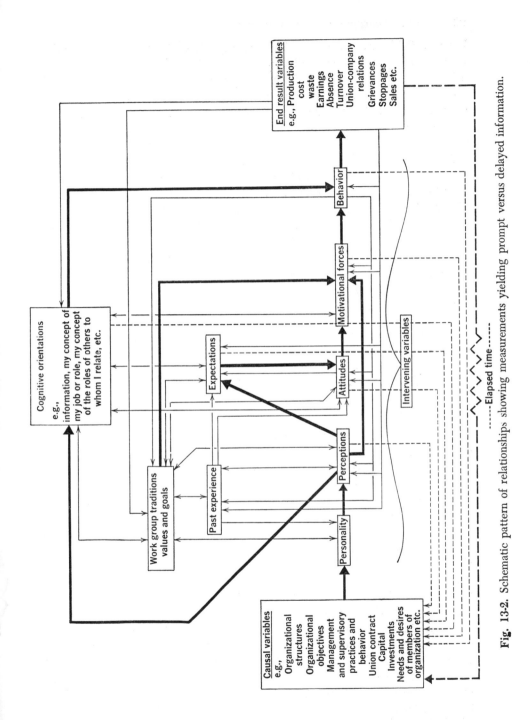

Fig. 13-2. Schematic pattern of relationships showing measurements yielding prompt versus delayed information.

have available are measures of the end-result variables, it is impossible
for them to appraise how well they are doing in building and maintaining
a highly effective interaction-influence system. Moreover, if the end-result
data indicate that the interaction-influence system is inadequate in some
way and so fails to achieve the performance desired, it is difficult to tell
where to take hold and what to do in order to bring about a desired improvement.

In Figure 13-2, the dashed arrow with "elapsed time" illustrates the
long time interval between changes in the causal variables and subsequent changes in the interaction-influence system which finally appear as
changes in the end-result measurements. There can be long delays, sometimes as much as a year or two, between a change in one of the causal
variables, such as the leadership principles used, and the resulting change
in the end results as shown by changes in the measurements of those
variables. Moreover, as the clerical experiment showed, the changes
which occur may have a curvilinear relationship through time to the
causal variables, and the changes in the intervening and end-result variables may be in opposite directions. Unless adequate measurements are
obtained, it is difficult to detect and interpret correctly what is happening.

These time delays, which may be of different length for different kinds
of changes, the curvilinear relationships, and the fact that often many
different changes occur in an organization within a relatively short span of
time, all make it virtually impossible to tell which changes in the end-
result variables occur as a consequence of particular changes in the
causal variables. Changes in competing organizations, of course, compli-
cate the matter even further.

An entirely different situation exists, however, when the intervening
variables are periodically measured. Changes in such variables as perceptions, expectations, attitudes, motivational forces, and cognitive orientation often occur much more rapidly in response to changes in the
causal variables than do changes in the end-result variables. When measurements of these intervening variables are regularly available, they will
show, with relatively little time delay, the impact on the intervening
variables of each change in the causal variables. Cause-and-effect relationships can be rapidly ascertained. The dashed arrows in Figure 13-2
are intended to depict this.

The rapid detection of cause-and-effect relationships enables members
of an organization to discover rapidly what, if any, improvements or adverse effects in the interaction-influence system occur as a result of
changes in the causal variables. Moreover, it is also possible to learn
from the measurements what kind of changes in the end-result variables
follows after a particular pattern of changes in the intervening variables.
The latter kind of analysis is not shown by arrows in Figure 13-2.

The suggested measurements and analyses enable the members of an organization to know at any time what the state of the interaction-influence system is, whether it is improving or deteriorating, and why and what to do to bring about desired improvements. They also reveal the levels of end results likely to be achieved from any particular state of the interaction-influence system.

Short Feedback Cycles

An organization which obtains periodic measurements of the intervening variables as well as those of the causal and end-result variables can make analyses of existing trends and relationships and use these data to shorten its "feedback" cycles (Lewin, 1947). An example may help to illustrate the concept of the shortened feedback cycle. A company which manufactures a heavy boardlike material for the siding of houses formerly tested the quality of the material as it came off a long machine. If something was wrong with the mixture at the beginning of the machine, more than six thousand square feet had to be scrapped when tests at the end of the machine showed that the quality was unsatisfactory. By relating the condition of the material shortly after it left the mixing chamber to its condition as it came off the end of the machine, the company was able to set up standards to test the board in the very early stages of the operation and to make the necessary corrections so that the final product met the desired standard. Using this shortened feedback cycle, only a few hundred square feet of material at most, instead of several thousand square feet, had to be scrapped when adjustments in quality were required.

Figure 13-3 shows in an oversimplified and schematic manner the way in which short feedback cycles can function in an organization. Figure 13-3 deals with a short cycle at the end-result portion of the causal, intervening, and end-result net of variables; that is, Figure 13-3 deals with the right-hand portion of Figure 13-1. As depicted schematically in both figures, the individual's job concept and his motivational forces combine to yield his actual behavior. His behavior, in turn, produces the results as measured in terms of the end-result variables. When measurements are obtained for individuals and work groups, analyses can be made of the relationships between particular job concepts, levels of motivational forces, the ensuing actual behavior, and the end results achieved. These relationships can be used to learn what modifications in actual behavior will yield improved end results. This knowledge, as suggested in Figure 13-3, can then be used to redefine job concepts and to describe modifications in the motivational forces, which, if achieved, would yield better end results. Tests of these changes can be run to see if they achieve the predicted improvement.

The regular measurement of the intervening variables makes possible quite short "feedback" cycles, such as shown in Figure 13-3, for each component part of the interaction-influence system. This enables each work group, as well as larger units in an organization, to test and improve every aspect of its own interaction-influence system. Each unit can discover what patterns of causal, intervening, and end-result variables work best for it.

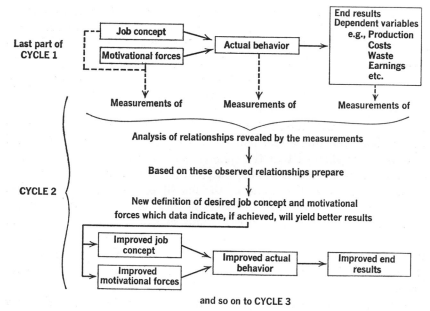

Fig. 13-3. Example of short feedback cycle.

Some Applications of Short Feedback Cycles

Short feedback cycles enable members of an organization to catch and to correct undesirable developments before they have become costly. Members can learn rapidly of any deviation from a desired state so far as each of the intervening variables is concerned. They also can learn promptly whether their efforts to improve the situation are yielding the desired results. If not, they can modify their efforts in directions indicated by the data so as to achieve the improvement desired. At all times, the members of the organization will have available precise information concerning the organization to guide them. They can thereby function in the most productive, least wasteful, and most satisfying manner.

The same process can be used for training in skills required by the interaction-influence system. Short feedback cycles can give each individual continuous information about his successes and failures. He can then concentrate on correcting his weaknesses and need not waste time learning what he already knows. This is a much more efficient training process than company-wide programs which assume that all individuals need the same training.

From time to time in organizations, favorable trends or developments occur which are not fully understood. Changes of this kind are especially likely in the interaction-influence system. The measurements and analyses proposed permit the early discovery of these trends and provide valuable information to help understand them. Moreover, the short feedback cycles permit controlled experimentation. Controlled changes can be made in the conditions which are believed to be producing the improved results, and their causes thereby detected. In this manner, the underlying causes of the favorable trends can be correctly comprehended at an early date and the factors responsible for the favorable developments extended to the rest of the organization rapidly and efficiently.

Short feedback cycles also provide a valuable resource for making technological changes. Plans can be developed based on the best available principles for introducing a desired change. As the changes are introduced, the process can be closely watched by measurements of all three kinds of variables. At such times, it may be desirable to obtain some of these measurements more frequently than usual. Adjustments can then be made in the change process as called for and guided by the measurements. In this way improvements can be achieved smoothly, rapidly, and efficiently and with a minimum of strain and adverse consequences.

Companies sometimes adopt new practices, on the assumption that whatever is new is better. Unfortunately, this assumption is not always correct. Adequate measurements and the use of short feedback cycles can save a great deal of time and money by providing objective evidence as to the value of a new idea or practice at an early stage in its application.

In a similar manner, the advice of experts can be tested and choices made between the conflicting suggestions of different experts. The experts' ideas can be tried on a small experimental basis with short feedback cycles to ascertain the validity of these ideas before they are applied to the total organization.

The preceding discussion of the relationship between causal, intervening, and end-result variables may have given the impression that the system is conceived as atomistic and mechanistic. This uncomplicated, direct cause-and-effect model was used to keep the discussion simple. There is actually a high degree of interrelationship among the variables. A more accurate concept would be that of a highly complex, highly interrelated system existing at any one moment in a state of equilibrium. Changes at any one point in the system bring about related changes in many variables throughout the system, resulting in a new equilibrium with a different pattern of relationships among the variables.

This complex pattern of interrelationships makes the research on or-ganizations much more difficult than would be the case if simple, direct cause-and-effect relationships existed. The entire system, in its various states of equilibrium, needs to be measured, analyzed, and studied as an interdependent whole. The organization must be viewed as an organic unity since subparts of the system when studied alone may function quite differently from the way they operate when part of the total system. This makes even more necessary adequate periodic measurements of the causal, intervening, and end-result variables.

Measurements for Guidance

Under the classical theories of management, all the information ob-tained from measurements, such as accounting, production, turnover, and similar data, goes primarily to the top of the organization. There is a rapid decrease in the amount available as one proceeds down the hierarchy. Under the newer theory, the flow of information yielded by measurements would be drastically altered. Each work group would regularly receive summary reports showing results for the organization as a whole and for the major units, such as plant, department, or region, of which the work group is a part.

Making the summary information available to each work group is a necessity if a sense of responsibility for costs, waste, performance, etc., is to be developed in the group and if the group is to react intelligently and constructively to over-all problems of the organization. Experience with the Scanlon Plan has demonstrated that work groups at all levels in the company can contribute in constructive and important ways to the over-all well-being of the organization, such as indicating how highly com-petitive business can be obtained and made profitable (Lesieur, 1959).

In addition to such summary information, each work group would also have regularly available all the measurements needed to enable it to see how well it is performing its part of the interaction-influence system. The data would enable the work group to evaluate its progress toward the goals to which it was committed, to appraise the strengths and weaknesses of is own methods and of its own interaction-influence processes, and to determine what steps to take to bring about desired improvements.

Work groups which perform overlapping and linking functions would receive, in addition to their own data, the measurements and analyses dealing with the work groups for which they have functional responsi-bility. This information would enable them to see how well they, themselves, are performing the linking function. It would also show them how successful they are in assisting the work groups which they link to the rest of the organization to develop into highly effective groups.

Any facts or measurements of legitimate interest to a member of the organization would not be withheld. To be denied access to information which he feels is relevant and important to him violates the principle of supportive relationships. On the other hand, to be given all the information to which he feels entitled, or to know that he can have access to it, increases his sense of personal worth.

The motivational effect of information freely given is illustrated by the response of the district sales managers of a large company to the behavior of their vice president for research. These sales managers had come to the home office of the company for one of their semiannual reporting and planning meetings with top management. The vice president told them about some of the research under way and about the resulting new and improved products soon to be available. In the discussion period, the district managers reported difficulties with an important product and suggested necessary improvements. The research department had developed an entirely new product to replace the product under discussion. It was going to take another year, however, before it was on the market. The company was eager to keep news of the development from its competitors until the product was marketed. In discussing the suggestions made about the existing product, the vice president did not withhold the fact that a new product was in the making. He told them all about it, but emphasized the importance to the company of keeping the information strictly confidential. His behavior in giving them the relevant facts significantly increased their sense of importance, their sense of belonging to the company, and their loyalty to it and its goals. His confidence was well warranted. No secrets were betrayed.

The people who are to use measurements for self-guidance should have a voice in deciding upon the measurements to be obtained. It is also desirable, in so far as possible, to have the same measurements for comparable units. This facilitates intelligent interpretation and use of the measurements by permitting each measurement to be related to a body of comparable results. Some such process as the following, consequently, should be used.

Upon the basis of its own needs, each work group should decide tentatively the measurements it wishes. These measurements should provide the information required for its own planning and operations. After tentative decisions have been made by each work group as to the data it needs, an effort should be made, via the linking pin process of representation, to reach an agreement among comparable units concerning the measurements which they all desire. This process should result in agreement on a manageable number of measurements. All these measurements should be those which the work groups at lower as well as higher hierarchical levels need and want.

Generally speaking, management uses measurements today for control purposes: to set objectives, appraise progress, and evaluate performance. Supervisory and nonsupervisory employees are rewarded or punished by what the measurements reveal. They feel "under the gun" much of the time. This evokes anxieties and resentment.

A valid application of the newer theory precludes a threatening and punitive use of knowledge obtained through measurements. This would tear down, rather than build, the effectiveness of the interaction-influence system. Punitive or policing use of measurements makes the theory inoperative and is, in fact, a return to the authoritarian system.

As a company starts to shift from its present system of management to a system based on the newer theory, it may be a great temptation for work groups and individuals in the middle and upper levels of the organization to use the information revealed by measurements as a device for applying pressure. If the newer theory is to be applied successfully, however, work groups and individuals throughout the organization must feel that the information obtained from measurements is used to help them, not hurt them; that the atmosphere is supportive, not threatening.

The supportive use of information does not mean that situations in which an individual clearly lacks the aptitude to perform his particular job successfully are ignored. Whenever it becomes clear to the members of his own work group, and to the other work groups to which his group is linked, that an individual does not have the aptitude to perform his task with reasonable competence, he should be transferred to an assignment which requires his particular strengths and abilities. If he lacks training, he should receive it, of course, but he should not be held indefinitely in a position for which he lacks the aptitude. Keeping him in such a position is unfair not only to him but to other members of his work group and to the whole organization.

Forces Distorting Measurements

Managerial, supervisory, and nonsupervisory employees all fear measurements used for policing purposes. They are, consequently, motivated to distort these measurements in directions favorable to themselves. Widespread distortion for protection at every hierarchical level has been demonstrated in many studies (Argyris, 1953; Argyris, 1959; Roethlisberger & Dickson, 1939; W. F. Whyte, 1955).

Shultz, (1951, pp. 209–210), for example, reports the following:

One of the departmental Production Committee's most vigorously-pressed suggestions concerned the scheduling of jobs. Workers complained that they often set up their equipment as scheduled, only to find that the particular paper needed for that job was not yet on hand. Though paper for other jobs was apparently available, they could not make a switch since setup time was generally great. This complaint involved people outside the department, however, so the Production Committee could do little about it themselves. They passed it on to the top Screening Committee, a group which included the company president.

The head of the scheduling department, of course, felt particularly concerned with this complaint, and so he did some "homework" in preparation for the meeting. For each job, the worker turns in to the scheduling department a time slip on which is tabulated the total elapsed hours in terms of "running time," "delays," and so on. The department head examined the file of these slips thoroughly and found that there was actually very little delay due to "insufficient paper." When the question came up in the meeting, he triumphantly produced these "facts" and discounted the complaint as of minor importance. This disclosure was greeted with an embarrassed silence. After a long half-minute, one of the workers spoke up: "Those time slips are way off. We fill them out. We were told by the foreman that he would get in trouble if we showed that delay time, so we usually added it to the running time. We've been doing it that way for years. We had no idea you were using the slips as a basis for planning."

When measurements are used primarily for self-guidance rather than policing, the motivation to distort the data is largely removed. In this situation people recognize that they need accurate information. Any distortion now is likely to hurt them rather than protect them. Under these conditions, the motivation is to strive for accurate measurements. Moreover, new kinds of measurements and better methods of obtaining them are much more likely to be suggested, welcomed, and used, rather than feared and resisted, as is now the case.

An organization operating under the newer theory would have available for its self-guidance more measurements of different kinds of variables, and the data would be appreciably more accurate.

Computers and Centralized Data Processing

The availability of the electronic computer can push large organizations in one of two directions and at an accelerating pace: toward centralization or toward decentralization. Persons well informed about programming large computers have pointed out that the computers may reverse the trend toward decentralization and bring about much greater centralization (Leavitt & Whisler, 1958). It is felt that this will occur because the large computer's capacity to process and analyze data will lead to a centralization of data processing and operations research analyses. This it is felt will lead, in turn, to a centralization of decision-making, with tighter and tighter controls on the operation of lower levels of the organization.

On the basis of the data presented in previous chapters, we would predict that such a development will be accompanied by hostile attitudes and resentment not only among nonsupervisory employees, but also among lower and middle levels of management. The latter will almost surely react adversely to the substantial reduction in their sense of importance and personal worth which this development will bring about. Hostile attitudes will lead not only to the poorer execution of decisions based on analyses provided by the computer, but also to feeding the computer distorted and inaccurate information and measurements. The people involved will alter the data to protect themselves. In so far as these developments occur, the value of the computer's analyses will be correspondingly decreased.

Fortunately, it is not necessary to centralize decision-making to obtain the full benefit of computers. In fact, companies operating under the newer theory would make more extensive use of computers than do companies whose operations are centralized.

In the first place, in companies applying the newer theory, computers would be used for all the kinds of data processing and analyses for which centralized companies use computers, but the decision processes involved in their use would be fundamentally different. Decisions would not be made by a few members of top management. The work groups affected by the analyses coming from the computer would participate directly, or through representation provided by the linking process, in the decisions as to what analyses and computations are to be made and how this information is to be used. They would be involved in the important decisions related to the use of the computer. For this reason, and because of their identification with the goals of the organization, there would be much higher motivation to feed the computer accurate data and to make the best possible use of the information that the computers can supply.

There is another important use to which computers would be put in companies operating under the newer theory. A few years ago, it would have been much too costly to provide each work group with the measurements and analyses needed for its own self-guidance. It would also have required so much time to process the measurements that much of the information would have been out of date and of little use by the time it became available.

The electronic computer has drastically changed this situation. The tremendous capacities of these machines make it easy and economical to process rapidly all the measurements and analyses each work group desires. Moreover, the data can be consolidated rapidly for middle- and higher-level work groups so that each of these higher-level groups can have a correct picture of the situation for departments, plants, and large units of the organization for which it performs the linking, coordinating, and organization-building functions. Computations of all the relevant interrelationships between causal, intervening, and end-result variables can also be made available rapidly. These analyses provide the information needed to help interpret the data and increase the likelihood that the best conclusions will be drawn from them.

Decisions, Motivation, Results

We have observed that the quality of the decisions of an organization rests squarely on the adequacy and accuracy of the facts available to those who make its decisions. There is another important conditon, however, which also profoundly affects the quality of the decisions, namely, that those who make the decisions need to be fully identified with the organization and its objectives and motivated to seek solutions which best help the organization achieve its objectives.

A few examples may help to clarify this point:

· In one company, a long assembly line with 1,100 employees assembled exactly 1,500 units on the day shift. The company scheduled higher production and sought to achieve it, but the volume stayed at 1,500 units. The hourly production often varied, and by midafternoon the number of units might be appreciably more or less than that required for a 1,500 day, but by the end of the shift there were always 1,500 units, no more and no less.

· In a plant manufacturing heavy equipment, the employees cut production on the final assembly for two weeks to exactly one-half of the normal volume scheduled by the company. At the end of these two weeks, they restored production to its normal level with as little fanfare as had occurred when they cut it in half.

· In a company with much of its work on either individual or group piece rates, virtually no employee produces above 150 per cent of standard. An appreciable number of workers are at the level of 145 to 149 per cent of standard, but the decision has been made—and not by management—that it is undesirable to reach or exceed 150 per cent of standard.

The reality of the present-day situation in complex industrial organizations is that their members at every hierarchical level, including nonsupervisory employees, are making decisions or participating in them in ways which profoundly affect the quality and quantity of production, waste, costs, earnings, etc. The newer theory of management takes this reality into account. If the goals of an organization are to be accomplished, the people making the decisions must have the interest of the organization at heart and must have before them all relevant facts. These are prerequisites for sound decisions and the effective execution of these decisions.

Without question, wise decisions are important and necessary to the success of an enterprise, but it is equally true that no decision is any better than the motivation used in carrying it out. An excellent decision poorly executed because of hostile or apathetic motivation is no better in its consequences for the organization than a poor decision. It is well to keep in mind the formula:

Results achieved = quality of the decision $\times$
$$\text{motivation to implement the decision}$$

If *either* term in the right half of the equation is low, the action performed will be unsatisfactory.

Adequate measurements coupled with participation in decision-making provide an organization with a twofold advantage: (1) better decisions, based on more accurate information, and (2) greater motivation to implement these decisions.

The potential power in using measurements for self-guidance was recognized and pointed to by Mary Parker Follett. Years ago she wrote (Metcalf & Urwick, 1940):

My solution is to depersonalize the giving of orders, to unite all concerned in a study of the situation, to discover the *law of the situation* and obey that. Until we do this I do not think we shall have the most successful business administration. This is what does take place, what has to take place, when there is a question between two men in positions of equal authority. The head of the sales departments does not give orders to the head of the production department, or vice versa. Each studies the market and the final decision is made as the market demands. This is, ideally, what should take place between foremen and rank and file, between any head and his subordinates. One *person* should not give orders to another *person*, but both should agree to take their orders from the situation. If orders are simply part of the situation, the question of someone giving and someone receiving does not come up. Both accept the orders given by the situation. Employers accept the orders given by the situation; employees accept the orders given by the situation. This gives, does it not, a slightly different aspect to the whole of business administration through the entire plant?

We have here, I think, one of the largest contributions of scientific management: it tends to depersonalize orders. From one point of view, one might call the essence of scientific management the attempt to find the law of the situation. With scientific management the managers are as much under orders as the workers, for both obey the law of the situation. Our job is not how to get people to obey orders, but how to devise methods by which we can best *discover* the order integral to a particular situation. When that is found, the employee can issue it to the employer, as well as employer to employee. This often happens easily and naturally. My cook or my stenographer points out the law of the situation, and I, if I recognize it as such, accept it, even though it may reverse some "order" I have given.

If those in supervisory positions should depersonalize orders, then there would be no overbearing authority on the one hand, nor on the other the dangerous *laissez-aller* which comes from the fear of exercising authority. Of course we should exercise authority, but always the authority of the situation.

In addition to the "law of the situation," Mary Parker Follett used another term in referring to this concept, namely, the "authority of facts." Both terms recognize that the decisions which are best for the organization are not dependent upon who makes them, but upon all the facts being taken into account and objectively appraised. When people in an organization have substantially the same goals and the same body of facts, they usually will make the same decisions, irrespective of who does the deciding. But who makes the decisions profoundly affects the motivation to implement the decision.

The law of the situation and the hard, objective realities (referred to on page 112 as *situational requirements*) can be used with far greater power today than when they were first proposed. Many variables such as attitudes, expectations, and motivations can be measured now which could not be measured in Mary Parker Follett's day and can provide objective data where previously only impressions and judgments were available.

The power of this new kind of measurement, when used as suggested by Miss Follett, is illustrated by the experience of the War Finance Division of the U.S. Treasury Department in its effort to sell Series E bonds to as many people as possible during World War II.

T. W. Gamble became National Director of the War Finance Division after the First War Bond Drive. Prior to this he had been Chairman of the Oregon State War Bond Committee. Under his leadership, Oregon had made an outstanding record. Only Hawaii and Alaska, both of which had been bombed by Japan, could compare with Oregon on a per capita basis.

From his experience, Mr. Gamble knew many of the important steps to be taken to assure the success of a war-bond drive. He had found it particularly important to have as many potential bond buyers as possible asked personally to increase their purchase of bonds. In laying the plans for the Second War Bond Drive, Mr. Gamble urged the chairman of every state war-bond committee to mobilize a large number of volunteers to solicit all potential buyers and ask them to buy. Everyone recognized that the recruiting and training of these volunteers was a tremendous task. Mr. Gamble nevertheless was convinced that it was necessary if a high level of sales of the Series E bonds were to be achieved. In spite of his outstanding record and his persuasiveness, he was unable to convince many of the state chairmen that the substantial task of recruiting a large number of volunteers to solicit potential buyers was necessary.

The typical reply was about as follows: "Mr. Gamble, personal solicitation may be necessary in Oregon in order to achieve a high level of sales, but in this state it is not the case. We don't need to go to all that trouble here. If we put on an intensive campaign through the mass media and with mass meetings, we will achieve and surpass our quota."

Although Mr. Gamble's persuasive abilities failed to move state chairmen who resisted using personal solicitation, he was successful when he marshaled the authority of facts. He arranged with a research organization [2] to conduct a national survey of the results of the Second War Bond Drive. A major purpose of the study was to learn what kinds of people did or did not increase their buying of war bonds during the campaign and why this was the case. Immediately after the Second War Bond Drive, about 1,800 persons were interviewed to appraise the drive and particularly to discover how to improve the third drive. The most important findings, as Gamble expected, concerned the effect of personal solicitation.

Since it was felt that personal solicitation might be a crucial variable affecting bond buying, the study was designed so that each respondent was specifically asked whether during the drive he had been asked personally to buy war bonds. At another point in the interview, he was asked how many bonds he had bought during the period of the drive and how many bonds he had been buying prior to the drive and would ordinarily buy.

When respondents were asked why they increased their buying of war bonds during the drive, most of them gave a patriotic reason. They would say, for example, that the government needed the money to buy war equipment. Only a small proportion answered that they bought because they were asked to buy. Yet when the data were analyzed, this reason was found to be of greatest importance. Of all gainfully employed people, 25 per cent reported that they had been asked personally to buy war

[2] The Division of Program Surveys of the Department of Agriculture, the staff of which later became the Survey Research Center of the University of Michigan.

bonds. When these people were grouped together, it was found that 47 per cent of this group bought *more* bonds during the Second War Bond Drive than they had been buying. Among the three-fourths of gainfully employed persons who had not been asked to buy, however, only 12 per cent had bought more than usual.

This relationship between bond buying and solicitation held for every income group, for every occupational group, and for every geographical region. No matter how the data were grouped, it was found that among those who were asked to buy, there were about thirty-five percentage points more buyers than among those who were not asked to buy.

Mr. Gamble then arranged a series of regional meetings attended by the state chairman, the members of the state committees, and the members of state staffs. The purpose of the meeting was to discuss the initial plans and promotional material for the Third War Bond Drive and to plan for the activities at the state and local levels.

After a brief introductory statement, Mr. Gamble had a member of the research organization which had conducted the study present a rather full summary of the major findings. The findings of the powerful influence of personal solicitation loomed large in the presentation because this variable had been found to be particularly effective in influencing buying behavior. In addition to the regional meetings, a short report of the findings was published and placed in the hands of every member of every state, county, and local war-bond committee.

Although Mr. Gamble made frequent reference to the research findings, he did not press state committees to make greater use of personal solicitation in the Third than in the Second War Bond Drive. He relied on the authority of facts.

The power of this approach is demonstrated by the results. In the survey following the Third War Bond Drive it was found that personal solicitation in the third drive had been doubled: 50 per cent of all gainfully employed persons were solicited. In this drive, 59 per cent of those who were personally solicited bought more bonds than usual. Among those who were not personally asked to buy, only 18 per cent bought additional bonds.

The major purpose of the war-bond drives was, of course, sales of bonds to individuals. This one finding on the importance of personal solicitation and its application in the Third War Bond Drive helped materially to increase the sale of Series E bonds and the total sale of all bonds to individuals. The doubling of personal solicitation in the third drive over the second was a major factor in almost doubling the amount of Series E bonds that were sold. In the second drive, $1.5 billion dollars of Series E bonds was sold; $2.5 billion dollars was sold in the third. Throughout all the bond drives, there was a close relationship between the amount of solicitation and the total amount of bonds sold to individuals. Moreover, under the continuing impact of the authority of facts, the total level of solicitation increased until two out of every three potential buyers were asked to buy, and of those who were asked to buy, approximately 64 per cent bought more bonds than they had been buying. This level of solicitation was reached by the Fifth War Bond Drive (Cartwright, 1947; Cartwright, 1949).

The preceding example illustrates the important contribution which objective, scientific data can make. A common body of facts replaces a variety of experiences. This increases the likelihood that the different persons involved will arrive at substantially the same decision. The contribution of a common body of data to group decision-making processes is shown schematically below:

Processes for Arriving at a Common Solution

1. Independent approach to achieving a common solution:

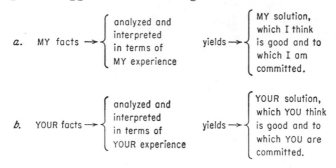

If the two persons above have to agree on a common solution, they can proceed as follows: Leave the fact-gathering and decision-making processes the same and seek only to reconcile the solutions. But each person thinks his solution is best; hence, there are only two courses of action:

a. Conflict: Where each person seeks to force his solution on the other. *Motivational consequences:* The person who wins will be highly motivated to carry out the solution well. The person who loses will be motivated to carry out the solution poorly, and if he possibly can, to sabotage the activity, at least partially, to show the solution was a poor one.

b. Compromise: Here each person modifies his solution as little as possible, seeking through bargaining to force the other to make the greater change. But each gives up some aspects of his own preferred solution. *Motivational consequences:* Neither person likes the final solution nor feels it is the best solution. Both will be inclined to endeavor to carry it out halfheartedly.

2. Coordinated fact-gathering approach to achieving a common solution:

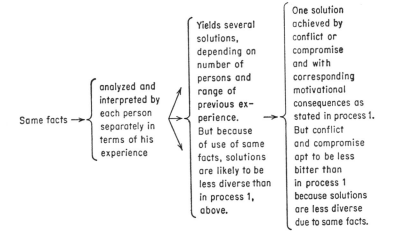

3. Approach based on coordinated fact-gathering coupled with group-decision process:

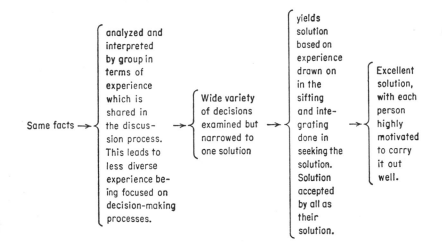

An Application Cycle

The full benefit from the periodic measurements of the causal, inter-vening, and end-result variables will be obtained only when they are used in a continuous series of cycles of planning, action, measurements, feedback, and planning again. The approach outlined below applies suggestions made earlier and is illustrative. The exact procedure which should be used in a particular company and with a particular work group or individual must necessarily be tailored to fit the traditions and practices of the organization and the background, expectations, and skills of the work group. Accordingly, only the basic dimensions will be discussed. These will be much the same from company to company and at low as well as high levels of supervision.

1. Each manager working with his subordinates as a group sets objectives for the next period ahead. The period we are most concerned with here is the short-term one—one month, three months, nine months, or whatever is the normal period used by the organization for planning and setting goals. Objectives might appropriately be set also for a longer term, but they would be more tentative and should be examined and readjusted at the end of each shorter period. Measurements of results for previous periods would be used as guides in setting or revising the objectives.

The plans and objectives prepared by each manager and his work group would specify such dimensions as:

- · · Performance objectives in terms of such end-result variables as have been suggested (e.g., a specified reduction in waste or a specified improvement in output).
- · · Organizational objectives dealing primarily with the interaction-influence system (e.g., specified improvement in the communication process or in the group interaction process).
- · · Processes and procedures to be used to attain these objectives.
- · · Specifications for measurements needed to ascertain how well each objective is reached, how well each procedure is followed, and what modifications, if any, are desirable to achieve further improvement. Managers would be encouraged to state the measurements which they feel they need to plan, guide, and improve their operation and their own performance.

In the developmental stages of these continuous cycles, it probably will be desirable to use measurements of only a modest number of variables. As experience is gained in using these measurements, their number and variety can be progressively increased.

2. The manager and his superior review the plans and objectives set by the manager and his work group. This review should be done in group meetings by the superior and all managers who report to him. When appropriate, representatives of staff departments should also be called in. In this way, the objectives of related units can be brought in balance and integrated, and the balance and integration achieved made satisfactory to all concerned. The objectives set should reflect the needs of the man-

ager and those below him in the organization as well as the over-all goals of the company. As necessary, the superior should also have personal sessions with the individual managers. The objectives should be high enough to really challenge the managers, but not so high as to put severe pressure upon them and their work groups.

3. At the end of each period for which plans and goals have been established, results are reported on all the variables measured. These results should be reported for the entire operation under each manager; where desired, they can also be reported separately for the different subunits under a manager. Along with his own results, each manager would receive data from comparable operations elsewhere in the company for evaluating his own performance. The other units may or may not be individually identified in the data, depending upon the procedures which have been agreed upon. Initially, the decision is likely to be not to identify them. After experiencing several cycles of applying the measurements and learning that data can be used in a supportive manner with constructive advice and help, the managers and the work groups learn that they have much to gain by being identified.

4. Each manager studies the results of his operation and evaluates his leadership and performance. What implications does he see? What insights can he gain? Which results surprise him? Following his own study, he should proceed to review the data with his subordinates in group sessions and examine such questions as:

· What was done well in relation to the objectives set?
· Where did performance fail to measure up?
· Which factors contributed to the successes achieved, and which contributed to the shortcomings?
· What should be done in the next period to extend the successes and to overcome the past shortcomings?

The manager should meet with his superior also and review the results reported, as well as the interpretations that he and his work group have placed on them. Most of this review should be done in group sessions, with the superior and with the other managers reporting to him so as to gain the benefit of their experience, insights, and suggestions and to assure coordination of the total operation.

5. At the same time that results of the previous period are being reviewed, objectives and plans are drawn for the period ahead. Existing procedures and methods can be improved or modified as called for by the data, and new approaches devised. The aim, of course, is to exploit all the data in order to bring about desirable improvements. All this work can go on individually and in groups: by managers working alone, by managers working with their subordinates in work groups, by the superior alone, and

by the superior working with the managers. The group meetings facilitate learning by sharing experiences, help to coordinate the plans and work of the different units, and increase the motivation to carry out the plans.

The complete cycle just described is carried out continuously so that each manager and his work group will have a constant flow of information coming to them about their operation and behavior. The process of planning, taking action, measuring results, feeding data back, and planning again must be a never-ending one if improvement is to go on continuously (Lewin, 1958).

A Note of Caution

A final note of caution might be appropriate for those about to undertake the measurement of causal and intervening variables for the first time. Whenever an organization suddenly and for the first time is given a large volume of measurements dealing with a wide array of variables, the members of the organization feel so completely overwhelmed that they find it difficult to analyze and use the data. They often reject the entire process as a consequence. As with so many good things, it is unwise to do too much too rapidly. Experience in introducing this kind of measurement into an organization has shown that it is desirable to start with measurements of a limited number of variables first. Additional variables can be added as the persons using the measurements acquire skill in interpreting and applying the measurements and want more data to help them in guiding their operation.

In selecting the different variables to be measured first, it is well to focus on those which deal with dimensions of greatest importance and which the members of the organization are best prepared at that time to interpret and apply. The data in Chapters 2, 3, 4, and 9 and the theory in Chapter 8 provide information which can help in this selection. Thus, for example, the information in these chapters would suggest that priority be given to the measurement of such variables as:

· The extent to which members of the organization have confidence and trust in each other and feel that the atmosphere of the organization is supportive and helps to maintain each individual's sense of importance and personal worth
· The extent to which the organizational structure consists of overlapping work group with well-defined functions and with roles understood and accepted by all.
· The extent to which these work groups are functioning well as groups with high group loyalty and are making efficient use of group methods of supervision

· The extent to which the group processes are working well as shown by the level of effectiveness of the communication processes, the influence processes, and the decision-making and goal-setting processes
· The character of the supervisory and managerial processes and the reaction of peers and subordinates to these processes as they experience them
· The level of performance goals; the clarity with which they are seen as setting both short-run and long-run targets; the motivation to achieve these goals; and the progress being made in accomplishing them

As the members of an organization acquire experience in the use of this new kind of measurement and learn how to interpret and apply it, we find that they want to get it regularly and they want to have more variables measured. Their experience in using the new measurements gives them insights into what can be measured and how this new information can help them to do their jobs more effectively.

Experience with use of the measurements also enables the members of an organization to discover what frequency of measurement is most useful for them. Some organizations find that the measurement of such intervening variables as the efficiency of communication is most useful if done once a year for the entire organization. Other organizations, or departments within an organization, find at times that measurements are needed more often. This is likely to be the case when efforts are being made to bring about improvement in a particular situation or to introduce a major change. These more frequent measurements may involve obtaining data for everyone each six months; or they may involve such steps as obtaining measurements from every fourth person each three months. With the latter procedure, measurements would have been obtained by the end of the year from every member of the organization, using only a 25 per cent sample at any one time.

An important development occurs as members of an organization gain experience with new measurements of causal and intervening variables. The body of data available after even a few cycles of measurement provides norms for interpreting the new measurements. The results of analyses also suggest the action to be taken. Experience in interpreting these measurements provides a background for their more insightful and constructive use.

Chapter 14

A COMPARATIVE VIEW
OF ORGANIZATIONS

All component parts of any system of management must be consistent with each of the other parts and reflect the system's basic philosophy. In an authoritative form of organization, decisions are made at the top; in a participative form, they are made widely throughout the organization. If the decision-making process of one system were grafted onto another, the effectiveness of the latter system would be impaired. Communication, motivation, and other processes related to decision-making would no longer fit the pattern. Necessary information would be lacking at the decision-making points, and the decisions, once made, would be inadequately communicated and executed.

The complex but internally consistent pattern of interrelationships among the various parts of any system of management which is working well becomes evident when we compare one system with another. A system can be arrayed along several different dimensions, as, for example, the amount of control which an organization exercises over its members. On this variable, forms of organization range from the completely laissez-faire, where no influence is exercised, to those with a large amount of control.

For our purposes here, we shall examine various systems of management arrayed along a dimension which is probably at a right angle to the variable representing the amount of control exercised by the system. This second dimension involves the character of the motivational forces used to control and coordinate the activity of people operating under the system, as shown in Table 14-1. The systems of organization represented in this table involve at least a moderate amount of control. The laissez-faire model is, consequently, not shown since it falls at another point in space.

The patterns depicted in Table 14-1 are intended to be illustrative. They do not attempt to cover all aspects of leadership and organizational behavior nor all characteristics of an organization. These patterns are

TABLE 14-1

ORGANIZATIONAL AND PERFORMANCE CHARACTERISTICS OF DIFFERENT MANAGEMENT SYSTEMS BASED ON A COMPARATIVE ANALYSIS

Operating characteristics	System of organization			
	Authoritative		Consultative	Participative
	Exploitive authoritative	Benevolent authoritative		Participative group
1. Character of motivational forces				
a. Underlying motives tapped	Physical security, economic security, and some use of the desire for status	Economic and occasionally ego motives, e.g., the desire for status	Economic, ego, and other major motives, e.g., desire for new experience	Full use of economic, ego, and other major motives, as, for example, motivational forces arising from group processes
b. Manner in which motives are used	Fear, threats, punishment, and occasional rewards	Rewards and some actual or potential punishment	Rewards, occasional punishment, and some involvement	Economic rewards based on compensation system developed through participation. Group participation and involvement in setting goals, improving methods, appraising progress toward goals, etc.

ORGANIZATIONAL AND PERFORMANCE CHARACTERISTICS OF DIFFERENT MANAGEMENT
SYSTEMS BASED ON A COMPARATIVE ANALYSIS (*Continued*)

Operating characteristics	System of organization			
	Authoritative		Consultative	Participative
	Exploitive authoritative	Benevolent authoritative	Consultative	Participative group
c. Kinds of attitudes developed toward oganization and its goals	Attitudes usually are hostile and counter to organization's goals	Attitudes are sometimes hostile and counter to organization's goals and are sometimes favorable to the organization's goals and support the behavior necessary to achieve them	Attitudes may be hostile but more often are favorable and support behavior implementing organization's goals	Attitudes generally are strongly favorable and provide powerful stimulation to behavior implementing organization's goals
d. Extent to which motivational forces conflict with or reinforce one another	Marked conflict of forces substantially reducing those motivational forces leading to behavior in support of the organization's goals	Conflict often exists; occasionally forces will reinforce each other, at least partially	Some conflict, but often motivational forces will reinforce each other	Motivational forces generally reinforce each other in a substantial and cumulative manner
e. Amount of responsibility felt by each member of organization for achieving organization's goals	High levels of management feel responsibility; lower levels feel less. Rank and file feel little and often	Managerial personnel usually feel responsibility; rank and file usually feel relatively little responsibility	Substantial proportion of personnel feel responsibility and generally behave in ways to achieve the or-	Personnel feel real responsibility for organization's goals and are motivated to behave in ways to im-

	System 1	System 2	System 3	System 4
(continued from previous page)	welcome opportunity to behave in ways to defeat organization's goals	for achieving organization's goals	ganization's goals	plement them
f. Attitudes toward other members of the organization	Subservient attitudes toward superiors coupled with hostility; hostility toward peers and contempt for subordinates; distrust is widespread	Subservient attitudes toward superiors; competition for status resulting in hostility toward peers; condescension toward subordinates	Cooperative, reasonably favorable attitudes toward others in organization; may be some competition between peers with resulting hostility and some condescension toward subordinates	Favorable, cooperative attitudes throughout the organization with mutual trust and confidence
g. Satisfactions derived	Usually dissatisfaction with membership in the organization, with supervision, and with one's own achievements	Dissatisfaction to moderate satisfaction with regard to membership in the organization, with supervision, and one's own achievements	Some dissatisfaction to moderately high satisfaction with regard to membership in the organization, supervision, and one's own achievements	Relatively high satisfaction throughout the organization with regard to membership in the organization, supervision, and one's own achievements
2. Character of communication process				
a. Amount of interaction and communication aimed at achieving organization's objectives	Very little	Little	Quite a bit	Much with both individuals and groups
b. Direction of information flow	Downward	Mostly downward	Down and up	Down, up, and with peers
c. Downward communication				

TABLE 14-1 (*Continued*)

ORGANIZATIONAL AND PERFORMANCE CHARACTERISTICS OF DIFFERENT MANAGEMENT SYSTEMS BASED ON A COMPARATIVE ANALYSIS (*Continued*)

| Operating characteristics | System of organization | | | |
| | Authoritative | | Consultative | Participative |
	Exploitive authoritative	Benevolent authoritative		Participative group
(1) Where initiated	At top of organization or to implement top directive	Primarily at top or patterned on communication from top	Patterned on communication from top but with some initiative at lower levels	Initiated at all levels
(2) Extent to which communications are accepted by subordinates	Viewed with great suspicion	May or may not be viewed with suspicion	Often accepted but at times viewed with suspicion. May or may not be openly questioned	Generally accepted, but if not, openly and candidly questioned
d. Upward communication				
(1) Adequacy of upward communication via line organization	Very little	Limited	Some	A great deal
(2) Subordinates' feeling of responsibility for initiating accurate upward communication	None at all	Relatively little, usually communicates "filtered" information but only when requested. May "yes" the boss	Some to moderate degree of responsibility to initiate accurate upward communication	Considerable responsibility felt and much initiative. Group communicates all relevant information

	System 1	System 2	System 3	System 4
(3) Forces leading to accurate or distorted information	Powerful forces to distort information and deceive superiors	Occasional forces to distort; also forces for honest communication	Some forces to distort along with many forces to communicate accurately	Virtually no forces to distort and powerful forces to communicate accurately
(4) Accuracy of upward communication via line	Tends to be inaccurate	Information that boss wants to hear flows; other information is restricted and filtered	Information that boss wants to hear flows; other information may be limited or cautiously given	Accurate
(5) Need for supplementary upward communication system	Need to supplement upward communication by spy system, suggestion system, or some similar devices	Upward communication often supplemented by suggestion system and similar devices	Slight need for supplementary system; suggestion system may be used	No need for any supplementary system
e. Sideward communication, its adequacy and accuracy	Usually poor because of competition between peers and corresponding hostility	Fairly poor because of competition between peers	Fair to good	Good to excellent
f. Psychological closeness of superiors to subordinates (i.e., how well does superior know and understand problems faced by subordinates?)	Far apart	Can be moderately close if proper roles are kept	Fairly close	Usually very close
(1) Accuracy of perceptions by superiors and subordinates	Often in error	Often in error on some points	Moderately accurate	Usually quite accurate

227

TABLE 14-1 (*Continued*)

ORGANIZATIONAL AND PERFORMANCE CHARACTERISTICS OF DIFFERENT MANAGEMENT
SYSTEMS BASED ON A COMPARATIVE ANALYSIS (*Continued*)

| Operating characteristics | System of organization | | | |
| | Authoritative | | Consultative | Participative |
	Exploitive authoritative	Benevolent authoritative	Consultative	Participative group
3. Character of interaction-influence process				
a. Amount and character of interaction	Little interaction and always with fear and distrust	Little interaction and usually with some condescension by superiors; fear and caution by subordinates	Moderate interaction, often with fair amount of confidence and trust	Extensive, friendly interaction with high degree of confidence and trust
b. Amount of cooperative teamwork present	None	Virtually none	A moderate amount	Very substantial amount throughout the organization
c. Extent to which subordinates can influence the goals, methods, and activity of their units and departments				
(1) As seen by superiors	None	Virtually none	Moderate amount	A great deal
(2) As seen by subordinates	None except through "informal organization" or via unionization	Little except through "informal organization" or via unionization	Moderate amount both directly and via unionization	Substantial amount both directly and via unionization

d. Amount of actual influence which superiors can exercise over the goals, activity, and methods of their units and departments	Believed to be substantial but actually moderate unless capacity to exercise severe punishment is present	Moderate to somewhat more than moderate, especially for higher levels in organization	Moderate to substantial, especially for higher levels in organization	Substantial but often done indirectly, as, for example, by superior building effective interaction-influence system
e. Extent to which an adequate structure exists for the flow of information from one part of the organization to another, thereby enabling influence to be exerted	Downward only	Almost entirely downward	Largely downward but small to moderate capacity for upward and between peers	Capacity for information to flow in all directions from all levels and for influence to be exerted by all units on all units
4. Character of decision-making process				
a. At what level in organization are decisions formally made?	Bulk of decisions at top of organization	Policy at top, many decisions within prescribed framework made at lower levels	Broad policy and general decisions at top, more specific decisions at lower levels	Decision-making widely done throughout organization, although well integrated through linking process provided by overlapping groups
b. How adequate and accurate is the information available for decision-making at the place where the decisions are made?	Partial and often inaccurate information only is available	Moderately adequate and accurate information available	Reasonably adequate and accurate information available	Relatively complete and accurate information available based both on measurements and efficient flow of information in organization

TABLE 14-1 (*Continued*)

ORGANIZATIONAL AND PERFORMANCE CHARACTERISTICS OF DIFFERENT MANAGEMENT SYSTEMS BASED ON A COMPARATIVE ANALYSIS (*Continued*)

Operating characteristics	System of organization			
	Authoritative		Participative	
	Exploitive authoritative	Benevolent authoritative	Consultative	Participative group
c. To what extent are decision-makers aware of problems, particularly those at lower levels in the organization?	Often are unaware or only partially aware	Aware of some, unaware of others	Moderately aware of problems	Generally quite well aware of problems
d. Extent to which technical and professional knowledge is used in decision-making	Used only if possessed at higher levels	Much of what is available in higher and middle levels is used	Much of what is available in higher, middle, and lower levels is used	Most of what is available anywhere within the organization is used
e. Are decisions made at the best level in the organization so far as (1) Having available the most adequate and accurate information bearing on the decision?	Decisions usually made at levels appreciably higher than levels where most adequate and accurate information exists	Decisions often made at levels appreciably higher than levels where most adequate and accurate information exists	Some tendency for decisions to be made at higher levels than where most adequate and accurate information exists	Overlapping groups and group decision processes tend to push decisions to point where information is most adequate or to pass the relevant information to the decision-making point
(2) The motivational	Decision-making con-	Decision-making con-	Some contribution by	Substantial contribution

230

consequences (i.e., does the decision-making process help to create the necessary motivations in those persons who have to carry out the decision?)	tributes little or nothing to the motivation to implement the decision, usually yields adverse motivation	tributes relatively little motivation	decision-making to motivation to implement	by decision-making processes to motivation to implement
f. Is decision-making based on man-to-man or group pattern of operation? Does it encourage or discourage teamwork?	Man-to-man only, discourages teamwork	Man-to-man almost entirely, discourages teamwork	Both man-to-man and group, partially encourages teamwork	Largely based on group pattern, encourages teamwork
5. Character of goal-setting or ordering *a.* Manner in which usually done	Orders issued	Orders issued, opportunity to comment may or may not exist	Goals are set or orders issued after discussion with subordinate(s) of problems and planned action	Except in emergencies, goals are usually established by means of group participation
b. To what extent do the different hierarchical levels tend to strive for high performance goals?	High goals pressed by top, resisted by subordinates	High goals sought by top and partially resisted by subordinates	High goals sought by higher levels but with some resistance by lower levels	High goals sought by all levels, with lower levels sometimes pressing for higher goals than top levels
c. Are there forces to accept, resist, or reject goals?	Goals are overtly accepted but are covertly resisted strongly	Goals are overtly accepted but often covertly resisted to at least a moderate degree	Goals are overtly accepted but at times with some covert resistance	Goals are fully accepted both overtly and covertly

TABLE 14-1 (*Continued*)

ORGANIZATIONAL AND PERFORMANCE CHARACTERISTICS OF DIFFERENT MANAGEMENT SYSTEMS BASED ON A COMPARATIVE ANALYSIS (*Continued*)

Operating characteristics	System of organization			
	Authoritative		Consultative	Participative
	Exploitive authoritative	Benevolent authoritative	Consultative	Participative group
6. Character of control processes				
a. At what hierarchical levels in organization does major or primary concern exist with regard to the performance of the control function?	At the very top only	Primarily or largely at the top	Primarily at the top but some shared feeling of responsibility felt at middle and to a lesser extent at lower levels	Concern for performance of control function likely to be felt throughout organization
c. How accurate are the measurements and information used to guide and perform the control function, and to what extent do forces exist in the organization to distort and falsify this information?	Very strong forces exist to distort and falsify; as a consequence, measurements and information are usually incomplete and often inaccurate	Fairly strong forces exist to distort and falsify; hence measurements and information are often incomplete and inaccurate	Some pressure to protect self and colleagues and hence some pressures to distort; information is only moderately complete and contains some inaccuracies	Strong pressures to obtain complete and accurate information to guide own behavior and behavior of own and related work groups; hence information and measurements tend to be complete and accurate

c. Extent to which the review and control functions are concentrated	Highly concentrated in top management	Relatively highly concentrated, with some delegated control to middle and lower levels	Moderate downward delegation of review and control processes; lower as well as higher levels feel responsible	Quite widespread responsibility for review and control, with lower units at times imposing more rigorous reviews and tighter controls than top management
d. Extent to which there is an informal organization present and supporting or opposing goals of formal organization	Informal organization present and opposing goals of formal organization	Informal organization usually present and partially resisting goals	Informal organization may be present and may either support or partially resist goals of formal organization	Informal and formal organization are one and the same; hence all social forces support efforts to achieve organization's goals
7. Performance characteristics			
a. Productivity	Mediocre productivity	Fair to good productivity	Good productivity	Excellent productivity
b. Excessive absence and turnover	Tends to be high when people are free to move	Moderately high when people are free to move	Moderate	Low
c. Scrap loss and waste	Relatively high unless policed carefully	Moderately high unless policed	Moderate	Members themselves will use measurements and other steps in effort to keep losses to a minimum
d. Quality control and inspection	Necessary for policing	Useful for policing	Useful as a check	Useful to help workers guide own efforts

233

based on a rough integration of results emerging from qualitative and quantitative research as well as material from general observation. They reflect historical trends as well as on patterns observed in different cultures. The characteristics as described are necessarily brief, general, and illustrative and are intended to indicate the general pattern only. No attempt is made to introduce the qualifications which might be appropriate at many points in the table.

Table 14-1 is organized as though there were four discrete types of organizational systems which fall at the four points shown on the suggested continuum. This oversimplifies the situation. The four different systems really blend into one another and make one continuum with many intermediate patterns.

When all the different management systems which involve at least a moderate degree of control or influence are examined, it becomes evident that they can be ordered, as is done in Table 14-1, along a continuum involving the kinds of controls and motivational forces used and the kinds of attitudinal responses evoked. When these different forms of organization are so arrayed, a significant and important observation emerges: *all the many operating procedures and the performance characteristics of the different management systems form an orderly pattern along every horizontal dimension.* There are also orderly relationships along the vertical dimensions which reflect the patterns of complementing interrelationships between the different operating procedures for each of the different forms of organization.

The orderly pattern displayed in this table reminds one of the periodic table in chemistry and apparently can serve some of the same purposes. It is possible to use it, for example, to *interpolate within* the table. Thus, for any organization which falls along the suggested continuum, it is possible, with minor deviations, to derive the probable patterns of leadership, organizational characteristics, and behavior which are typical of that system of organization when it is functioning at an optimum level.

Organizations which do not fall along the continuum shown in Table 14-1, because they involve different amounts of control from that shown, or which differ in the degree of specificity of behavior prescribed can be plotted, as suggested previously, in three-dimensional space. When this is done, the same process of interpolation can be applied as has been suggested for Table 14-1.

A much more important use than interpolation can be made of the orderly relationships revealed in Table 14-1. These relationships can be used for *extrapolation* to discover both the leadership and interactional patterns and the organizational and operating characteristics of a form of organization which we have not yet found fully developed in the business world, namely, the participative-group form of organization. The entries in Table 14-1 are based in part upon extrapolation. They are also based upon the research on small groups (Cartwright & Zander, 1960; Hare et al., 1955; Thibaut & Kelley, 1959) and upon the data from studies showing what the highest-producing managers do and the kinds of organizations they develop (Chapters 2 to 4).

Table 14-1 can be expanded substantially by adding to it broad categories not now included, such as training, and also by adding items under the broad categories already shown. Adding items to Table 14-1 can be an interesting and illuminating process. It helps to throw light on how each system of management can be expected to function and the results it is likely to achieve. Such items as the following can be added:

1. What leadership skills does each system require?

2. What interpersonal, interactional skills does each system demand from its members as well as from its leaders?

3. How complex are these skills? How hard are they to learn? To what extent does the system assist leaders and members to develop leadership and membership skills?

4. How efficient is each form of organization in training and developing the particular kind of leader required by that system? What kind of training does each system of organization demand? What training opportunities and resources does each offer? How limited or extensive are these opportunities with regard to what can be learned?

5. How much integrity must the leader have if the system is to work well? How much emotional maturity?

6. To what extent does each system tend to develop integrity in the members of the organization? To what extent does it develop emotional maturity?

Other categories and variables which might be added are those dealing with compensation, the form of the organizational structure (man-to-man versus group), planning, mental health, the manner in which the organization functions under stress or strain, the effect of stress upon it, and the capacity of the organization to adapt to technological and other changes.

As one adds items to Table 14-1 and examines the operating characteristics and performance qualities of the different forms of organization, two facts emerge. The first is that to function at its best each system of organization requires personalities, skills, and characteristic ways of interacting on the part of leaders and members which fit that particular system. For instance, authoritarian organizations require dependent personalities on the part of all except those in control (Argyris, 1957c). Participative organizations require emotionally mature personalities (Morse & Reimer, 1956; Tannenbaum & Allport, 1956; Vroom, 1960c).

The second fact about these different forms of organization is that each tends to produce people suited to function well within that system.

Each system tends to mold people in its own image. Authoritarian organizations tend to develop dependent people and few leaders. Participative organizations tend to develop emotionally and socially mature persons capable of effective interaction, initiative, and leadership.

Table 14-1, especially when greatly expanded by adding broad categories and many additional items under each category, can yield a substantial body of information on the performance characteristics of the participative-group form of management. Since this is essentially the management system called for by the newer theory, Table 14-1 indicates the general pattern of operating characteristics an organization should achieve under the newer theory.

This information can be used to assess how well the newer theory is being applied in any situation. Whenever the performance characteristics do not reach the level called for by the derivations in Table 14-1, this is clear evidence of deficiencies in its application. The discrepancies between the operating characteristics called for by the derivations and the results actually achieved—as revealed by the periodic measurement of the intervening and end-result variables—can point to the changes required in operations in order to reach the potential level of performance which Table 14-1 shows is possible. Moreover, the derivations in Table 14-1 can be helpful in suggesting ways of modifying procedures to achieve the desired performance characteristics.

Chapter 15

LOOKING TO THE FUTURE

As background for a discussion of the problems an organization will face in shifting to a full-scale application of the newer theory, it will be helpful to review briefly the general character of an organization when it is based upon a full application of the theory:

I. Nature of the organization
    A. Integrated system
        It is an integrated, internally consistent management system. The operating procedures for all such processes as selection, training, compensation, communication, decision-making, and supervision required to apply it to any particular company or plant need to be complementary in the manner indicated in Chapter 14.
    B. Structure
        The overlapping group form of organization appears to come closest to the requirements specified by the principle of supportive relationships. In addition, there is substantial research to show that the communication and influence processes are most effective in groups to which an individual feels highly loyal and is highly attracted. The highly effective communication and influence processes called for by the newer theory require an organizational structure which will facilitate these processes. The evidence, both theoretical and experimental, indicates that the overlapping group form of organizational structure meets these requirements better than any other form of organization now known. Consequently, the overlapping group structure is the basic pattern of the newer theory and is applied fully by our model organization.
    C. Character of work groups
        The work groups of the organization are highly effective groups and have all the performance characteristics typical of such groups.
    D. Leadership
        The leadership of the organization has all the technical and mangerial skills ordinarily required. In addition, the philosophy of

management and leadership skills required to build and operate an interaction-influence system consisting of highly effective groups is present.

E. Atmosphere

To function as specified by the principle of supportive relationships, the organization provides a supportive, ego-building atmosphere, one in which people feel valued and respected and in which confidence and trust grow. The atmosphere is permeated by ego-enhancing rather than ego-deflating and threatening points of view toward people.

F. Personnel

The organization is staffed by persons with appropriate aptitudes and training to perform the different functions for which they are responsible. In addition to the abilities and skills usually required, the members of the organization have adequate interpersonal and group-process skills. They have accurate sensitivity to the reactions of others and a satisfactory level of skills in the leadership and membership roles necessary for functioning well in face-to-face groups.

G. Cooperative working relationships

In a friendly and supportive atmosphere, the members of the organization have sufficient interaction with the other members of the work groups and units of which they are part to achieve a high level of confidence and trust and an effective flow of information and of influence. This requires at least a minimum level of stability in personnel assignments. Rapid turnover and shifts in personnel tend to prevent the establishment of a high level of cooperative working relationships.

H. Measurements

The members of the organization have available to them accurate, current measurements which reflect the internal state of the organization, the relevant dimensions of its environment, and its present performance. These measurements are available to those members of the organization whose decisions affect each of the different variables. In this manner, these measurements facilitate sound decisions based on accurate, objective information and thereby permit the "authority of facts" and the "law of the situation" to prevail.

II. Operating characteristics

A. The principle of supportive relationships which has been proposed for the newer theory specifies conditions that lead to a full and efficient flow of all relevant information in all directions—

upward, downward, and between peers—throughout the organization. This full and open flow of useful and relevant information provides at all points in the organization accurate data to guide action, to call attention to problems as they arise, and to assure that sound decisions based on all available facts are made.

B. The principle of supportive relationships calls for an exercise of influence comparable with the flow of information. In organizations which effectively use the newer theory, consequently, every person feels, and is correct in his feeling, that he can and does exercise influence upon the decisions and behavior of all those with whom he is in more or less regular contact. Through them he exerts at least some influence upon the entire organization.

Persons in organizations operating under the newer theory, in comparison with those in most existing organizations, exercise greater influence upon what happens in the organization. This is true at every hierarchical level from nonsupervisory employees to the head of the organization. The application of the newer theory results in a greater total amount of influence being exercised throughout the organization. As a consequence, the organization can more fully mobilize and focus all its resources to accomplish its goals than can present-day organizations.

C. This efficient flow of communication and exercise of influence throughout the organization has important consequences for decision-making. All the relevant information and technical knowledge existing in the organization on a particular problem usually flow to the point or points where the decisions on the problem are made. Not only does information flow efficiently, but in addition, ideas, experience, and suggested solutions also flow to the decision-making points as a result of the influence process required by the newer theory. As a consequence, sound decisions are made based on more adequate facts than is usually the case today.

The substantial amount of accurate information flowing through the organization also results in the relevant parts of the organization being promptly aware of problems and able to deal with them rapidly and effectively.

The participation provided by the influence process has important consequences. The over-all objectives of the organization are a satisfactory integration of the needs and desires of the members of the organization and of all persons functionally related to it, such as consumers, shareholders, and suppliers. Moreover, the over-all objectives of the organization, the objectives of the various departments, and the goals of work groups and of individuals in work groups are in general harmony, and all are polarized toward achieving the objectives of the organization. This results in behavior efficiently focused on achieving the organization's objectives.

D. A high level of effective, coordinated motivation is achieved. This uses fully and in an additive manner all motivational forces which are accompanied by favorable attitudes. The principle of supportive relationships is used as a guide to accomplish this.

1. The organization's objectives are embraced by its members. Each endeavors to implement these objectives since he sees them as objectives which, in part at least, he has helped create. He is aware that he has influenced them or can do so and that these objectives reflect his own needs and desires.

2. The reward system of the organization, like its objectives, is established through a process of interaction and influence. In this way a system of financial and related rewards is developed which has a high probability of: (a) being viewed as equitable by all interested parties; (b) helping to build highly effective groups; and (c) rewarding behavior which helps the organization achieve its goals.

3. Each member recognizes that the more adequately the organization's objectives are met, the greater is the extent to which his own goals and desires are fulfilled. This results in the members setting high performance goals for themselves and their work group. The full motivational force of the goals of highly effective groups is present.

III. Over-all performance characteristics

An organization should be outstanding in its performance if it has competent personnel, if it has leadership which develops highly effective groups and uses the overlapping group form of structure, and if it achieves effective communication and influence, decentralized and coordinated decision-making, and high performance goals coupled with high motivation. We should expect such an organization to have high productivity; products of high quality; low costs; low waste; low turnover and absence; high capacity to adapt effectively to change; a high degree of enthusiasm and satisfaction on the part of its employees, customers, and stockholders; and good relations with unions. In short, the theoretical model called for by the newer theory appears to be an ideal organization. Existing organizations can move toward this model with benefit to all. This appears to be the direction in which the high-producing managers are, in fact, moving.

From Theory to Practice

There is, however, a wide gulf between a statement of general theory and the development of specific operating procedures to make possible a satisfactory and valid application of the theory in a specific situation. To move from the newer theory, as stated in this volume, to a full-scale application will require a great deal of experimentation and development. The situation, in many ways, is similar to the problems encountered when a major finding of physical science research is moved through developmental research and engineering to a pilot plant before launching a full-scale operation of the new product or process. The developmental work and the pilot plant require substantial amounts of time and money.

An organization about to apply the newer theory, whether it be a business enterprise, a governmental agency, a hospital, a union, an educational system, or a voluntary association, needs to conduct a substantial amount of developmental research before embarking upon a full-scale application. This process may also require a small pilot project to eliminate the usual difficulties before a completely successful application is achieved. Although an adequate discussion of this process is the subject of another book, it may be useful to examine very briefly here some of the major steps involved in applying the theory in any particular company.

The best way to proceed in any organization will depend upon many factors unique to the situation. In some companies, it will be better to introduce the newer theory gradually, on a company-wide basis. In others, a pilot project will be desirable. Size will be one factor in determining the steps to be taken. Small organizations may have little need for a pilot project; large corporations may find it essential. A pilot project will enable a large company to develop and test an operation on a small and manageable scale. This experience can then be used to guide the application of the theory to the entire organization.

During the developmental research and especially during any pilot phase, mistakes will be made. It is well to be prepared for them and to be in a position to handle them constructively. It would be desirable, consequently, to carry out much of the developmental research and all the pilot-plant experiment in a relatively small operation and preferably in one which is self-contained. In a small unit, everyone can know that the experiment is under way and what its nature and objectives are. When errors are made, they can be caught promptly and everyone informed about them. Members of the unit frequently will take part in detecting mistakes and in helping to correct them.

In staffing the pilot operation, it would be highly desirable to pick persons whose present methods of management most nearly approach the principles and practices called for by the newer theory. In early experiments this was not done either for managers or nonsupervisory employees. It has since been found, however, that staffing pilot projects with persons whose skills and expectations come as close as possible to the conditions to be created increases the likelihood that success will be achieved in the least time and at the least cost.

The pilot project should develop the general model of the procedure to be used in operating the particular plant or company under the newer theory. This should deal with selection, training, communication, compensation, decision-making, supervision, and all other procedures required by the operation. In this process, attention should be focused on the general rather than the highly specific. General principles and a general model will be widely applicable, but specific techniques are likely to vary from department to department.

If a pilot project is used, it can become a valuable training resource after the imperfections are removed. There is no better way to train personnel at every organizational level in the philosophy and skills required for operating under the newer theory than to have them participate as members in a pilot project. Rotating people into and out of this operation will be highly effective as a training procedure.

Controlling the Magnitude of Change

In conducting the pilot project and in the later steps of shifting the entire organization to the newer system of management, it is important to keep in mind that any change will be apt to work best if it does not require too drastic a shift at any one time in leadership or interaction skills. If the changes are too sudden or too great, the members of the organization will react with fear and psychological, if not physical, flight.

The process of participation can be used to illustrate the adverse consequences of changes which are too great. It frequently is stated that participation will increase employee motivation and productivity and that the greater the amount of participation, the greater the beneficial effect. There is substantial evidence to support this point of view, but there is also evidence pointing to the fact that the amount and character of participation need to be geared to the values, skills, and expectation of the people involved if productive results are to be obtained (French, Israel, & Aas, 1960; Tannenbaum, 1954; Tannenbaum & Allport, 1956; Vroom, 1960c). Participation should not be thought of as a single process or activity, but rather as a whole range of processes and activities. It is even possible to describe participation tentatively as a continuum of processes, crudely shown in the figure on page 243:

$$\underline{a \quad b \quad c \quad d \quad e \quad f \quad g \quad h \quad i \quad j \quad k \quad l}$$

Little   Much
participation   participation

Some of the points on the above continuum might be described roughly as follows:

a. No information given to employees, either about the current situation or in advance of proposed changes.

b. Some information given about the current situation, but never about a proposed change until the change occurs.

c. Brief notice of a proposed change given shortly before the change occurs.

d. Brief notice of a proposed change given shortly before the change, along with a few reasons for the change.

e. Reports sought from employees of problems they encounter in doing their work.

f. Notice of proposed change and full explanation for this change given well in advance.

g. Employees notified of a proposed change in advance, and an opportunity offered to employees to express reactions and suggestions on the proposed change if they desire to do so.

h. Employees' ideas or suggestions sought generally.

i. Employees notified in advance of a proposed change, and group discussions arranged so that employees can comment on whether the proposed change is the best plan or whether some modification would result in a better plan.

j. Employees (or subordinates) told of a problem, and group discussions conducted to discover the best way to handle the problem, but the final decision made by the head of the unit in the light of the ideas and suggestions advanced by the group.

k. Subordinates and leader tackle problem as a group and after consideration and discussion decide upon solution, but leader (or a higher authority) holds right of veto power.

l. Leader and subordinates functioning as a group tackle the problem and solve it, using the best available methods for group functioning.

These statements are intended only to illustrate the range of possibilities so far as the process of participation is concerned. All the above points may or may not fall on a single continuum. As described here, they probably are a rough approximation of the correct order or position.

In the above statements, it is assumed that the giving or sharing of information is an essential step in the process of participation and one of the first in moving toward more complete participation. There appears to be ample evidence, both observational and experimental, for relating the sharing of information to participation.

Available research data suggest that the people within each social or industrial organization are accustomed to some degree of participation in its functioning. It may be at a very low level, such as points a or b, or at a very high level, such as points j or k. Every company has a modal point. The data also provide evidence that while the total organization is accustomed to a certain level of participation, the subparts of the organization differ somewhat in the amounts of participation they employ. Some departments or units use more participation, others use less, but almost none spans the entire possible range suggested in a to l above.

These differences in the amount of participation between the subparts of an organization tend to be related to differences in productivity and job satisfaction. Within the range of participation that ordinarily exists in the organization, the greater the amount of participation which occurs within a unit, the greater tends to be the productivity of that unit and the greater the satisfaction of its members. [French et al. (1960), also showed that participation, to be effective, had also to be seen as "legitimate."]

At every level of participation, a moderate increase usually results in improved performance. This increase, however, must not be too great nor occur too suddenly, as, for example, a sudden shift from level c to l. Whenever the increase in participation goes appreciably beyond the habits, values, and expectations of the persons involved, they seem to feel that it is not "legitimate," seem unable to cope with it successfully, and often become insecure. Whenever this occurs, the positive value of participation is lost.

A relatively high level of participation in itself tends to yield high levels of motivation and performance. It does not appear necessary at these high levels to increase the amount of participation to achieve high motivation and high performance.

In introducing the newer system of management, it is important to know the range of expectations and the leadership and membership skills among members of the organization and to restrict the initial changes to this range. If this range is less than that required to achieve a complete application of the newer theory, the process of moving from the present management system to the newer can be done in a series of steps. As the members of the organization become experienced and at ease with the changes in interactional processes introduced in the first step, further changes can be gradually introduced.

A company can choose between alternative paths in moving toward a full-scale operation of the newer theory. It can begin with a pilot project, or it can make gradual applications of the theory on a company-wide basis. No matter which way is chosen, certain actions must be taken as part of a successful application of the theory: measurements must be obtained periodically of the causal, intervening, and end-result variables, the overlapping form of organization must be established, group methods of supervision introduced, group leadership and membership skills acquired, and the like. Therefore a company beginning with a pilot project does not have to wait until the pilot work is completed to take preparatory steps. Such steps as those just suggested can be gradually undertaken on a company-wide basis when the pilot project is started. When experience with the pilot project indicates that the time is ripe, a gradual shift to a full-scale application of the newer theory can be made, benefitting from the preparatory steps already taken.

Aggressive Acts against Leadership

Organizations operating under tight controls will have more difficulty in changing to the newer theory than will those companies whose present operations more nearly conform to it. The former not only will have to make greater changes in interactional processes and often in a series of steps, but they are also likely to run into apathy, indifference, and even aggressive responses. One might expect that any movement away from authoritarian control would be greatly appreciated by employees. Experience has shown, however, as have experiments (White & Lippitt, 1960) that when a management relinquishes tight controls and moves toward participative management, the *initial* response of members of the organization at every hierarchical level may be apathy or open hostility and aggressive responses against their superiors. This can be a shocking and distressing experience to managers. Unless they are forewarned, top management may be tempted to halt the introduction of the new theory at this point and revert to its former practices.

Two major causes of this aggressive reaction seem to be the need to release bottled-up animosity and the need to test the superior's sincerity. A company making a major shift in its management practices, therefore, must expect either hostility and aggression or indifference as part of the first stage in the developmental program.

Not only does the top management of a tightly controlled company need to be prepared for the release of animosity, it has to be prepared for resistance to change itself (Coch & French, 1948; Lewin, 1947; Lewin, 1951; Lippitt, 1949; Lippitt, Watson, & Wesley, 1958; Mann, 1957; Mann & Likert, 1952; White & Lippitt, 1960). This is true of technological change (Mann & Hoffman, 1960), and it is especially true of changes in the organization as a human and social entity. Change which takes place slowly enough to permit participation can come smoothly, successfully, and with the kind of motivation which accelerates change. But changes which are made rapidly or which are superimposed by authority meet with strong resistance (Coch & French, 1948; Smith & Nyman, 1939). The company president who issued orders to "push cooperation aggressively" failed to accomplish his purpose.

It is important to keep in mind also that the larger the organization, the more difficult it is to achieve significant change within a given period of time without undue strain. As a consequence, large organizations should expect to take appreciably longer than small organizations in shifting their operations to the newer theory.

Start at the Top of the Organization

It would be well if the president and other top officers started to apply the newer theory to their own operations before the program moves from the pilot project into actual operation in the company. This could be a valuable part of the developmental program and also would smooth the way for acceptance by other levels of the organization.

The top officers must be convinced of the validity of the theory and must play a major role in its introduction if it is to succeed. As the research examined in this volume shows, subordinates reflect their superior's managerial principles and practices. Consequently, members of an organization are not likely to use a theory of management for any length of time if it deviates substantially from that of the head of the organization.

Errors are likely to be made in introducing any major change. If the top officers of a company have been fully involved in introducing the newer system of management, they will be prepared for mistakes and psychologically will have written off the costs. Therefore their behavior toward those running the pilot project when mistakes are made will continue to be supportive and encouraging. If top management is not thoroughly committed to the newer theory and prepared for the cost of errors, those whom top management holds responsible may find themselves in hot water. This will abruptly stop any change in the management system.

There is an aspect of the newer theory which may be of interest to companies with overseas operations. It is probable that the theory will prove to be applicable in other countries and cultures. People in all cultures seem to respond favorably to treatment which, in terms of their values, contributes to their sense of personal worth and importance. Since this is the essential concept of the principle of supportive relationships, it appears to be applicable to company management in cultures quite different from that in the United States. The research on leadership and management in countries less developed industrially supports the view that the principle of supportive relationships has wide applicability (Abegglen,

1958; Bose, 1957; Bose, 1958a; Bose, 1958b; Chowdhry, 1953; Chowdhry, 1960; Chowdhry & Pal, 1957; Chowdhry & Trivedi, 1953; Chowdhry & Trivedi, 1958; Ganguli, 1956; Ganguli, 1957; Ganguli, 1958; Rice, 1958).

It is probable that the newer theory, and such material as that in Table 14-1, may correctly indicate the general direction in which management theories and practices are likely to develop in a country. For each country or for a company within a country, its present management system can be located along the horizontal axis in Table 14-1. The available research findings obtained in the United States, in other industrialized countries, and in less industrialized countries indicate that in each country those organizations whose management systems deviate more toward the participative-group form tend to be more productive than those organizations whose management systems tend more to resemble the exploitive-authoritative end of the continuum. These findings suggest that in each company and country there will be competitive and experiential forces tending to shift the management systems gradually toward the participative-group form of organization. This trend is likely to occur unless there are powerful forces in the company or country restraining such development. This information can be useful in guiding a company's plans as to staffing, training, and management development. The ability to know today the general direction of development for the next decade or two can be helpful.

The rate of development will, of course, be influenced by many different factors and is more difficult to estimate. Those in control in some states may strive to prevent any change in the management systems used in their country. If this happens, it will not only affect the trend in leadership and management principles but will also affect adversely the trend in productivity of the industries in the countries involved.

In Conclusion

Two or three years is usually required to introduce a major technological change in an organization smoothly and without excessive stress. The time-consuming problems in making such a shift do not usually involve the technological processes, but the people. Introducing a substantially different management system is a far more complex undertaking so far as the people are concerned and, consequently, will require an appreciably longer period of time.

Field experiments conducted by the Institute for Social Research in several companies indicate that at least three or four years is likely to be necessary to develop and test the application of the newer theory in a particular company. In companies with more than two or three hundred employees, an additional five years or more may be required to shift the organization to a full-scale application of the newer theory. In large corporations, even more time will be necessary.

Neither the testing of the theory nor the shifting of an organization to a full-scale application of the theory can be hurried. Haste is self-defeating because of the anxieties and stresses it creates. There is no substitute for ample time to enable the members of an organization to reach the level of skillful and easy, habitual use of the new leadership and membership principles and methods required for an application of the newer theory.

The decisions a company makes today, consequently, with regard to the extent it uses social science research and experimentally tests new theories, principles, and practices will exert a major influence on the character and effectiveness of its management system a decade hence.

BIBLIOGRAPHY

Abegglen, J. C. *The Japanese factory*. Glencoe, Ill.: Free Press, 1958.

Acton Society Trust. *Size and morale*. London: Author, 1953.

Acton Society Trust. *Size and morale*, part II. London: Author, 1957.

Argyris, C. Human problems with budgets. *Harvard Business Rev.*, 1953, **31**(1), 97–110.

Argyris, C. The individual and organizational structure: recent research findings in human relations research. Amer. Mgmt Asso., *Personnel Ser.*, No. 168, 1956, 3–11.

Argyris, C. The individual and organization: some problems of mutual adjustment. *Administrative Sci. Quart.*, 1957, **2**(1), 1–24. (a)

Argyris, C. Organization and the human being. *Product Engng*, Dec. 30, 1957. (b)

Argyris, C. *Personality and organization*. New York: Harper, 1957. (c)

Argyris, C. Some propositions about human behavior in organizations. In *Symposium on preventive and social psychiatry*. Washington: Walter Reed Army Institute of Research, 1957. Pp. 209–230. (d)

Argyris, C. Understanding human behavior in organizations: one viewpoint. In M. Haire (Ed.), *Modern organization theory*. New York: Wiley, 1959.

Asch, S. *Social psychology*. Englewood Cliffs, N.J.: Prentice-Hall, 1952.

Bakke, E. W. Concept of the social organization. In M. Haire (Ed.), *Modern organization theory*. New York: Wiley, 1959.

Bales, R. F. *Interaction process analysis: a method for the study of small groups*. Reading, Mass.: Addison-Wesley, 1950.

Barnard, C. I. *Functions of the executive*. Cambridge, Mass.: Harvard Univer. 1948. (a)

Barnard, C. I. *Organization and management*. Cambridge, Mass.: Harvard Univer., 1948. (b)

Bass, B. M. *Leadership psychology and organizational behavior*. New York: Harper, 1960.

Baumgartel, H. J., Jr. Leadership, motivation and attitudes in twenty laboratories. Unpublished doctoral dissertation, Univer. of Michigan, 1955.

Baumgartel, H. J., Jr. Leadership, motivations and attitudes in research laboratories. *J. soc. Issues*, 1956 **12**(2), 24–31.

Bendix, R. *Work and authority in industry*. New York: Wiley, 1956.

Benne, K. D., & Sheats, P. Functional roles of group members. *J. soc. Issues*, 1948, **4**(2), 42–45.

Bennis, W. G., & Shepard, H. A. A theory of group development. *Human Relat.*, 1956, **9**(4), 415–437.

Blake, R. R., & Mouton, J. S. *Training for decision-making in groups.* Austin, Tex.: Univer. of Texas, 1956.

Bolda, R. A., & Lawshe, C. H. The use of training case responses in management training evaluation. *Educ. psychol. Measmt,* 1959, **19,** 549–556.

Bose, S. K. A psychological approach to productivity improvement. *Conf.* of Psychologists, Bombay, 1957.

Bose, S. K. Group cohesiveness as a factor in industrial morale and productivity. *J. Sci. Club* (Bangalore, India), 1958, 11. (a)

Bose, S. K. Industrial motivation for higher productivity. Lecture, Indian Institute of Technology, Kharagpur, India, 1958. (b)

Brooks, E. What successful executives do. *Personnel,* 1955, **32**(3), 210–225.

Brown, W. *Exploration in management.* London: Heinemann, 1960.

Browne, C. G., & Neitzel, B. J. Communication, supervision, and morale. *J. appl. Psychol.,* 1952, **36,** 86–91.

Bruner, J. S., & Tagiuri, R. Perception of people. In G. Lindzey (Ed.), *Handbook of social psychology.* Reading, Mass.: Addison-Wesley, 1954. Pp. 634–655.

Campbell, A. Administering research organizations. *Amer. Psychologist,* 1953, **8**(6), 225–230.

Campbell, A. Operations research and human behavior. In *Operations research,* II. Ann Arbor, Mich.: Univer. of Michigan, Coll. of Engineering Industry Program, 1958. Pp. 119–127.

Campbell, A., Converse, P., Miller, W., & Stokes, D. *The American voter.* New York: Wiley, 1960.

Campbell, A., Gurin, G., & Miller W. *The voter decides.* Evanston, Ill.: Row, Peterson, 1954.

Campbell, A., & Katona, G. The sample survey: a technique for social science research. In L. Festinger & D. Katz (Eds.), *Research methods in the behavioral sciences.* New York: Holt, Rinehart and Winston, 1953. Pp. 15–55.

Cannell, C. F., & Kahn, R. L. The collection of data by interviewing. In L. Festinger & D. Katz (Eds.), *Research methods in the behavioral sciences.* New York: Holt, Rinehart and Winston, 1953. Pp. 327–380.

Cannell, C. F., & Kahn, R. L. Nobody tells me anything. *Dun's Rev. and Modern Industry,* 1957, **70**(5), 36–38, 98–107.

Cannell, C. F., & Kahn, R. L. Interviewing: an essential executive function. In Davis & Scott (Eds.), *Readings in human relations.* New York: McGraw-Hill, 1959.

Cartwright, D. Surveys of the war finance program. *Proc. Conf. on Consumers' Interests.* Philadelphia: Univer. of Pennsylvania, 1947.

Cartwright, D. Some principles of mass persuasion. *Human Relat.,* 1949, **2,** 253–267.

Cartwright, D. Achieving change in people: some applications of group dynamics theory. *Human Relat.,* 1951, **4,** 381–392.

Cartwright, D. Social psychology and group processes. *Annu. Rev. Psychol.,* 1957, **8,** 211–236.

Cartwright, D. (Ed.) *Studies in social power.* Ann Arbor, Mich.: Institute for Social Research, 1959. (a)

Cartwright, D. The potential contribution of graph theory to organization theory. In M. Haire (Ed.), *Modern organization theory.* New York: Wiley, 1959. (b)

Cartwright, D., & Harary, F. Structural balance: a generalization of Heider's theory. *Psychol. Rev.,* 1956, **63**(5), 277–296.

Cartwright, D., & Lippitt, R. Group dynamics and the individual. *Int. J. Group Psychother.*, 1957, 7(1), 86–102.

Cartwright, D., & Zander, A. (Eds.) *Group dynamics: research and theory* (2d ed.) Evanston, Ill.: Row, Peterson, 1960.

Chase, S. *Roads to agreement.* New York: Harper, 1951.

Chowdhry, Kamla. An analysis of the attitudes of textile workers and the effect of these attitudes on working efficiency. *ATIRA Res. Note* (Ahmedabad, India), 1953.

Chowdhry, Kamla. *Human relations, a review: background and current trends.* Ahmedabad, India: ATIRA Human Relations Division, 1960.

Chowdhry, Kamla, & Pal, A. K. Production planning and organization morale: a case from India. *Human Organization*, 1957, 15(5).

Chowdhry, Kamla, & Trivedi, V. R. Motivation to work: improvement in motivation to work of winders and warpers and its effect on loomshed efficiency. *ATIRA Res. Note* (Ahmedabad, India), 1953.

Chowdhry, Kamla, & Trivedi, V. R. *Four cases on training: introducing a new function in a mill.* Ahmedabad, India: ATIRA Human Relations Division, 1958.

Coch, L., & French, J. R. P., Jr. Overcoming resistance to change. *Human Relat.*, 1948, 1(4), 512–532.

Comrey, A. L., High, W. S., & Wilson, R. C. Factors influencing organizational effectiveness, VI. *Personnel Psychol.*, 1955, 8(1), 79–99. (a)

Comrey, A. L., High, W. S., & Wilson, R. C. Factors influencing organizational effectiveness, VII. *Personnel Psychol.*, 1955, 8(2), 245–257. (b)

Converse, P. E. Group influence in voting behavior. Unpublished doctoral dissertation, Univer. of Michigan, 1958.

Cordiner, R. J. *New frontiers for professional managers.* New York: McGraw-Hill, 1956.

Coser, L. A. The functions of small group research. *Soc. Problems*, 1955, 3(1).

Dahlstrom, E. *Management, unions and society.* Stockholm: Studieforbundet Naringsliv och Samhalle, 1954.

Dalton, M. *Men who manage.* New York: Wiley, 1959.

Davis, R. C. Commitment to professional values as related to the role performance of research scientists. Unpublished doctoral dissertation, Univer. of Michigan, 1956.

Dent, J. K. Managerial leadership styles: some dimensions, determinants, and behavioral correlates. Unpublished doctoral dissertation, Univer. of Michigan, 1957.

Donald, Marjorie. Some concomitants of varying patterns of communication in a large organization. Unpublished doctoral disseration, Univer. of Michigan, 1958.

Dubin, R. *Human relations in administration.* Englewood Cliffs, N.J.: Prentice-Hall, 1951.

Estes, H. Some considerations in designing an organizational structure. Paper read at Foundation for Research on Human Behavior seminar, Ann Arbor, Mich., December, 1960.

Evans, C. E. Supervisory responsibility and authority. Amer. Mgmt Asso., *Res. Rep.* No. 30, 1957.

Festinger, L. Informal social communication. *Psychol. Rev.*, 1950, 57, 271–282.

Festinger, L., & Katz, D. (Eds.) *Research methods in the behavioral sciences.* New York: Holt, Rinehart, and Winston, 1953.

Fiedler, F. E. *Leader attitudes and group effectiveness*. Urbana, Ill.: Univer. of Illinois, 1958.

Fleishman, E. A. Leadership climate, human relations training, and supervisory behavior. *Personnel Psychol.*, 1953, 6, 205–222.

Fleishman, E. A., Harris, E. F., & Burtt, H. E. Leadership and supervision in industry. *Ohio State Business Educ. Res. Monogr.*, 1955, No. 33.

Follett, Mary Parker. See Metcalf & Urwick, 1950.

Foundation for Research on Human Behavior. *Leadership patterns and organizational effectiveness*. Ann Arbor, Mich.: Author, 1954. (a)

Foundation for Research on Human Behavior. *Training in human relations*. Ann Arbor, Mich.: Author, 1954. (b)

Foundation for Research on Human Behavior. *Planning and training for effective leadership*. Ann Arbor, Mich.: Author, 1955.

Foundation for Research on Human Behavior. *Training foreign nationals in the United States*. Ann Arbor, Mich.: Author, 1956.

Foundation for Research on Human Behavior. *Assessing managerial potential*. Ann Arbor, Mich.: Author, 1958. (a)

Foundation for Research on Human Behavior. *Creativity and conformity: a problem for organizations*. Ann Arbor, Mich.: Author, 1958 (b)

Foundation for Research on Human Behavior. *Performance appraisal and review*. Ann Arbor, Mich.: Author, 1958. (c)

Foundation for Research on Human Behavior. *The adoption of new products: process and influence*. Ann Arbor, Mich.: Author, 1959. (a)

Foundation for Research on Human Behavior. *Communication in organizations: some new research findings*. Ann Arbor, Mich.: Author, 1959. (b)

Foundation for Research on Human Behavior. *Communication problems in superior-subordinate relationships*. Ann Arbor, Mich.: Author, 1960. (a)

Foundation for Research on Human Behavior. People are your business. *Newsletter* No. 6, July 31, 1960. (b)

Foundation for Research on Human Behavior. *Seven year report: 1952–1959*. Ann Arbor, Mich.: Author, 1960. (c)

Foundation for Research on Human Behavior. *An action research program for organization improvement*. Ann Arbor, Mich.: Author, 1960. (d)

Foundation for Research on Human Behavior. *Managing major change in organizations*. Ann Arbor, Mich.: Author, 1960. (e)

French, J. R. P., Jr. Role-playing as a method of training foremen. *Sociometry*, 1945, 8, 410–425.

French, J. R. P., Jr. A formal theory of social power. *Psychol. Rev.*, 1956, 63(3), 181–194.

French, J. R. P., Jr., Israel, J., & Aas, D. An experiment on participation in a Norwegian factory. *Human Relat.*, 1960, 13(1), 3-19.

French, J. R. P., Jr., & Raven, B. H. The bases of social power. In D. Cartwright (Ed.), *Studies in social power*. Ann Arbor, Mich.: Institute for Social Research, 1959. Pp. 150–167.

French, J. R. P., Jr., Ross, I. C., Kirby, S., Nelson, J. R., & Smyth, P. Employee participation in a program of industrial change. *Personnel*, November-December, 1958, 16–29.

French, J. R. P., Jr., & Zander, A. The group dynamics approach. *Psychol. labor-management relat*, IRRA, 1949, 71–80.

Friedmann, G. *Industrial society: the emergence of human problems of automation*. Glencoe, Ill.: Free Press, 1948.

Ganguli, H. C. Attitudes of union and non-union employees in a Calcutta electrical engineering factory. *J. appl. Psychol.*, 1956, **40**, 78–82.

Ganguli, H. C. *A study on supervision in a government engineering factory.* Kharagpur, India: Indian Institute of Technology, 1957.

Ganguli, H. C. Mental health problems of automated and nonautomated workers with reference to accelerated industrialization. Geneva: World Health Organization, 1958.

Georgopoulos, B. S. The normative structure of social systems: a study of organizational effectiveness. Unpublished doctoral dissertation, Univer. of Michigan, 1957.

Georgopoulos, B. S., Mahoney, G., & Jones, N. A path-goal approach to productivity. *J. appl. Psychol.*, 1957, **41**(6), 345–353.

Georgopoulos, B. S., & Tannenbaum, A. S. A study of organizational effectiveness. *Amer. sociol. Rev.*, 1957, **22**, 534–540.

Gerard, R. W. *Mirror to physiology: a self-survey of physiological science.* Washington: American Physiological Society, 1958.

Goodacre, D. M. Group characteristics of good and poor performing combat units. *Sociometry*, 1953, **16**(2), 168–179.

Goodwin, H. F. Work simplification. *Factory Mgmt and Maintenance*, July, 1958, 72–106.

Gordon, T. *Group-centered leadership.* Boston: Houghton Mifflin, 1955.

Gross, N., Mason, W. S., & McEachern, A. *Explorations in role analysis.* New York: Wiley, 1958.

Haire, M. *Psychology in management.* New York: McGraw-Hill, 1956.

Haire, M. (Ed.) *Modern organization theory.* New York: Wiley, 1959.

Haire, M., & Grunes, W. F. Perceptual defenses: processes protecting an organized perception of another personality. *Human Relat.*, 1950, **4**, 403–412.

Hamann, J. R. Panel discussion. Amer. Mgmt Asso. *Gen. Mgmt Ser.*, No. 182, 1956, 21–23.

Harary, F. Structural duality. *Behavioral Science*, 1957, **2**, 255–265.

Harary, F. A criterion for unanimity in French's theory of social power. In D. Cartwright (Ed.), *Studies in social power.* Ann Arbor, Mich.: Institute for Social Research, 1959. (a)

Harary, F. Graph theoretic methods in the management sciences. *Mgmt Sci.*, 1959, **5**, 387–403. (b)

Harary, F. On the measurement of structural balance. *Behavioral Sci.*, 1959, **4**, 316–323. (c)

Harary, F. Status and contrastatus. *Sociometry*, 1959, **22**, 23–43. (d)

Harary, F., & Norman, R. *Graph theory as a mathematical model in the social sciences.* Ann Arbor, Mich.: Institute for Social Research, 1953.

Harary, F., & Ross, I. C. A procedure for clique detection using the group matrix. *Sociometry*, 1957, **20**(3), 205–215.

Harary, F., & Ross, I. C. A description of strengthening and weakening group members. *Sociometry*, 1959, **2**, 139–147.

Hare, P., Borgatta, E. F., & Bales, R. F. *Small groups.* New York: Knopf, 1955.

Harris, E. F. Measuring industrial leadership and its implications for training supervisors. Unpublished doctoral dissertation, Ohio State Univer., 1952.

Havron, M. D. The contribution of the leader to the effectiveness of small military groups. In L. Petrullo & B. M. Bass (Eds.), *Leadership and interpersonal behavior.* New York: Holt, Rinehart and Winston, 1961.

Hemphill, J. K. *Group dimensions: a manual for their measurement.* Columbus: Ohio State Univer., Bureau of Business Research, 1956.

Herzberg, F., Mausner, B., & Snyderman, Barbara. *The motivation to work.* (2d ed.) New York: Wiley, 1959.

Hill, J. M. M. A consideration of labor turnover as the resultant of a quasi-stationary process (the Glacier project—IV). *Human Relat.,* 1951, 4, 255–265.

Hoffman, L. R. Homogeneity of member personality and its effect on group problem-solving. *J. abnorm. soc. Psychol.,* 1959, 58(1), 27–32.

Homans, G. C. *The human group.* New York: Harcourt, Brace, World, 1950.

Hood, R. C. Concern for cost: a participative approach. *Amer. Mgmt Asso., Manufacturing Ser.,* No. 221, 1956, 24–40.

Hoppock, R. *Job satisfaction.* New York: Harper, 1935.

Houser, J. D. *What people want from business.* New York: McGraw-Hill, 1938.

Hovland, C. I., Janis, I. L., & Kelley, H. H. *Communication and persuasion.* New Haven, Conn.: Yale Univer., 1953.

Hovland, C. I., et al. (Eds.) *The order of presentation in persuasion.* Vol. 1. *Yale studies in attitude and communication.* New Haven, Conn.: Yale Univer., 1957.

Hovland, C. I., & Janis, I. L. (Eds.) *Personality and persuasibility.* Vol. 2. *Yale studies in attitude and communication.* New Haven, Conn.: Yale Univer., 1959.

Hovland, C. I., & Rosenberg, M. J. *Attitude, organization and change.* Vol. 3. *Yale studies in attitude and communication.* New Haven, Conn.: Yale Univer., 1960.

Human Sciences Research, Inc. *Annotations of small group research studies.* Arlington, Va.: Author, October, 1960.

Indik, B. P. Organization size and member participation. Unpublished doctoral dissertation, Univer. of Michigan, 1961.

Institute for Social Research. *Factors related to productivity.* Ann Arbor, Mich.: Author, 1951.

Institute for Social Research. *Publications: 1946–1956.* Ann Arbor, Mich.: Author, 1956.

Institute for Social Research. *Publications: Sept. 1956–Jan. 1960.* Ann Arbor, Mich.: Author, 1960.

Jackson, J. M. Analysis of interpersonal relations in a formal organization. Unpublished doctoral dissertation, Univer. of Michigan, 1953. (a)

Jackson, J. M. The effect of changing the leadership of small work groups. *Human Relat.,* 1953, 6(1), 25–44. (b)

Jackson, J. M. The organization and its communication problems. In *Hlth Educ. Monogr.,* 1957, No. 1, *Communication,* Society of Public Health Educators.

Jackson, J. M., & Saltzstein, H. D. *Group membership and group conformity processes.* Ann Arbor, Mich.: Institute for Social Research, 1956.

Jacobson, E. Foreman-steward participation practices and worker attitudes in a unionized factory. Unpublished doctoral dissertation, Univer. of Michigan, 1951.

Jacobson, E. The growth of groups in a voluntary organization. *J. soc. Issues,* 1956, 12(2), 18–23.

Jacobson, E., Kahn, R. L., Mann, F. C., & Morse, N. (Eds.) Human relations research in large organizations. *J. soc. Issues,* 1951, 7(3).

Jacobson, E., & Seashore, S. Communication practices in complex organizations. *J. soc. Issues,* 1951, 7(3), 28–40.

Jaques, E. *The changing culture of a factory.* London: Tavistock Publications, 1951.

Jaques, E. *Measurement of responsibility.* London: Tavistock Publications, 1956.

Jaques, E., Rice, A. K., & Hill, J. M. M. The social and psychological impact of a change in method of wage payment (the Glacier project—V). *Human Relat.*, 1951, 4, 315–341.

Jenkins, W. O. A review of leadership studies with particular reference to military problems. *Psychol. Bull.*, 1947, 44(1), 54–79.

Kahn, R. L. The prediction of productivity. *J. soc. Issues*, 1956, 12(2), 41–49.

Kahn, R. L. Employee motivation. In *Addresses on industrial relations, 1957 series.* Ann Arbor, Mich.: Univer. of Michigan, Bureau of Industrial Relations, 1957.

Kahn, R. L. Human relations on the shop floor. In E. M. Hugh-Jones (Ed.), *Human relations and modern management.* Amsterdam: North-Holland Publishing Co., 1958. Pp. 43–74.

Kahn, R. L. Productivity and job satisfaction. *Personnel Psychol.*, 1960, 13(3), 275–278.

Kahn, R. L., & Cannell, C. F. *The dynamics of interviewing: theory, techniques, and cases.* New York: Wiley, 1957.

Kahn, R. L., & Katz, D. Leadership practices in relation to productivity and morale. In D. Cartwright & A. Zander (Eds.), *Group dynamics: research and theory* (2d ed.) Evanston, Ill.: Row, Peterson, 1960. Pp. 554–571.

Kahn, R. L., & Mann, F. C. Uses of survey research in policy determination. *Proc., Ninth Annu. Meeting, IRRA*, 1957. Pp. 256–274.

Kahn, R. L., Mann, F. C., & Seashore, S. E. (Eds.) Human relations research in large organizations, II. *J. soc. Issues*, 1956, 12(2).

Kahn, R. L., & Tannenbaum, A. S. Union leadership and member participation. *Personnel Psychol.*, 1957, 10, 277–292.

Katona, G. *Psychological analysis of economic behavior.* New York: McGraw-Hill, 1951.

Katona, G. *The powerful consumer.* New York: McGraw-Hill, 1960.

Katz, D. Morale and motivation in industry. In W. Dennis (Ed.), *Current trends in industrial psychology.* Pittsburgh: Univer. of Pittsburgh, 1949. Pp. 145–171.

Katz, D. Satisfactions and deprivations in industrial life. In A. Kornhauser, R. Dubin, & A. M. Ross (Eds.), *Industrial conflict.* New York: McGraw-Hill, 1954. Pp. 86–106.

Katz, D., & Kahn, R. L. Human organization and worker motivation. In L. Reed Tripp (Ed.), *Industrial productivity.* Madison, Wis.: Industrial Relations Research Association, 1951. Pp. 146–171.

Katz, D., & Kahn, R. L. Some recent findings in human relations research. In E. Swanson, T. Newcomb, & E. Hartley (Eds.), *Readings in social psychology.* New York: Holt, Rinehart and Winston, 1952. Pp. 650–665.

Katz, D., Maccoby, N., Gurin, G., & Floor, L. G. *Productivity, supervision and morale among railroad workers.* Ann Arbor, Mich.: Institute for Social Research, 1951.

Katz, D., Maccoby, N., & Morse, Nancy. *Productivity, supervision and morale in an office situation.* Ann Arbor, Mich.: Institute for Social Research, 1950.

Katz, E., & Lazarsfeld, P. F. *Personal influence: the part played by people in the flow of mass communications.* Glencoe, Ill.: Free Press, 1955.

Kennedy, J. L., A transition-model laboratory for research on cultural change. *Human Organization,* 1955, **14**(3), 16–18.

Kish, L. Selection of the sample. In L. Festinger & D. Katz (Eds.), *Research methods in the behavioral sciences.* New York: Holt, Rinehart and Winston, 1953. Pp. 175–240.

Krulee, G. K. The Scanlon plan: co-operation through participation. *J. Business, Univer. of Chicago,* 1955, **28**(2), 100–113.

Lawshe, C. H., Bolda, R. A., & Brune, R. L. Studies in management training evaluation. I. Scaling responses to human relations training cases. *J. appl. Psychol.,* 1958, **42**(6), 396–398.

Lawshe, C. H., Bolda, R. A., & Brune, R. L. Studies in management training evaluation. II. The effects of exposure to role-playing. *J. appl. Psychol.,* in press.

Lawshe, C. H., Bolda, R. A., & Brune, R. L. Studies in management training evaluation. III. A note on attitudes toward training. *J. appl. Psychol.,* in press.

Lawshe, C. H., Brune, R. L., & Bolda, R. A. Studies in management training evaluation. IV. Observations on frequency of participation in group discussion. *J. appl. Psychol.,* in press.

Leavitt, H. J. *Managerial psychology.* Chicago: Univer. of Chicago, 1958.

Leavitt, H. J., & Whisler, T. L. Management in the 1980's. *Harvard Business Rev.,* 1958, **36**(6), 13–27.

Lesieur, F. G. *The Scanlon plan.* New York: Wiley, 1959.

Lewin, K. Frontiers in group dynamics. *Human Relat.,* 1947, **1**, 5–41.

Lewin, K. *Resolving social conflict.* (Gertrud Lewin, Ed.) New York: Harper, 1948.

Lewin, K. *Field theory in social science.* (D. Cartwright, Ed.) New York: Harper, 1951.

Lewin, K. Group decision and social change. In E. E. Maccoby, T. M. Newcomb, & E. L. Hartley (Eds.), *Readings in social psychology.* (3d ed.) New York: Holt, Rinehart and Winston, 1958. Pp. 197–211.

Lieberman, S. The relationship between attitudes and roles: a natural field experiment. Unpublished doctoral dissertation, Univer. of Michigan, 1954.

Lieberman, S. The effects of changes in roles on the attitudes of role occupants. *Human Relat.,* 1956, **9**(4), 385–402.

Likert, Jane. *Leadership for effective leagues.* Washington: League of Women Voters, 1958.

Likert, Jane. *The member and the league.* Washington: League of Women Voters, 1960.

Likert, R. A technique for the measurement of attitudes. *Arch. Psychol., N.Y.,* 1932, **140**, 1–55.

Likert, R. The sample interview survey. In W. Dennis (Ed.), *Current trends in psychology.* Pittsburgh: Univer. of Pittsburgh, 1947. Pp. 196–225.

Likert, R. The basis of good performance review techniques. *The periodic review of employee performance and progress.* Chicago: Univer. of Chicago Industrial Relations Center, 1949. Pp. B1–B9.

Likert, R. Findings of research on management and leadership. *Proc. Pacific Coast Gas Asso.,* 1952, **43**, 28–35. (a)

Likert, R. Motivational dimensions of administration. *America's manpower crisis.* Chicago: Public Administration Service, 1952. Pp. 89–117. (b)

Likert, R. Motivation: the core of management. Amer. Mgmt Asso., *Personnel Ser.,* No. 155, 1953, 3–21. (a)

Likert, R. Public relations and the social sciences. *Publ. Relat. J.*, 1953, 9(2), 3–6, and 9(3), 11–15. (b)

Likert, R. The contribution of human relations research to improved productivity. *Human relations in industry.* Paris: European Productivity Agency, 1955. Pp. 45–49. (a)

Likert, R. Developing patterns of management. I. Amer. Mgmt Asso., *Gen. Mgmt Ser.*, No. 178, 1955, 32–51. (b)

Likert, R. Developing patterns of management. II. Amer. Mgmt Asso., *Gen. Mgmt Ser.*, No. 182, 1956, 3–29. (a)

Likert, R. Motivation and productivity. *Mgmt Rec.*, 1956, 18(4), 128–131. (b)

Likert, R. Organizational aspects of human behavior. *Industry and the human being in an automatized world.* Ann Arbor, Mich.: Univer. of Michigan, 1957. Pp. 23–28.

Likert, R. Effective supervision: an adaptive and relative process. *Personnel Psychol.*, 1958, 11(3), 317–352. (a)

Likert, R. Measuring organizational performance. *Harvard Business Rev.*, 1958, 36(2), 41–50. (b)

Likert, R. An emerging theory of management applicable to public administration. In D. L. Bowen & R. H. Pealy (Eds.), *Administrative leadership in government: selected papers.* Ann Arbor, Mich.: Institute of Public Administration, 1959. Pp. 1–15. (a)

Likert, R. Management, measurement and motivation. In F. E. May (Ed.), *Increasing sales efficiency: conference on sales and marketing management, 1959.* Ann Arbor, Mich.: Univer. of Michigan, Bureau of Business Research, 1959. Pp. 102–131. (b)

Likert, R. Motivational approach to management development. *Harvard Business Rev.*, 1959, 37(4), 75–82. (c).

Likert, R. A motivational approach to a modified theory of organization and management. In M. Haire (Ed.), *Modern organization theory.* New York: Wiley, 1959. Pp. 184–218. (d)

Likert, R. An emerging theory of organization, leadership and management. In L. Petrullo & B. M. Bass (Eds.), *Leadership and interpersonal behavior.* New York: Holt, Rinehart and Winston, 1961.

Likert, R., Argyris, C., March, J., & Shepard, H. Management implications of recent social science research—a symposium. *Personnel Adminstration*, 1958, 21(3), 5–14.

Likert, R., & Hayes, S. P. (Eds.) *Some applications of behavioural research.* Paris: UNESCO, 1957.

Likert, R., & Katz, D. Supervisory practices and organizational structures as they affect employee productivity and morale. Amer. Mgmt Asso., *Personnel Ser.*, No. 120, 1948, 14–24.

Likert, R., & Pelz, D. C. Group motivation of research teams. *Proc. tenth national conf. on administration of res.* University Park, Pa.: Pennsylvania State Univer., 1957. Pp. 59–65.

Likert, R., & Seashore, S. E. Employee attitudes and output. *Monthly Labor Rev.*, 1954, 77(6), 641–648.

Likert, R., & Seashore, S. E. Motivation and morale in the public service. *Publ. Personnel Rev.*, 1956, 17(4), 268–274.

Likert, R., & Willits, J. M. *Morale and agency management.* Hartford, Conn.: Life Insurance Agency Management Asso., 1940. 4 vols.

Lionberger, H. F., & Coughenour, C. M. Social structure and diffusion of farm innovation. Univer. of Missouri, Agricultural Experiment Station, *Bull.* 631, 1957.

Lippitt, R. *Training in community relations.* New York: Harper, 1949.

Lippitt, R., & Bradford, L. Role-playing in supervisory training. *Personnel,* 1946, 22, 3–14.

Lippitt, R., Watson, Jeanne, & Westley, B. *The dynamics of planned change: a comparative study of principles and techniques.* New York: Harcourt, Brace and World, 1958.

Lombard, G. F. F. *Behavior in a selling group.* Boston: Harvard Business Sch., 1955.

McAnly, L. C. Maytag's program of expense reduction. Amer. Mgmt Asso., *Manufacturing Ser.,* No. 221, 1956, 24–40.

McGregor, D. Conditions of effective leadership in industrial organization. *J. Consult. Psychol.,* 1944, 8, 56–63.

McGregor, D. Changing patterns in human relations. *Conference Bd Mgmt Rec.,* 1950, 12(9), 322ff.

McGregor, D. An uneasy look at performance appraisal. *Harvard Business Rev.,* 1957, 35(3), 89–94.

McGregor, D. *Human side of enterprise.* New York: McGraw-Hill, 1960.

McGregor, D., & Knickerbocker, I. Industrial relations and national defense. *Personnel,* 1941, 18(1), 49–63.

McMurry, R. N., The case for benevolent autocracy. *Harvard Business Rev.,* 1958, 36, 82–90.

Maccoby, E. E., Newcomb, T. M., & Hartley, E. L. (Eds.) *Readings in social psychology.* (3d ed.) New York: Holt, Rinehart and Winston, 1958.

Maier, N. R. F. *Principles of human relations.* New York: Wiley, 1952.

Maier, N. R. F. *Psychology in industry.* (2d ed.) New York: Houghton Mifflin, 1955.

Maier, N. R. F. *The appraisal interview.* New York: Wiley, 1958.

Maier, N. R. F., & Hoffman, L. R. Overcoming superior-subordinate communication problems in management. Amer. Mgmt Asso., in press.

Maier, N. R. F., Hooven, J. G., Hoffman, L. R., & Read, W. H. Communication problems in superior-subordinate relationships. Amer. Mgmt Asso., in press.

Maier, N. R. F., Solem, A. R., & Maier, Ayesha. *Supervisory and executive development: a manual for role playing.* New York: Wiley, 1957.

Make committee work effective. *Nation's Business,* May, 1958.

Mann, F. C. Putting human relations research findings to work. *Mich. Business Rev.,* 1950, 2(2), 16–20.

Mann, F. C. Changing superior-subordinate relationships. *J. soc. Issues,* 1951, 7(3), 56–63.

Mann, F. C. Studying and creating change: a means to understanding social organization. In *Research in industrial human relations.* Madison, Wis.: Industrial Relations Research Asso., 1957. Pp. 146–167.

Mann, F. C., & Baumgartel, H. J. *Absences and employee attitudes in an electric power company.* Ann Arbor, Mich.: Institute for Social Research, 1953. (a)

Mann, F. C., & Baumgartel, H. J. *The supervisor's concern with costs in an electric power company.* Ann Arbor, Mich.: Institute for Social Research, 1953. (b)

Mann, F. C., & Dent, J. *Appraisals of supervisors and attitudes of their employees in an electric power company.* Ann Arbor, Mich.: Institute for Social Research, 1954. (a)

Mann, F. C., & Dent, J. The supervisor: member of two organizational families. *Harvard Business Rev.*, 1954, **32**(6), 103–112. (b)

Mann, F. C., & Hoffman, L. R. Individual and organizational correlates of automation. *J. soc. Issues*, 1956, **12**(2), 7–17.

Mann, F. C., & Hoffman, L. R. *Automation and the worker: a study of social change in power plants.* New York: Holt, Rinehart and Winston, 1960.

Mann, F. C., & Likert, R. The need for research on the communication of research results. *Human Organization*, 1952, **2**(4), 15–19.

Mann, F. C., Metzner, H., & Baumgartel, H. The supervisor and absence rates. *Supervisory Mgmt*, 1957, **2**(7), 7–14.

Mann, F. C., & Sparling, J. E. Changing absence rates: an application of research findings. *Personnel*, January, 1956, 3–19.

Mann, F. C., & Williams, L. K. Observations on the dynamics of a change to electronic data processing equipment. *Administrative Sci. Quart.*, 1960, **5**(2), 217–256.

March, J. G., & Simon, H. A. *Organizations.* New York: Wiley, 1958.

Marcson, S. *The scientist in American industry.* Princeton, N.J.: Princeton Univer. Industrial Relations Section, 1960.

Marrow, A. J. *Making management human.* New York: McGraw-Hill, 1957.

Marvick, D. *Career perspectives in a bureaucratic setting.* Ann Arbor, Mich.: Institute of Public Administration, 1954.

Mathewson, S. B. *Restriction of output among unorganized workers.* New York: Viking, 1931 .

Mayo, E. *The human problems of an industrial civilization.* New York: Viking, 1931.

Mayo, E., & Lombard, G. Teamwork and labor turnover in the aircraft industry of Southern California. *Bus. Res. Studies*, No. 32. Cambridge, Mass.: Harvard Univer., 1944.

Mayo, E. *The social problems of an industrial civilization.* Cambridge, Mass.: Harvard Univer., 1945.

Mellinger, G. D. Interpersonal trust as a factor in communication. *J. abnorm. soc. Psychol.*, 1956, **52**(3), 304–309.

Meltzer, L. Scientific productivity in organizational settings. *J. soc. Issues*, 1956, **12**(2), 32–40.

Meltzer, L. Consequences of the joint consideration of individual and aggregate data in correlational social research. Unpublished doctoral dissertation, Univer. of Michigan, 1958.

Merton, R. K., & Lazarsfeld, P. F. (Eds.) *Continuities in social research.* Glencoe, Ill.: Free Press, 1950.

Metcalf, H. C., & Urwick, L. (Eds.) *Dynamic administration: the collected works of Mary Parker Follett.* New York: Harper, 1940.

Metzner, H., & Mann, F. C. Employee attitudes and absence. *Personnel Psychol.*, 1953, **6**(4), 467–485.

Millett, J. D. *Management in the public service.* New York: McGraw-Hill, 1954.

Milward, G. E. (Ed.) *Large-scale organisation.* London: Institute of Public Administration, 1950.

Morse, Nancy. *Satisfactions in the white-collar job.* Ann Arbor, Mich.: Institute for Social Research, 1953.

Morse, Nancy, & Reimer, E. The experimental change of a major organizational variable. *J. abnorm. soc. Psychol.*, 1956, **52**, 120–129.

Morse, Nancy, & Weiss, R. The function and meaning of work and the job. *Amer. soc. Rev.*, 1955, **20**(2), 191–198.

National Training Laboratories. *Explorations in human relations training.* Washington: National Education Asso., 1953.

National Training Laboratories. *An annotated bibliography of research, 1947–1960.* Washington: National Education Asso., 1960.

Newcomb, T. M. *Social psychology.* New York: Holt, Rinehart and Winston, 1950.

Nyman, R. C., & Smith, E. D. *Union-management cooperation in the "stretch-out."* New Haven, Conn.: Yale Univer., 1934.

O'Donnell, C. The source of managerial authority. *Political Sci. Quart.,* 1952, 67, 573.

Olmstead, M. *The small group.* New York: Random House, 1959.

Patchen, M. The effect of reference group standards on job satisfactions. *Human Relat.,* 1958, 11(4), 303–314.

Patchen, M. Absence and employee feelings about fair treatment. *Personnel Psychol.,* 1960, 13(3), 349–360.

Patchen, M. *The choice of wage comparisons.* Englewood Cliffs, N.J.: Prentice-Hall, 1961.

Pelz, D. C. The influence of the supervisor within his department as a conditioner of the way supervisory practices affect employee attitudes. Unpublished doctoral dissertation, Univer. of Michigan, 1951.

Pelz, D. C. Influence: a key to effective leadership in the first-line supervisor. *Personnel,* November, 1952, 3–11.

Pelz, D. C. Some social factors related to performance in a research organization. *Administrative Sci. Quart.,* 1956, 1(3), 310–325.

Pelz, D. C. Motivation of the engineering and research specialist. Amer. Mgmt Asso., *Gen. Mgmt Ser.,* No. 186, 1957, 25–46.

Pelz, D. C. Social factors in the motivation of engineers and scientists. *Sch. Sci. and Math.,* June, 1958, 417–429.

Pelz, D. C. The influence of anonymity on expressed attitudes. *Human Organization,* 1959, 18(2), 88–91, (a)

Pelz, D. C. Interaction and attitudes between scientists and auxiliary staff. I. Viewpoint of staff. *Administrative Sci. Quart.,* 1959, 4(3), 321–336. (b)

Pelz, D. C. Interaction and attitudes between scientists and auxiliary staff. II. Viewpoint of scientists. *Administrative Sci. Quart.,* 1960, 4(4), 410–425.

Pepitone, Emmy. Responsibility to the group and its effects on the performance of members. Unpublished doctoral dissertation, Univer. of Michigan, 1952.

Petrullo, L., & Bass, B. M. (Eds.) *Leadership and interpersonal behavior.* New York: Holt, Rinehart and Winston, 1961.

Pfiffner, J. M., & Sherwood, F. P. *Administrative organization,* Englewood Cliffs, N.J.: Prentice-Hall, 1960.

Read, W. H. Some factors affecting the accuracy of upward communication at middle management levels in industrial organizations. Unpublished doctoral dissertation, Univer. of Michigan, 1959.

Reid, P. Supervision in an automated plant. *Supervisory Mgmt,* August, 1960, 2–10.

Revans, R. W. The analysis of industrial behaviour. *Automatic production—change and control.* London: Institution of Production Engineering, 1957.

Revans, R. W. *Operational research and personnel management,* part II. London: Institute of Personnel Management, 1959.

Rice, A. K. An examination of boundaries of part institutions (the Glacier project—VI). *Human Relat.,* 1951, 4, 393–401.

Rice, A. K. *Productivity and social organization.* London: Tavistock Publications, 1958.

Rice, A. K., & Trist, E. L. Institutional and sub-institutional determinants of change in labor turnover (the Glacier project—VIII). *Human Relat.*, 1952, **5**, 347–373.

Roethlisberger, F. J. *Management and morale*. Cambridge, Mass.: Harvard Univer., 1941.

Roethlisberger, F. J., & Dickson, W. J. *Management and the worker*. Cambridge, Mass.: Harvard Univer., 1939.

Rogers, C. R. *Counseling and psychotherapy*. Boston: Houghton Mifflin, 1942.

Rogers, C. R. *Client-centered therapy*. Boston: Houghton Mifflin, 1951.

Ronken, H. O., & Lawrence, P. R. *Administering changes*. Boston: Harvard Graduate Sch. of Business Adminstration, 1952.

Rose, A. M. The social psychology of desertion from combat. *Amer. soc. Rev.*, 1951, **16**, 614–629.

Rose, I. A. Discussion. Amer. Mgmt Asso., *Gen. Mgmt Ser.*, No. 182, 1956, 18–29.

Ross, I. C. Role specialization in supervision. Unpublished doctoral dissertation, Columbia Univer., 1957.

Ross, I. C., & Harary, F. On the determination of redundancies in sociometric chains. *Psychometrika*, 1952, **17**, 195–208.

Ross, I. C., & Harary, F. Identification of liaison persons of an organization using the structure matrix. *Mgmt Sci.*, 1955, **1**, 251–258.

Ross, I. C., & Zander, A. Need satisfactions and employee turnover. *Personnel Psychol.*, 1957, **10**(3), 327–338.

Seashore, S. E. *Group cohesiveness in the industrial work group*. Ann Arbor, Mich.: Institute for Social Research, 1954.

Seashore, S. E. Administrative leadership and organizational effectiveness. In R. Likert & S. P. Hayes (Eds.), *Some applications of behavioural research*. Paris: UNESCO, 1957. Pp. 44–80. (a)

Seashore, S. E. The training of leaders for effective human relations. In R. Likert & S. P. Hayes (Eds.), *Some applications of behavioural research*. Paris: UNESCO, 1957. Pp. 81–123. (b)

Seashore, S. E., Aas, D., & Soltvedt, M. *Piecerates in industry: a study of role relations in the setting of piecerates*. Oslo: Institutt for Samfunsforshning, 1957.

Seashore, S. E., Indik, B. P., & Georgopoulos, B. S. Relationships among criteria of job performance. *J. appl. Psychol.*, 1960, **44**(3), 195–202.

Selznick, P. *Leadership in administration*. Evanston, Ill.: Row, Peterson, 1957.

Shartle, C. L. *Effective performance and leadership*. Englewood Cliffs, N.J.: Prentice-Hall, 1956.

Shultz, G. P. Worker participation on production problems. Amer. Mgmt Asso., *Personnel*, 1951, **28**(3), 201–211.

Simon, H. A. *Administrative behavior*. New York: Macmillan, 1947.

Simon, H. A. *The new science of management decision*. New York: Harper, 1960.

Smith, E. D., & Nyman, R. C. *Technology and labor*. New Haven, Conn.: Yale Univer., 1939.

Sofer, C., & Hutton, G. *New ways in management training*. London: Tavistock Publications, 1958.

Stock, Dorothy, & Thelen, H. A. *Emotional dynamics and group culture*. Washington: National Training Laboratories (NEA), 1958.

Stogdill, R. M. *Individual behavior and group achievement*. New York: O- Press, 1959.

Stogdill, R. M., & Shartle, C. L. *Patterns of administrative performance.* Columbus, Ohio: Ohio State Univer., Bureau of Business Research, 1956. (a)

Stogdill, R. M., & Shartle, C. L. *Methods in the study of administrative leadership.* Columbus, Ohio: Ohio State Univer., Bureau of Business Research, 1956. (b)

Stouffer, S. A., Lumsdaine, A. A., Lumsdaine, M. H., Williams, R. M., Jr., Smith, M. B., Janis, I. L., Star, S. A., & Cottrell, L. S., Jr. *The American soldier: combat and its aftermath.* Vol. 2. Princeton, N.J.: Princeton Univer., 1949.

Stouffer, S. A., Suchman, E. A., DeVinney, L. C., Star, S. A., & Williams, R. M., Jr. *The American soldier: adjustment during Army life.* Vol. 1. Princeton, N.J.: Princeton Univer., 1949.

Super, D. Occupational level and job satisfaction. *J. appl. Psychol.,* 1939, **23,** 547–564.

Tannenbaum, A. S. The relationship between personality and group structure. Unpublished doctoral dissertation, Syracuse Univer., 1954.

Tannenbaum, A. S. Control structure and union functions. *Amer. J. Sociol.,* 1956, 61(6), 536–545. (a)

Tannenbaum, A. S. The concept of organizational control. *J. soc. Issues,* 1956, 12(2), 50–60. (b)

Tannenbaum, A. S. The application of survey techniques to the study of organizational structure and functioning. *Publ. Opinion Quart.,* 1957, **21**(3), 439–442. (a)

Tannenbaum, A. S. Personality change as a result of an experimental change of environmental conditions. *J. abnorm. soc. Psychol.,* 1957, **52,** 404–406. (b)

Tannenbaum, A. S. *A study of the League of Women Voters of the United States: factors in league effectiveness.* Ann Arbor, Mich.: Institute for Social Research, 1958.

Tannenbaum, A. S. Mechanisms of control in local trade unions. In J. Barbash (Ed.), *Unions and union leadership.* New York: Harper, 1959.

Tannenbaum, A. S., & Allport, F. H. Personality structure and group structure: an interpretative study of their relationship through an event-structure hypothesis. *J. abnorm. soc. Psychol.,* 1956, **51**(3), 272–280.

Tannenbaum, A. S., & Donald, Marjorie. *A study of the League of Women Voters of the United States: factors in league functioning.* Ann Arbor, Mich.: Institute for Social Research, 1957.

Tannenbaum, A. S., & Georgogopulos, G. S. The distribution of control in formal organizations. *Soc. Forces,* 1957, 36(1), 44–50.

Tannenbaum, A. S., & Kahn, R. L. Organizational control structure: a general descriptive technique as applied to four local unions. *Human Relat.,* 1957, 10(2), 127-140.

Tannenbaum, A. S., & Kahn, R. L. *Participation in union locals.* Evanston, Ill.: Row, Peterson, 1958.

Taylor, F. W. *The principles of scientific management.* New York: Harper, 1911.

Thelen, H. A. *Dynamics of groups at work.* Chicago: Univer. of Chicago, 1954.

Thibaut, J. W., & Kelley, H. H. *The social psychology of groups.* New York: Wiley, 1959.

andis, H. C. Categories of thought of managers, clerks, and workers about jobs and people in an industry. *J. appl. Psychol.,* 1959, **43,** 338–344. (a)

dis, H. C. Cognitive similarity and interpersonal communication in industry. *J. appl. Psychol.,* 1959, **43**(5), 321–326. (b)

Triandis, H. C. Differential perception of certain jobs and people by managers, clerks, and workers in industry. *J. appl. Psychol.*, 1959, **43**, 221–225. (c)

Triandis, H. C. Cognitive similarity and communication in a dyad. *Human Relat.*, 1960, **13**, 175–183.

Trist, E. L., & Bamforth, K. W. Some social and psychological consequences of the longwall method of coal-getting. *Human Relat.*, 1951, **4**(1), 3–38.

Viteles, M. S. *Motivation and morale in industry.* New York: Norton, 1953.

Vroom, V. H. The effects of attitudes on the perception of organizational goals. *Human Relat.*, 1960, **13**(3), 229–240. (a)

Vroom, V. H. Employee attitudes. In R. Gray (Ed.), *Frontiers of industrial relations.* Pasadena, Calif.: California Institute of Technology, 1960. (b)

Vroom, V. H. *Some personality determinants of the effects of participation.* Englewood Cliffs, N.J.: Prentice-Hall, 1960. (c)

Vroom, V. H., & Mann, F. C. Leader authoritarianism and employee attitudes. *Personnel Psychol.*, 1960, **13**(2), 125–140.

Walker, C., & Guest, H. *The man on the assembly line.* Cambridge, Mass.: Harvard Univer., 1952.

Walker, C., Guest, H., & Turner, A. N. *The foreman on the assembly line.* Cambridge, Mass.: Harvard Univer., 1956.

Watson, Jeanne, & Lippitt, R. *Learning across cultures.* Ann Arbor, Mich.: Institute for Social Research, 1955.

Weiss, R. *Processes of organization.* Ann Arbor, Mich.: Institute for Social Research, 1956.

Weiss, R., & Kahn, R. L. Definitions of work and occupation. *J. soc. Problems,* Fall-Winter, 1960.

Westerlund, G. *Group leadership and field experiment.* Stockholm: Nordisk Rotogravyr, 1952.

White, R., & Lippitt, R. *Autocracy and democracy: an experimental inquiry.* New York: Harper, 1960.

Whitehead, T. N. *The industrial worker.* Cambridge, Mass.: Harvard Univer., 1938.

Whyte, W. F. *Patterns for industrial peace.* New York: Harper, 1951.

Whyte, W. F. (Ed.) *Money and motivation.* New York: Harper, 1955.

Whyte, W. F. Human relations theory—a progress report. *Harvard Business Rev.,* 1956, **34**(5).

Whyte, W. H., Jr. *The organization man.* New York: Simon and Schuster, 1956.

Williams, L. K., Hoffman, L. R., & Mann, F. C. An investigation of the control graph: influence in a staff organization. *Soc. Forces.,* 1959, **37**(3), 189–195.

Wilson, A. T. M. Some aspects of social process. *J. soc. Issues,* Supplement Ser. No. 5, November, 1951, 5–23.

Zaleznik, A. *Worker satisfaction and development.* Boston: Harvard Business Sch., 1956.

Zaleznik, A., Christenson, C. R., & Roethlisberger, F. *The motivation, productivity, and satisfaction of workers: a predictive study.* Boston: Harvard Graduate Sch. of Business Administration, 1958.

Zander, A., Cohen, A. R., & Stotland, E. *Role relations in the mental health professions.* Ann Arbor, Mich.: Institute for Social Research, 1957.

Zander, A., & Heyns, R. Observation of group behavior. In L. Festinger & Katz (Eds.), *Research methods in the behavioral sciences.* New York: Holt, Rinehart and Winston, 1953. Pp. 381–418.

Zander, A., Thomas, E. J., & Natsoulas, T. Personal goals and the group's for the member. *Human Relat.,* 1960, **13**(4), 333–344.

NAME INDEX

Aas, Dagfinn, 93, 94, 242, 244
Abegglen, J. C., 246
Acton Society Trust, 38
Allport, F. H., 235, 242
American Management Association, viii
American Philosophical Society, viii
American Psychological Association, viii
Argyris, Chris, 2, 30, 36, 60n., 102, 208, 235
Asch, S., 92

Bales, R. F., 164, 175n., 235
Bamforth, K. W., 37, 38
Barnard, C. I., 60n.
Baumgartel, H. J., 14, 18, 35, 93
Benne, K. D., 172, 173, 175
Borgatta, E. F., 164, 235
Bose, S. K., 7, 29, 43, 247
Bowen, H. G., vii
Brooks, E., 19
Browne, C. G., 53
Bruner, J. S., 92
Burtt, H. E., 19, 89

Campbell, Angus, viii, 134
Carnegie Corporation, 5n.
Cartwright, Dorwin, viii, 36, 55, 102, 105, 134, 164, 216, 235
Chowdhry, Kamla, 247
Christenson, C. R., 30, 36
Coch, Lester, 39, 40, 41, 42, 43, 245, 246
Conrad, V. A., viii
Converse, Philip, 134
Coughenour, C. M., 134

Dalton, M., 90, 92
Dent, James, 9, 18, 21, 28, 54
DeVinney, L. C., viii, 30, 36
Dickson, W. J., 30, 92, 208
Donald, Marjorie, 140
Dubin, R., 30

Estes, Hugh, 9
Evans, C. E., 53

Fleishman, E. A., 19, 89
Floor, L. G., 12, 16, 29, 33
Follett, Mary Parker, 60n., 212, 213
Foreman, C. W. L., viii
French, J. R. P., Jr., viii, 30, 36, 39–43, 93, 94, 242, 244–246

Gamble, T. W., 213–215
Ganguli, H. C., 7, 247
Gault, H. M., viii
Georgopoulos, Basil, 8, 9, 32, 38, 119
Gerard, R. W., 21
Gerhard, F. B., viii
Goodacre, D. M., 36
Goodwin, H. F., 87
Gordon, T., 19
Grant, Donald, viii
Grunes, W. F., 92
Guest, H., 16, 80
Gurin, Gerald, 12, 16, 29, 33, 134

Haire, Mason, viii, 60n., 92
Hamann, J. R., 51
Hare, P., 164, 235
Harper & Brothers, viii
Harris, E. F., 19, 70, 89
Hoffman, L. R., 16, 53, 245
Holt, Rinehart and Winston, Inc., viii
Hooven, J. G., 53
Hoppock, R., 16
Hovland, C. I., 44

Indik, B. P., 176
Institute for Social Research, vii, viii, 43, 62, 119, 140, 164, 247
Israel, J., 93, 94, 242, 244

265

SUBJECT INDEX

Absence, 197, 201
    affected by group forces, 38
    and attitudes toward organization, 14
    under authoritarian leadership, 69
    as criterion, of effectiveness, 6
        of performance, 19, 25
    and goals of "informal" organization, 30
    and group solidarity, 35
    in group system of organization, 112
    and productivity, related to group loyalty, 35
    related to supervisory behavior, 18
    in repetitive work, 81
    and size, of organization, 38
        of work group, 38
    of supervisor, and performance, 28–29
        and productivity, 65
Accidents, and size, of organization, 38
    of work group, 38
Anxiety, in effective work groups, 167
    and group loyalty, 33–34
Attitude-toward-men score of superior,
    and complaints, 122
    and perceived expectations, 121
    and productivity, 119
    and recognition, 121
    and responsibility of workers, 121
    and tension, 122
    and work assignments, 121
Attitudes, under authoritarian leadership, 69
    changes in, 66–68
        effect on production, 42
    consumer, need for measurement, 73
    as criterion of performance, 25
    effect on communications, 44–45
    and expectations, 1–2, 93–94
    and experience, 2, 70, 94–95, 198
    favorable, and characteristics of supervisor, 101
    in group system of organization, 112
    toward high producer, 65–66
        and group loyalty, 33

Attitudes, job-related, and group meetings, 26
    frequency, 43
    of managers toward organization's goals, 11
    motives influencing, 98, 100
    toward objectives of organization, and communication, 30
    and productivity, 30
    toward organization, 14
        related, to absence, 14
            to individual productivity, 14
            to recruiting new employees, 14
            to turnover, 14
        and toward supervision, 32
    and participation, 93
    and peer-group loyalty, 124–139
    and performance, in repetitive work, 79–80
        in varied work, 78–79
    toward performance ratings, 15
    and personality of supervisor, 93
    toward piece-rate system and supervision, 90
    and principle of supportive relationships, 103
    toward production, 66
        and group loyalty, 32
    and productivity (see Productivity)
    related to other variables, 197–201
    toward supervision and toward organization, 32
    toward supervisor, 66–67
        and group loyalty, 32–33
    supervisory, and performance, 19
    and supervisory behavior, 16–20, 89–90, 95
    and "treating people as human beings," 101
    and upward influence of superior, 9 113
    and work simplification, 87
Authority, delegation, 56–57
"Authority of facts," 213–216, 238